PRAISE FOR *THE CLINIC*

"*The Clinic* drew me in from its tense first page and left me thinking long after I finished it. It's a twisty mystery with feeling that kept me turning the pages until well into the night."

—Sara Ochs, author of *The Resort*

"With relentless writing and twists around every corner, Cate Quinn weaves a gripping mystery through the world of luxury rehab that will have you saying 'one more chapter' until you hit the final page. So be warned: once you step foot in *The Clinic*, the doors lock behind you."

—Tony Wirt, author of *Just Stay Away*

"Cate Quinn's propulsive thriller *The Clinic* reads like an edge-of-your-seat page-turner, with clever twists and turns and redirections, all while taking place at an unconventional rehab clinic in the wilds of the Pacific Northwest coast. But at its core, this is a haunting story of addiction, long-lasting trauma, and the power of transformative change—I absolutely loved it."

—Ashley Tate, author of *Twenty-Seven Minutes*

"*The Clinic* weaves moving portrayals of rehab into a twisty, beautifully written mystery. With enigmatic characters and a vivid atmosphere, Cate Quinn delivers a pitch-perfect page-turner. I devoured it."

—R. J. Jacobs, author of *Always the First to Die* and *This Is How We End Things*

"An absolutely propulsive read that grabbed me by the throat and never let me go until the final page."

—Cass Green, author of *In a Cottage in a Wood*

THE
CLINIC

CATE QUINN

ORION

This edition first published in Great Britain in 2024 by Orion Fiction
an imprint of The Orion Publishing Group Ltd
Carmelite House, 50 Victoria Embankment
London EC4Y 0DZ
An Hachette UK Company

1 3 5 7 9 10 8 6 4 2

A CIP catalogue record for this book is
available from the British Library.

ISBN (Hardback) 978 1 3987 2045 9
ISBN (Export Trade Paperback) 978 1 3987 2046 6
ISBN (eBook) 978 1 3987 2048 0

Printed and bound in Great Britain by Clays Ltd, Elcograf S.p.A.

www.orionbooks.co.uk

Author's Note

This is the first book I have written sober.

In 2020, I checked into rehab, simultaneously the scariest and most rewarding thing I have ever done. I was terrified of all kinds of things, but uppermost in my mind was I might never write another book. For fifteen books, I'd used alcohol for creative insights and bouts of introspection. It seemed invaluable to the process. Suffice to say, I did go on to write another book, and this is the one I'm most proud of. *The Clinic* is dedicated to anyone anywhere struggling with addiction. And to Sam, T, D, L, J, H and M, the original do or die crew.

Prologue

The clinic was usually loud at night. Addicts, detoxing, shouting. But this part was quiet, the disinfectant smell less pervasive.

No one had said rehab would be easy. But Haley hadn't counted on it being this hard. Her agent had painted it as a vacation. A break from the drugs before returning to the recording studio and celebrity parties. They hadn't mentioned how Haley would have to perform an Oscar-worthy set of panic attacks and tearful breakdowns to avoid therapy getting personal. Because Haley couldn't go there. She really couldn't. At twenty-seven she had enough bad memories to last a lifetime.

That was why she was padding barefoot along the squeaky, bleached floor of this dark corridor at night, headed for the medical store. And here it was. Haley's painted toes came to a halt outside.

Rehab went on and on about not trusting addicts and keeping everything locked away. But a security system is only as effective as the people who run it, and with her trademark charm, Haley had needed barely a minute to win over the guard. Sometimes she was so good she impressed herself.

The door was plain. Unmarked. Electronic key code. Stupid. All that plate glass and double locks for the daily pharmacy, and then they keep ten times the drugs behind this flimsy panel of wood. Haley had kicked holes in bigger doors during fights with her manager.

She breathed out. Zipped her pink velour onesie a little higher over her chin—designer label, naturally, bought especially for rehab. The cute loungewear clung to her pixie frame, with a useful hood for pulling down low over her eyes.

Tapping the override code, she almost paused. Haley had been clean for over three weeks. She'd sworn to herself she would stick to a few lines at parties from now on. No crazy weeklong binges. She'd get acting work too. That was why she'd gotten the singing contract anyway. "We can autotune your voice, kid. It's the looks and sweet country-girl charm we need."

Maybe it would be nice to get through the full month without anything. Just to prove she could.

But the lock was whirring as Haley remembered how addicts in group therapy had been ragging on her. There was this guy. OK, two guys, in actual fact, who never let up. Admittedly she had played them during her first days there, when she had been going out of her mind with detox and boredom. What else was going to keep her occupied?

So these guys couldn't get over that she'd ditched them, basically. Trying to get to the bottom of why she was here, who she was. But there was some stuff she would never tell anyone. Stuff she really, *really* didn't appreciate being reminded of.

Which was why when the door swung open, Haley at first only had eyes for the rows upon rows of white cardboard boxes arranged neatly on shelves.

Relief hit her in a golden wave.

She'd come for a little something to help her sleep through the bad thoughts. Get through the last few nights of rehab. Now that she was here, she figured she might as well take a couple extra servings from the all-you-can-eat buffet of annihilators. How much fun it would be to float through those therapy sessions without caring. It was such a nice idea that she could feel herself physically wriggling into it, like a cozy blanket. After all that raw pain, she'd be armored up in a fluffy padded suit of couldn't-care-less. A smile tugged itself onto her face. So many names she recognized on the boxes. Haley hardly knew where to start.

It was only when she reached for the first package that she saw… In the corner of the room. Her hands flew to her mouth.

"Oh my God…" Bile rose in her throat.

Footsteps sounded in the corridor outside.

Haley knew no drug could help her now.

This would be the room she would die in.

CHAPTER ONE

MEG

The high-roller pits in Luckie's Casino have fancier bathrooms than any LA five-star hotel. And at 3:00 a.m., no one is in here but me, leaning over the crisp square lines of the porcelain sink.

The girl looking back at me in the gold-tiled mirror needs some work. She's altogether too neat and groomed with her blond chignon, professional makeup, and designer shoes.

Sliding a package of white powder from my bra, I tap the tiniest dab neatly under my nose and another little touch to my black cocktail dress. Taking in the effect, I take an eyedropper from my purse and drip the contents fast into both blue eyes.

"Shit!" I recoil reflexively, grabbing my face, hunched over. I uncurl, wincing. My pupils have dilated to double the size. One of my colored contact lenses has slipped, revealing a half-moon of deep-green iris. I nudge the lens back and take a breath before tidying my smudged mascara enough to show I've tried. A little spritz of water to make my forehead look sweaty, and a few strands pulled from the neat wig covering my own dark, wavy hair. The girl in the mirror is drug fueled. Wired. She's perfect.

"Showtime," I tell her.

The casino floor looks different through my bloodshot eyes. Golden palm trees are blurry. I scan the crowded pits of high rollers.

As I return to the table, I see it. The slight relaxing of the body language of the two men I'm playing against.

"Hey, Francine," says Charlie, the guy I lost two grand to an hour ago. "Powdering your nose?"

I wipe self-consciously with the edge of a knuckle. Charlie is an oily little man with a loan shark for a boss. He's probably been shuffling poker cards since he was old enough to shake a can for dimes on skid row. Same as me. Give or take.

"Gotta stay sharp for y'all," I tell him with my best country-girl twang. "Win it all back."

The dealer gives us the nod. "Ready?"

"Sure." I beam. "Let's play."

He slides out cards. Three each. I pull mine up, feeling the eyes on me, waiting for the tell. I flatten the cards back a little too quickly before breaking a wide smile.

"I'm in," I say.

Charlie eyes me. "You know," he says slowly, "you remind me of someone." He thinks some more. "That girl." He clicks his fingers. "What's her name? That country singer. Haley. Haley Banks. The party girl."

"Yeah?"

Took you long enough, asshole. I've been channeling my messed-up sister all night.

My whole life I've been compared unfavorably to Haley. She was the blond, blue-eyed princess; I was dark. She got lithe little curves; I grew up wiry. There are similarities though. Arched brows and an elf-like slant to our eyes and cheekbones. A certain disregard for the rules and an ability with accents.

"I'll take that as a compliment." I frown at the table. "I'm in."

"I'm gonna do you a favor," Charlie says. "How 'bout I give you a chance to win everything back? Double or quits."

"Sounds good." I twitch an eyelid.

"How about you?" Charlie turns to the other player, who I've quietly dubbed the Viking, on account of his large stature, blond hair, and strong, silent method of play.

The Viking eyes Charlie. "I'll sit this one out. You guys are too crazy for me." He leans his long body back against the chair.

"Looks like it's only you and me who still got balls, toots." Charlie winks at me, and gestures without thanks for the dealer to issue more cards. I pull a wide smile.

"My luck is about to change, fella. You just wait and see."

Charlie peels back his cards, face completely neutral. Some people will tell you that reading tells is an art. But it isn't an art; it's a science. Faces tell you nothing. You've got to blank them out entirely. Hands tell you a lot. Feet too if you can get a look. The way legs are crossed. Breathing.

Cross-reference that with patterns of past behavior, assess what cards are down, and run a probability matrix. You need all this, even if you're trying to lose.

I collect my cards and make an exaggerated glance at my chips. An amateur giveaway that I like what I see and my brain is telling me to bet high.

"You know what," I tell him. "I'm all in."

It's impossible to tell what Charlie's thinking. He caught that chip glance. Question is this. Does he buy my act? He riffles chips thoughtfully.

Come on, Charlie. I know it's you who's been setting up loan sharks in here. Say something incriminating.

Eight hours of continuous play are hitting me now. I wonder if that chip glance was too obvious.

"Know what?" he says. "I'll raise."

I lower my eyes. "Um. I think… Can I bet this?" I hold up my wrist. "It's a Rolex."

The dealer shakes his head firmly.

Charlie leans toward me, then hesitates.

Come on, Charlie, I beg silently. *Offer me a loan.*

It takes every ounce of self-control to keep my face sweetly clueless.

Charlie lowers his voice. "You want me to help you out? I can get you a number of a guy who can wire you two thousand right away. Ten if you need."

Yes!

"Really?" I reply in an uncertain whisper. My heart is soaring. *Finally.* "You'd give me the chance to stay in the game?"

He leans back, his eyes sliding to the dealer. Then he pushes a card across with digits scrawled on it.

"Make a trip to the bathroom. Use your phone," he says. "The money will be in your account by the time you get back to the table."

I stand. Smile.

"You know what?" I tell the dealer. "I need another bathroom break. I'll be back in one little minute."

As I walk away and give the signal, two security guards peel from the sides of the room, moving to take Charlie in. Loan sharks aren't welcome at Luckie's.

Shame. He was a good player. And I had a winning hand.

I exit the casino floor as a TV blares early-morning news. An anchor announces urgently to the camera, "World-famous singer Haley Banks checked in to the world's most expensive rehab last month…"

I roll my eyes as I pass. Not bothering to listen to the rest.

Typical. I catch bad guys. But my big sister, Haley, is the one who makes headlines.

CHAPTER TWO

CARA

Through the lobby window of the Clinic, I watch for the police car. My manicured hand drops to discreetly rub where my designer heel catches.

Outside, the Pacific Northwest morning is the same as yesterday and the day before. Our oceanfront resort lives under an unremitting wash of salt mist. Not freezing, but fresh, dappling everything in a green fuzz of moss and punky shoots of emerald grass. Even the firs look larger and darker here, with low branches trailing lichen garlands and tree bark wrinkled so deep you could fit a fist in the folds.

It's still hard to believe that only a few months ago I was in sunny LA, managing an extremely basic hotel, with no idea that the mysterious cream-colored envelope on my desk was about to change my life. I had opened it to discover a handwritten invitation to a job interview.

The position I was invited to try for was simply stated as "manager," and the facility was described as a "luxury addiction rehabilitation clinic."

Printed plane tickets were included. To an airport I later discovered was midway between Seattle and San Francisco.

There were no other details besides a name. Dr. Alexander Lutz. I'd never heard of him.

It has only crossed my mind recently that another person might have declined Mr. Lutz's understatedly glamorous invitation. Personally, I didn't have a whole heap of options. I wonder if I would have chosen differently if I'd have known what would happen to Haley Banks.

On the lobby window, there's a small streak on the outside of the glass. With the lemony morning sun casting its low light, the smear looks like an outline of a girl's face. Curved chin. Closed eyes.

A blaze of shock memories flicker like wildfire. The dormitory where Haley was found two days ago. Patients clustered around the bed in a white noise of terror and grief. I seem to recall someone was shaking the body. A last-ditch attempt at CPR maybe.

I tap the smeared glass with a glossy fingernail, then lift the bulky radio from a clip on my waist.

"Housekeeping? Could we attend to lobby window three, please?"

A distorted "Yes, ma'am" has me stow the radio. I check my scheduler and return to my desk—a huge polished-wood structure like an upturned boat in the large lobby.

A panel of lights shows the occupation status of various areas in the facility: Spa. Therapy rooms. Treatment suite.

I pick up the phone receiver and begin pressing buttons in rapid succession, working through tasks. Fresh hot towels for the spa. Aromatherapy oils in the treatment suite. We have a sound-healing session this afternoon, and I ensure the correct cleaning schedule for the acoustic cave has been followed.

Plenty of work to be getting on with. I return my attention to the panel. One "occupied" light flared for the first time ever this week. My eyes match it to the corresponding location.

Morgue.

Dark images crowd in. A gurney. Bloodstained surgical gloves. Yesterday, when I came to let the pathologist out, he hadn't yet covered the body. The naked corpse, with its brutal autopsy cuts, had the singer's expensively colored blond hair and the notorious "Heartbreaker" tattoo on her slender, tanned hipbone. But the slack face was empty of that signature blend of charisma and mischief. The girl who'd lit up stages around the world was a nobody. It occurred to me at the time that you don't truly understand what *lifeless* means until you see the remains of a person like Haley Banks.

I check my slim gold wristwatch. Straighten my notepad. Spritz the client-facing side of my desk with lavender-scented spray. Adjust my computer screen. I can't help but feel nervous about what the police might ask.

My mind conjures an imaginary squad car navigating the route I took on my first arrival.

Having risen early, I'd driven the pretty coastal road, taking in all the little towns with their clapboard houses, ice-cream and fishing stores, old-fashioned boardwalks, and poetically named landmarks. Squirrel Cove. Redwood Bay. Thunder Point. Abruptly, the towns ran out.

I made a sharp turn back inland, shedding the sea view for winding fir-lined roads and then a peat dirt track through boggy forest.

It was a long, long drive to nowhere.

Several times I was sure I must have the wrong route. I seemed to be driving away from the coast. But eventually, the road turned back to asphalt, and the world ran out. I was on the rocky edge of a cliff face, with wild ocean crashing beyond.

Perched on the summit was a very large, very grand old house. Victorian, with turrets and fish-scale sidings; magnificent, flawlessly finished, with no indication the squalling ocean weather affected it at all. A high metal fence sealed it from the road, with a discreet brass sign saying, "The Clinic."

Through the car window, I had watched for a long moment, taking it all in. The quiet majesty and gleaming grandeur of the exterior. This was the kind of property I had always dreamed of managing. A picture of perfect luxury, completely removed from the dirt and disorder of the outside world. From the glossy slate tiles of the roof to the high polish of the entry sign, every last inch was impeccable.

I decided right then and there to overlook the strangeness of the invitation.

Whoever this Mr. Lutz was, he knew how to run things right.

An engine sound jolts me out of my thoughts. I glance toward the window. The police are here.

I stand. Smooth my skirt. Adjust where my waistband digs in. As my heels click over the shining lobby, I try not to imagine what the police might ask. Or rather, *who* they might ask about.

Haley Banks was our most famous patient.

Platinum hair, impish blue eyes, and tanned little legs in a denim skirt and cowboy boots. Smiles like butter wouldn't melt. Right from the second I checked her in, I knew she was trouble.

CHAPTER THREE

MEG

I push through a set of doors marked "Staff only" and cross into the backstage world of the casino. It's a warren of ultrasecure corridors with card-accessed areas. The Los Angeles golden-orange dawn is rising in its slow heat. Tiredness is hitting me, along with the throb of my old shoulder injury. I reach for my medication and realize eight hours at the tables has almost worn me out. Two tablets left. I swallow them both without water.

Ahead is a cupboard labeled, "Electricity. Danger. Do Not Open." I stop by it, flash my ID at the hidden sensor, and push it to pass through into the next level. Two more coded doors take me to the inner circle of casino security. A huge room banked by walls of camera screens showing the gaming tables. Green baize, red diamonds and hearts, and black clubs and spades as far as the eye can see.

"Meg!" Harry comes to greet me, loping over with his usual half grin. We work together on casino sting operations, which given our hours means he's basically my best friend. This despite his terrible fashion sense. He dresses like a New York cop on vacation who forgot to swap his boots. The no-nonsense clothes downplay the tall, broad-shouldered frame, thick crop of bouncy curling black

hair and deep-brown eyes. Harry is what I call "stealth cute"—
good-looking but he doesn't know it.

"You did it." He grins, drawing me into a tight hug, then
stepping back and clearing his throat. "We got him!"

"So it was a Saint-Clair man?"

"Yep. One of Saint-Clair's loan sharks. That's the last of 'em.
Revenge is sweet, right?"

I nod. Another wave of tiredness hits, and my mind moves to
the now-empty pack of medication. As I pull off the blond wig and
let my unruly black hair spill free, I notice a stocky, balding man
loitering behind Harry, staring.

"Oh." Harry stands aside. "This is our new camera guy, Randy."

Randy moves forward, pointing incredulously. "I recognize you
from the casino floor. The girl from Ohio, hoping to win big in
LA. You were a redhead." I remember him too. He headed security
on slots.

I extend a hand. "That was last week. Today I was coked-up
Francine from Texas. But my real name is Meg. Welcome to the
secret service."

"Yeah." I can see him still trying to process my total change in
accent and demeanor.

"It's an act I put on for the casino floor," I explain. "Helps flush
out certain types. It's not only hustlers and loan sharks we go after.
Some of our stings are for casino staff. We don't want regular staff
to know too much about us."

He shakes my hand limply. "Sure was a good act. So…you're
ex-NYPD like Harry?"

"Nope."

"Meggy always winds up sounding like the last person she
talks to," fills in Harry. "It's a thing she does." He looks at me.

"Right now she sounds like me. In actual fact, she's Hollywood royalty."

I fix him with a warning glance and he winks, unapologetic.

"Can't believe I had no idea what went on up here," says Randy, oblivious to my steely-eyed glare at Harry.

"We got the same resources as an undercover police operation," I agree. "Except most of us have records." I flash him a smile. "Apart from Harry. He got unlucky. Someone on the force realized his family had mob connections."

"It was news to me too," growls Harry, who never likes to be reminded of his unfair dismissal. "Least this joint serves better coffee."

I cross the floor to a series of whiteboards showing which operative is on which detail.

My name isn't there.

My eyes track back and forth. "I thought I was on Pit 5 tomorrow?" I turn to Harry. He shrugs.

"Boss is in his office. Ask him."

"Must be a mistake," I decide, heading from the room. But I have a bad feeling about this.

My shoulder is killing me. Distractedly, I pull out my phone, checking if my dealer has dropped my oxycodone already.

There's a message.

Oxy will be there in 20 min. You can pay me later.

I fire a quick text back.

Think I'm stupid enough to owe a drug dealer? I'll leave you cash.

I'm about to close my screen when I notice a slew of earlier messages.

They arrived almost two days ago, in the middle of the night. Must have missed them as I was starting my epic twenty-hour shift.

The screen shows a run of text messages all from the same person.

Haley: Call me.
Haley: Call me NOW.
Haley: I have to speak with you NOW.
Haley: Call me.

I roll my eyes. My big sis likely did a forgiveness therapy session and wants to reach out. Either that or she's mixed my number up with her dealer.

Since she sent the texts almost a day ago and has now gone silent, I guess she found someone to supply her drama.

I consider replying. Don't know what to write.

Probably not a good idea to rile her up again.

Pushing the phone back in my pocket, I head to my boss's office.

CHAPTER FOUR

CARA

The police have parked at an untidy angle on the deep-green lawn. I trot out to greet them, pausing to straighten a fan of magazines in the lobby as I pass.

I'm fast at navigating the complicated access system for the exterior gate. But opening the gigantic wooden door is usually a two-man job. I manage it the best I can and head into the courtyard. Walking past the tall fence are a man and a woman in uniform. Both wear trooper hats, and the woman has an ill-advised shoulder-length cut to her thick, curly brown hair that sends it projecting almost horizontally from the wide brim.

The man has piercing eyes, the biggest graying mustache I've seen outside a Wyatt Earp movie, and a way of standing with his thumbs in his belt loops, feet pointing outward. I can picture him on his downtime in a flannel shirt and trapper's cap with a can of beer in one hand, fishing rod in the other.

"Good day to you, ma'am." He tips his hat. "You're Cara? The manager here?"

"Manager, housekeeper, butler, accountant." I smile at him. "Plenty to do."

"Can't get the staff somewhere so remote?" he suggests.

"We keep hire numbers small to protect the privacy of our guests. You're Police Chief Hanson?" I supply.

"Correct." His giant mustache jumps in agreement. "And this is Officer Meyers." He talks slowly, moves slowly, like a mountain growing moss.

Meyers is short, squat, and beaming, with a bulky flak vest and enormous sunny smile of untidily applied pink lipstick. If the ever-present mist could be chased away by sheer ebullience and a hasty slick of Maybelline, she would be the woman to do it.

My mom always told me, there's no excuse for a plain woman. Taught me to contour my long nose, fill in my narrow brows, shade the blue eyes that are my best feature. Meyers is like a lesson in how not to use makeup. Or fix hair. I touch my own honey-blond highlights, wondering at the fright wig beneath her hat.

It's only as she closes in that I realize the flak jacket around her chest is a sling.

With a baby inside.

What the...?

I unintentionally take a step back.

"Don't worry about him," Meyers says, smiling and registering my surprise. "He's sleeping. My oldest got his thumb caught in a raccoon snare, and it was all hands on deck."

Explains the bad haircut and the milk stain on her shoulder.

"Nothing for it but to bring the little guy for a ride-along," supplies Hanson, in a noncommittal tone that makes me wonder if he's entirely on board.

Hanson moves to help me open the door, and I realize I must look pretty silly to these outdoorsy, baby-wearing folk, in my high-shouldered dress, pin-sharp makeup, and Marilyn Monroe styled waves. Teetering in designer shoes as I yank the handle with French-manicured nails.

"Thanks." We lever back the gate, me standing awkwardly to one side. "I hope the drive over wasn't too long."

Hanson considers this. "Glad we're here, I'll say that much," he decides. "Meyers and I, we had something of a set-to in the car, finding the route. Fought like an old married couple."

I'm never quite sure how to deal with admissions of this nature. My eyes dart back and forth at them uncertainly. Moments like this, I wonder how it feels just saying whatever's on your mind.

"GPS says you don't exist," fills in Meyers, with a sideways glance that suggests the animosity on her part is not entirely dispelled.

I nod. "Dr. Lutz requested the address be removed from mapping systems."

A jolt of uncertainty hits me as I question whether this is legal, but Hanson makes no further comment. Maybe because Meyers is cutting him an I-told-you-so glance.

I walk them through the next tall gate and finally through the interior oak doors.

"Sierra Johnson is a patient here. Did the newspapers get that right?"

"We don't disclose the names of our patients," I say tightly.

"My daughter owns every last one of her band's albums," says Meyers. "Won't stop singing that one... What's that one?"

I give her a politely noncommittal smile.

"Quite the security system," adds Hanson, taking in the wider setup. "What do we have? Double entry. Fingerprint access. Cameras. And did I spy an electric fence outside?"

"Yes," I say. "Dr. Lutz is careful to use the very best. On account of our famous guests."

There's an awkward pause.

Because the failure of Dr. Lutz's comprehensive security is why the police are here.

For all the processes and checks, something has gone badly wrong. The famous singer Haley Banks—the one who always struck me as a drama queen—got the override code somehow.

She was a lot smarter than she seemed, because she found the medication room without being seen. It's incredibly sad, not to mention disruptive for the other patients. Privately, I have real concerns about their ongoing recovery.

CHAPTER FIVE

MEG

The door to Sol's office is a very basic security model that I know for a fact will be modified, since the boss is paranoid with good reason.

I push it open without knocking. Inside is a mix of plush chair and plain desk, latest computer and stained coffee cup with "World's Best Dad" emblazoned across it. The office is never quite neat, as though a world of chaos is only inches from spilling out.

Sol gives a tired smile when he sees me. He's showing his age now.

"Hey, Meg." His tone says it all. He raises his hands before I can speak. "Yeah. I moved you. You'll have to survive on comps that aren't lobster."

"Don't give me that bullshit, Sol. What's going on? You got Corinne's name on there. *Corinne.* She can work a small-town hustler act, but she's never going to make it on the big tables."

Sol meets my eye. "She knows when to fold."

"What?" I'm completely thrown for a second—until I remember. I throw my hands up in frustration.

"*That* game? C'mon! I handed you Saint-Clair's last loan shark. The guy before was an asshole."

"And you should know enough not to let that rile you. You were tilting like fucking crazy."

Tilt. It's a poker term meaning you're out of control of your emotions. The insult must show in my face, because Sol's hard expression loosens.

"Meg. Losses happen. Even to our best players." He inclines his head to show I'm included in the definition. "But that guy was practically dancing on the table, begging you to call. And you served him up thousands of dollars on a silver platter. We have to pay that out, Meg."

"I know, I know."

"*Do* you?" He looks fierce. "Even before the Saint-Clair case, when have you *ever* folded a hand, Meg?"

A flash of anger. "I fold all the time!"

He waves an annoyed hand. "I don't mean in the shallows. I mean when it matters."

I swallow.

"You still living in that hotel?" he asks.

"It's a serviced apartment."

"Anyplace got a breakfast buffet, that's a hotel. We pay you enough to get your own place, right?"

"Sure, you pay me plenty."

"OK. 'Cause you know that's important to me. I like to take care of my best staff."

"I'm good. Really."

He shrugs, perplexed as ever by anyone's choice to live alone, when his family have inhabited the same block in LA since two generations before he was born.

"I just wonder if you're OK all alone there, Meg."

I'm caught off guard. "I... Yeah. Sure. I got new pills."

"Your bar spend is double any other undercover."

I try for a winning smile. "That's why you hired me. Bad guys drink to keep up with me."

"I hired you because you're the best poker player I've ever seen. Look. Meg. I'm no doctor, but even I know pills and fifteen shots of JD don't mix."

I flush, ready to defend myself, but he stands and walks over to me, placing a paternal hand on my arm. "What happened to you with Saint-Clair's men in the warehouse was fucked up. No shame if you're not over it."

"Give me a break, Sol. That was almost a year ago!" Without me meaning to, my hand reaches for my injured shoulder. Sol's eyes follow the movement.

"Yeah. Well. A few of our guys are still messed up about that and they didn't even… They didn't go through half what you did." He nods, massages the bridge of his nose. "I heard you didn't take up our offer of therapy."

I hunch my shoulders in a shrug. "My mom was an actress, Sol. She dragged me and my sister through every known therapist in LA. All that crying and hugging it out was a lot of fun for them. Never saw the point myself."

He hesitates. "OK, sure. I never understood why rehashing all the bad stuff was a good idea, either."

I nod. "We got the last guy tonight. It's all over."

Sol gives me a long look. "The therapy is there if you want it. OK, Meg? Best money can buy."

I give an earnest expression, knowing I'm never going to take him up on that.

Finally he heaves up a sigh. "You're slipping, Meg. You need to cut down on the booze and pills. Take a couple days off. Get some sleep. I'll call you Friday."

I nod fast, realizing this is a reprieve. Sort of. Unless I shape up, I'm going to lose the best job I ever had. My injured shoulder burns.

As I walk out through the camera room, a radio is blaring.

"Troubled singer Haley Banks checked in to a luxury rehab center last month," begins the announcer. "The platinum-selling megastar has struggled with addiction…"

Typical. No matter how hard my day is, big sister Haley is frontline news.

I shoot out a hand and kill the sound as I blaze past. "Can people just do their jobs instead of listening to celebrity shit?" I demand. I know I'm being an asshole, but I don't care.

"Sheesh, Meg. Who yanked your chain?" says Harry.

I ignore him, and as soon as I'm out of sight, I pull out my phone and drop a text.

Coming to collect oxy. Usual place?

CHAPTER SIX

CARA

I pass the police through the secure vestibule and toward the main lobby.

"This was a prison back in the day?" asks Meyers.

"That's right," I say. "Prisoners were brought by tall ship. There were two hundred small cells, but when the beaver trade collapsed, the prison was left derelict."

"Not derelict anymore," says Meyers meaningfully.

"No," I say proudly. "Dr. Lutz restored every square inch. You'll see inside. It's very impressive."

"Dr. Lutz. That's the man we're here to see?" asks Hanson.

"Yes. He's the owner."

They troop dutifully behind me as we enter the lobby. Inside is an explosion of carved wood. The effect reaches triple height, with a grand central staircase, sweeping curved banisters, and elaborately tooled balustrades and pillars.

"I guess small wasn't in fashion, back in the day," observes Hanson dryly.

"The lobby was the old governor's house," I explain.

"This whole house. This is the lobby?" Hanson asks.

"That's right," I say proudly. "The Clinic is a very large facility."

Meyers moves from foot to foot, rocking the baby, craning her neck up at the mahogany flourishes in a way that pushes her crazed sideways hair out at an even more bizarre angle. Her eyes follow the intricate dark-teak cornucopias of fruit, laurel wreaths, swags, and bows on the walls and the pitched ceiling.

"I can maybe make a little makeshift crib with towels?" I suggest. "Dr. Lutz will be here soon."

"No need," Meyers says cheerfully. "He'll only wake up if I set him down." Right when I thought her smile couldn't get any wider, she proves me wrong. "First baby, you watch 'em while they sleep. By the fourth, you pay 'em the same mind as a bag of groceries."

I try for a smile, feeling a little sorry for the groceries-baby, wondering how Dr. Lutz will respond to the newborn. I check my pager nervously.

"You been working here long?" Meyers asks conversationally.

"A few months," I admit. "It's been a steep learning curve."

"You come down from Seattle?"

"I grew up in Maine," I reply, faintly insulted. "Was in San Francisco for a while before moving to a basic hotel in Los Angeles."

I glance at Meyers's face, waiting for the next question. The one about me, my boss, and the viral meme. Surely she uses social media?

"Maine, huh." Meyers beams, jiggling. "Yuh cahn't git theah from heah." She uses the *r*-less native accent I had taken pains to shed.

I smile politely, relieved. *Never heard that one before.*

Mercifully, my pager sounds. I check it.

"Follow me, please," I tell them. "Dr. Lutz is waiting for you inside the Clinic."

We troop together toward the back of the lobby.

The governor's house backs onto a huge glass atrium, enclosing what was once an outside courtyard.

"This part is what connects us to the old prison building," I explain.

Beyond is a heavy-walled building made of hand-cut stone, with a polished concrete floor and soft, warm lighting.

Meyers sniffs the scorched-smelling air as we make multiple turns in the warmly lit corridors.

"Sauna and spa rooms," I explain. "We're passing our Chumash Indian sweat lodge." I point to a sign showing an igloo-shaped clay construction. "It has lemongrass-infused steam for inhaling and healing herbs and mud for your skin." In my nervousness, I've switched into tour-guide mode.

We reached the breakout area where Dr. Lutz asked us to meet him. Moroccan-style low seating and lamps.

A potted plant near one of the doors is growing at an odd angle. I adjust it so the leaves spread more tidily, then check my watch.

"Dr. Lutz will be here shortly," I say, wondering where he could be. Dr. Lutz is never late.

"You worked in fancy hotels before?"

"I've been lucky enough to work at some luxurious facilities," I say. "I got on the Beaumont Hotels fast track."

My voice can't help but betray my pride. Even Hanson and Meyers will have heard of the Beaumont Group.

Meyers's mouth pinches. "Fast track, but they put you in charge of a basic hotel in LA?"

I hesitate. "I imagine you've seen my face on social media," I say with as much dignity as I can muster.

Meyers shakes her head slowly. "Nope," she says. "Can't say we caught that one down here. Did we, Hanson?"

"We don't do much in the way of twittering and whatnot," confirms Hanson in his slow, rumbling voice.

"Cara is far too modest to tell you herself." A friendly voice breaks loudly into our conversation. "But we were incredibly lucky to steal her away."

We all turn to see Dr. Lutz has made an entrance from a direction I wasn't expecting.

Meyers stares with undisguised surprise. Even Hanson's gunmetal-gray eyes tighten slightly above his huge mustache. On first appearance, Dr. Lutz could be an aging Seattle hipster. Full beard, sideways-combed hair, and roomy jeans around a slight paunch.

He wears a clean-pressed T-shirt with the words "Addiction Recovery Warrior" set in angel wings, flip-flops on his leathery feet, and at his wrists, a curation of woven bracelets. His Swiss accent, however, is pure old-world European.

"Cara transformed a dingy LA hotel of junkies and hobos into a profitable premises in under a year. Prior to that, she beat ten thousand applicants to make the Beaumont fast track. Her eye for detail is unsurpassed."

I smile gratefully at the interruption. "This is Dr. Lutz," I explain, realizing they must be as surprised by his appearance as I was when we first met.

In answer, Dr. Lutz folds his hands together in prayer and bows, brown eyes twinkling. With his stocky limbs and soft belly, he is a teddy bear of a man.

"*You* are Dr. Lutz?" Hanson's tone delivers what his face doesn't.

"I *am*." Dr. Lutz treats Hanson to a charming smile.

"Owner of…this resort?" confirms Hanson.

"Owner. Designer. Architect. Clinical manager." Dr. Lutz's Swiss inflection is clearer now. "This facility is my life's work." His eyes land on Meyers's baby, sleeping in the sling. There's a pause before he decides to simply ignore this bizarre actuality.

Meyers is sniffing the air. Dr. Lutz has brought with him the spicy scent of tiger eye and Balinese oils.

"My meditation-blend incense," says Dr. Lutz, noticing. "Forgive me. I was deep in mantras when you arrived."

"Dr. Lutz," says Hanson, recovering himself by degrees. He stands belt loops stance. "Do you know why we're here, sir?"

Dr. Lutz is eyeing Hanson. With his heavy boots and outsized salt-and-pepper mustache, the officer looks particularly provincial in contrast to Dr. Lutz's curling beard and slogan shirt.

"I admit I am curious," Dr. Lutz says, pursing his lips and nodding slowly.

There's a pause. Meyers's baby issues a sudden earsplitting shriek. She jiggles back and forth as she and Hanson exchange glances.

"Cases like this, we like to look over the premises," Hanson says finally. "Check things are being done right."

Dr. Lutz is silent, parsing this information. His hands fold again in prayer, this time under his bearded chin. "What is it you should like to see?"

Hanson's face is steady.

"We'd like to see the bed, sir. The one Haley Banks died in."

CHAPTER SEVEN

MEG

I've changed from my work costume into jeans and a black T-shirt. Standard casual wear for a girl who doesn't care about fashion.

The best place for a drugs drop in a casino is the metal amnesty box. No cameras and no security. My guy, Dean, tapes my pills to the bulky box. I approach as usual and slide my hand casually round the back.

Three boxes of oxy. I peel them free, dizzy from the long night's work, lack of food, and shoulder pain. Pop three. Even before they hit my stomach, I feel better.

Casinos never have clocks, but I figure it must be 9:30 a.m. Time for a drink.

I message Harry. Figure he'll want to celebrate Saint-Clair's final demise with me.

Ten minutes later, we're both sitting on barstools. I always liked that the rest of LA are picking up Starbucks while we wind down from our night shift.

"What'll it be?" I ask Harry. "Tequila shot?" I watch his face. He shakes his head, so I smile like it was a joke.

"Coffee. I'm buying."

"Coffee? C'mon, Harry. Have a beer with me. Bud is basically a soft drink. I have that on my cornflakes."

He sighs. "Fine. Two beers."

The drinks arrive. I take a long pull.

"So, what's up with you, Meg?" asks Harry. "Getting Saint-Clair's guy making you nervous?"

My hand jerks, and a puddle of beer forms on the table. "Jeez," I say crossly, jabbing around the spillage with a napkin. "Why does everyone keep going on about that fucking gangster?"

Harry shrugs, his eyebrows rising. "Maybe because you ditched that guy you were crazy about right after it happened?"

He gives me a long, searching look.

"I never said I was crazy about you." But I can't meet his eyes.

"Yeah you did, Meg." He sighs. "Maybe you forgot. Around the time you started working twenty-hour shifts and taking oxy?"

"Wait." I hold my hands up. "You think I take oxy because of some fucking low-rent loan shark?"

He opens his mouth to reply.

"I take oxy because my fucking shoulder hurts, Harry. Nothing to do with Saint-Clair. Nothing." I raise my hand. "Bartender? Could I get a tequila shot over here?"

"If you say so." Harry's eyes turn steely. "So what's your excuse for what happened to us, Meg?"

"Jesus. Make that two tequilas." I turn to Harry and let out an exasperated sigh. "For fuck's sake, Harry. Enough already. I told you. I'm not the sort of girl you take to dinner."

"I don't buy that."

"You know the work we do. Relationships leave you vulnerable. That's the end of it. At the poker table, all emotions are tilt, right? Good or bad, they affect your play. Relationships are the tilt of life."

"You've started thinking of relationships in poker game terminology?" He looks away toward the nonexistent windows.

"In this job it's better to turn things off," I say. "Feelings and stuff," I add because he looks confused. "It's a gift I learned, growing up in Hollywood." I meant it as a joke, but his expression is pained.

"You know, Meg, sometimes you're kind of a sociopath."

"Because I work damn hard catching bad guys? No one calls James Bond a sociopath."

"They do call him a sociopath. Nowadays at least." Harry lifts his beer and swigs. "And Bond did want to settle down. His wife got killed. By Blofeld."

I down my tequila. "Then I'm one step ahead. No dead husbands."

There's a pause. "Is that honestly what you think?" says Harry quietly. "You'd put me in danger?"

"Do you honestly think I wouldn't?" I tip back the second shot.

"This is the Saint-Clair thing," Harry says. "I knew it."

"Could we drop it? Please?"

He spreads his hands. "Look, all I'm saying is you've been different since it happened."

I wouldn't take this from anyone else. But there *have* been differences, haven't there?

I roll my beer glass thoughtfully. We sit in silence for a moment.

"Harry. Do you ever have nightmares?"

"Sure, I have this dream about a woman. She's pretty unique, and I think we could be really something. But she keeps jerking me around."

"Ha-ha."

I frown at the polished bar and pick up a beer coaster emblazoned with a loud advertisement for Lady Luck Slots.

Harry takes a pull of his beer and fixes me with a look I sometimes like and sometimes don't. He sees too much.

"You not sleeping good, Meg?"

I shred the edges of the cardboard coaster.

"Not so much." I'm relieved at not having to explain.

Suddenly, I don't want to go home.

"Sure you don't want a tequila?" I ask Harry.

He looks weary. "Another morning. You want a ride?"

"I might stick around here."

He gives me a long look.

"Stay," I tell him.

He shakes his head slowly. "I wouldn't be doing you any good."

Tequila on an empty stomach is hitting me now. "Stay and drink with me. We'll have fun." I try for a wink but the tequila is mismatching my reflexes.

Harry tilts his head to one side, and his mouth twists. There's a loaded silence. "I'll catch you later."

"Plenty of guys in this bar who'd be happy to join me," I tell him petulantly.

He leans in and kisses me slowly on the cheek. I feel the hairs on my neck stand on end.

"Sometimes it's the hands you don't play that win you the game." He says it quietly into my ear, then stands to leave.

I watch him walk away, still hoping he'll turn around. He doesn't. The footage of Harry leaving skips. One minute he's there, then he's gone.

I catch my face reflected back in the shiny steel bar top. Sad green eyes with makeup smudged underneath, strands of dark hair sticking to the sweat on my face.

I try to focus. My eyes settle on a little TV high up in the corner of a bar. There's a familiar face on it.

Haley.

You forget how pretty Haley is until you see a good shot of her like this.

There's something wrong with that, I realize slowly. Haley is usually televised staggering out of limos. Throwing drinks at the Grammys. This is a still of her smiling face. A cold feeling pools in my stomach. A knowing that doesn't quite connect with my mind.

This is the kind of picture you show when something bad has happened.

My eyes bring the written headline into focus.

COUNTRY SINGER HALEY BANKS DIES IN REHAB, AGE 27

CHAPTER EIGHT

CARA

Dr. Lutz is smiling at the police officers in polite confusion. He strokes his curling beard, woven bracelets dropping down his aging wrist.

"You'd like to see the bed where Haley Banks was found?" he asks finally, tilting his head. "But a verdict of suicide has already been issued."

Hanson looks at Meyers, then nods slowly. "Well, sir. Here's the thing. In all my years of policing, I have never known an autopsy to happen so quickly. You have a mortuary on-site? Correct?"

"Sadly, this is standard in rehab," replies Dr. Lutz, nodding in an understanding way as if Hanson had shared a personal truth. "Rehabilitation is dangerous. As is drug addiction. Perhaps we moved a little faster than you felt comfortable with."

I notice Hanson's mustache curl inward.

"Oh, that is true enough," Hanson agrees without emotion, glancing at Meyers. "We certainly have our own pace out here. Isn't that right, Meyers?"

"We sure *do*," Meyers treats us to an unevenly lipsticked grin.

"Least...three, four days for an autopsy. Right?" confirms Hanson.

Meyers jiggles the baby. "I've known it take up to seven," she says.

"Right," Hanson says. "I'm sure you city folk find us all very backward. But slow and steady wins the race. We'd like to check the scene of death. If you don't mind."

Dr. Lutz's mouth flicks up in a smile.

For a moment I expect him to refuse.

"Of course," he says. "Please follow me."

Without pausing for confirmation, Dr. Lutz turns on his flip-flopped foot and heads for the spa. We follow behind in his trail of spicy incense.

The back of Dr. Lutz's shirt reads: "One Day at a Time."

"You like my building?" Dr. Lutz asks the police, beaming at them encouragingly as we take a different route from the one we came in by.

"It's...very impressive, sir," begins Hanson in his low voice.

"As you will see, the Clinic is one of the largest of its kind," continues Dr. Lutz, gratified. "I left Switzerland in my twenties and spent a decade in Indian drug treatment facilities. Ever since, I have dreamed of a world-class facility. Somewhere that can offer the holistic treatments of the East, with the progressive science of the West. And I have done it. Here. My masterpiece."

He fans out his hands as if expecting applause.

"I'm amazed you folk can find your way around," Meyers says, eyeing the maze of passages spun out in every direction.

"This part was built by convicts using rocks from the coast," Dr. Lutz explains, running a loving hand over the refurbished walls. "Many died during construction. Each stone was hand polished during the renovation, at a cost of one million dollars."

Hanson's giant mustache twists a few degrees.

"Takes a lot of money to cure addiction, huh?" he observes neutrally.

Dr. Lutz hesitates. "Yes," he says. "If only the government would realize how much it takes to help addicts," he adds sadly.

"Guess a place like this is outside the public purse," says Meyers.

"They said it would take two years to renovate and complete," agrees Dr. Lutz proudly. "I said, with my high standards, it would take three. In the end it took four." He holds up triumphant fingers and giggles, apparently delighted with this evidence of his unreasonableness.

Dr. Lutz's flip-flops are slapping the polished concrete, taking us quickly toward the dormitory. But Hanson slows to a sudden halt outside a door cordoned off by warning tape.

"This is Haley's room?"

"You are very observant," Dr. Lutz says.

"But she didn't die here, right?" Meyers cocks her head to one side, smiling pleasantly.

"Correct." Dr. Lutz's tone is icy.

"That's the part we wanted clarification on," says Hanson. He flips slowly through a pad of neat handwriting. Dr. Lutz eyes the unhurried pace with distaste.

"Security footage shows Miss Banks breaking into a medication room and stealing a quantity of medical-grade heroin around 1:00 a.m., correct?"

"You have the footage," confirms Dr. Lutz.

"Any reason a rehab facility would keep heroin on the premises?"

"This, again, is standard," Dr. Lutz says. "Rehabs carry FDA-approved pharmaceuticals for all eventualities. Detox can be life threatening."

Hanson nods. "And after raiding the medication room, Haley next went to the spa." Hanson looks at me.

"Right." I nod slowly. "There's a camera outside the spa. You can see Haley's face clearly. She entered in the early hours of the morning. Right after leaving the medication room."

"Any thoughts on why she might have done that, ma'am?"

"I suppose…she had shot up medical-grade heroin in the medication room. Decided the spa was a good place to enjoy the effects."

Hanson nods. "But Haley didn't die in the spa? Or in her room. She was found dead in a shared dormitory room."

Dr. Lutz makes a small sound of frustration. "We have already explained this at length. Several times."

"Apologies, sir," Hanson replies unapologetically. "I want to be sure I understand. Haley had her own room. Here." He points. "While others shared?"

"Rehabs maximize group camaraderie to aid recovery," Dr. Lutz explains. "Shared bedrooms, bathrooms, therapy sessions. But… Ms. Banks was very insistent about having a room and bathroom to herself."

The baby issues another high-pitched yelp, and Meyers adopts a wide-legged stance, lunging back and forth like a baseball player fixing to swing.

"Shall we go to the shared dormitory now?" suggests Hanson.

Dr. Lutz checks his watch pointedly. "It's this way," he says.

"*Female* dormitory, right?" Meyers glances at me.

It takes me a beat to catch up to his meaning.

"Yes," I reply hastily. "Patients weren't permitted in opposite-sex dormitories."

Meyers wrinkles her glossy pink mouth, taking her cue and turning to Dr. Lutz.

"Probably I'm not getting enough sleep these days," she says, rocking the sling. "Because I still can't make sense of why Haley Banks decides, after the spa, not to return to her own private bedroom. She went to where *other* people are." Meyers looks at me, polite, questioning, one hand on her baby's pink head. "Almost as if she's trying to get help."

CHAPTER NINE

CARA

The police are inside the female dormitory, standing over the bed where Haley was found.

"Fancy room," observes Meyers, glancing around the artfully contrasted taupes and greens. "King beds."

"We offer the same standard as a luxury hotel," I explain. "Egyptian cotton sheets, double-depth mattress, everything is natural materials, and there's a pillow menu for guests to select their own preference. Rice husk, feather, and so forth."

Meyers's eyebrows rise fractionally. I'm guessing her own pillows are Walmart's finest.

"Three different interior designers—from New York, Singapore, and London—conceptualized the decor," says Dr. Lutz. "They took inspiration from the luxury coastal location. Belowdecks in a luxury yacht is the broad theme."

Meyers eyes a brass light hanging on a burlap rope. Hanson is making slow, careful notes with a stubby pencil. Dr. Lutz is watching with narrow-eyed annoyance.

"You don't prefer a pen?" suggests Dr. Lutz.

Hanson's mustache rises and falls, but he doesn't look up, his gray eyes locked on the slow script taking shape on the page.

"A pen leaked in his pocket once," Meyers supplies. "He never got over it." She turns to me.

"Patients still sleep here?" she asks.

I hesitate.

"Better for them not to be moved," says Dr. Lutz.

"And…a patient named Sierra found Haley's body. Round about 6:00 a.m.?" continues Meyers.

"Correct," Dr. Lutz says. His eyes close. "Extremely regrettable."

"By patient, we're talking about *the* Sierra Johnson here? Sweet little girl band singer, Audrey Hepburn eyebrows? Flips out after a vodka martini?"

I stare at her. Is Meyers this unprofessional? Or is she deploying some kind of quirky interview technique? Judging by her haircut, it could be either.

"I can't confirm that," Dr. Lutz says, smiling slightly.

Hanson frowns deeper. "Meyers. You read the gossip columns. Isn't Sierra Johnson archenemies with Haley Banks?" He glances across for confirmation. "What is it they say? Cat fight?"

The baby sneezes. "Diva battle," fills in Meyers, patting its head.

Hanson snaps his fingers. "Diva battle." His mustache jerks up then down again. "Meyers. Can you imagine those two crammed in a tight space together?"

Meyers is shaking her head. "No, sir, I cannot. Haley Banks and Sierra Johnson. Hoo-eey."

"You shouldn't believe everything you read," Dr. Lutz says.

Hanson returns to his notepad. "So…who else shared this dormitory?"

"We can't tell you that." Dr. Lutz stands a little firmer in his flip-flops. "Our clients are extremely well known. They rely on us for discretion."

"All five?" Meyers tilts her head to look out the door. "That's the male dorm. Right over there?"

"Yes," I say. "They heard Sierra's screams. Came running to help. The alarm was sounded. Then Max and I…"

"Wait. Who is Max?"

"Max is the therapist here," I explain. "He managed to calm all the guests down while I contacted the police. He's the first person the police spoke to."

Hanson resumes his slow page turning.

"So he is," he says. "Max Reynolds." He whistles. "Lots of letters after his name."

"Our star psychologist," says Dr. Lutz, pulling at his curling beard. "Max's work on addiction is award winning."

"An award-winning psychologist and a manager from Beaumont Hotel Group," Hanson observes in his deep, ruminating tone. "I have to commend your recruitment strategy, Dr. Lutz."

Dr. Lutz puts his hands together in a praying gesture and bows.

Hanson's mustache flicks up and down in what might be a polite smile. "Would you be kind enough to take us to the medication room now, please?"

"I'm afraid that is where our help for you must end." Dr. Lutz's brow crinkles in sorrow. "Cause of death has been issued. Circumstances are not suspicious. I have no reason to risk upsetting my guests further."

There's a long, loaded pause as the shock of the refusal reverberates.

"Cause of death hasn't yet been written up," Hanson says. "You house vulnerable people here, sir. We would like to confirm they're not being placed at risk."

"Which is exactly why I must decline to let you see the medication room," Dr. Lutz says. "Your presence would be disruptive." He smiles a soft teddy-bear smile. "If you believe you can get a warrant, then by all means. Come back. Until that unlikely occurrence, I wish you good day, Chief Hanson."

CHAPTER TEN

MEG

"Meg? Meg?"

A familiar voice is speaking into my ear. I drag myself through a sludge of exhaustion and try to focus.

"OK, Meg. Time to wake up."

"What time is it?" I think I say it aloud, though I can't be certain. Someone answers, but the words fall between the gaps in my concentration.

Things come into focus. I'm in bed. Harry is here.

"Oh, hello." I smile. "Look who decided to stay the night." I'm relieved to know I can still work the charm when it matters.

Harry frowns. "What the hell are you talking about, Meg? I took you home from the bar. You tried to throw a chair at a TV. You need to tell me what boxing gym you use, by the way. That left hook is deadly. I had to use a police hold."

"You didn't sleep over?" I'm piecing things together too slowly. He's fully dressed, I realize now.

"I slept on the couch. After I took you back to your show home." He throws out a hand to indicate my serviced apartment with its immaculate wooden floors and sparse collection of muted furnishings. "Lots of real personal touches here, Meg. Now I know why you never invited me back to your apartment. Those actual people in the photo frames, or did you keep the ones they came with?" He points to pictures. A glamorous woman mugging for the camera. Two elfin-faced girls. One blond, one dark-haired.

"That's my mom as an actress. And that's me and Haley as little kids."

His face darkens. "You seriously don't remember yesterday?"

I try to think, but there are no images. Only a sense of something bad. A hard nugget of pain and regret is nestled far back in my head like an unexploded bomb. I retreat from it fast, in case it explodes.

"I came looking for you when I heard about your sister. I figure that's what you're throwing chairs about, right?"

Haley.

It hits me right in the solar plexus. A winding shot. Like all the air has been sucked out of my body. Because I'd forgotten. Completely forgotten. It's hard to say if it's worse remembering or being the kind of person who could forget.

"Meg?"

I lean forward, trying to breathe. "Just. Oh my God."

And there it is. The explosion. There's a ringing in my ears. A deafening, overwhelming pain. Because it can't be true. Yesterday the world had Haley in it. Today it doesn't.

Haley can't have left me. Not again.

I press both hands to my face. "Harry, is my purse in here?"

"You looking for your pills by any chance?"

A number of hard emotions ricochet through me. Mostly betrayal.

"You been checking up on me, Harry?"

"I went into your bachelor kitchen to fetch you some water. By the way, those fancy cupboards of yours? You're supposed to put food inside."

"If you were getting water, why were you opening my cupboards?"

"Jesus, Meg. I thought I'd help you out and take the trash, OK? I knew you took Oxy. But that's a lot of empty boxes. I couldn't exactly miss them. Oxy's really addictive." He looks at me meaningfully.

"Yeah, that's why they only prescribe small quantities now," I say defensively.

"Prescribe? I might be a lapsed detective, Meg, but even a dumb civilian like me knows that pharmacies don't package up ten boxes with duct tape."

"Cut it out, Harry. This isn't the time."

He frowns, then switches subjects. "By the way, some feral cat got into your kitchen from the stairwell, and I think you're going to need pest control to get it out." Harry holds up an arm striped with savage claw marks.

It takes me a second to process. "The striped cat? That's Tequila. She's got trust issues."

"She's *your* cat? That thing is fifty percent teeth and claw."

"She's not mine, but no one else can deal with the aggression and fleas."

My phone rings. Like a person in a trance, I pick it up.

There are forty-two missed calls and texts.

Mom. Dad. Unknown numbers.

The caller is "Mommy Dearest." Haley and I gave her that nickname when we were kids, and it stuck.

I click to kill the call. There's no way I can deal with Mom right now.

Not without Haley.

The thought brings acute, painful misery. To distract myself, I take the chance to scroll through the news on my phone. Looks like the press is much kinder to Haley in death than they were in life. Headlines read:

HALEY BANKS SUICIDE

HALEY BANKS, HEROIN OVERDOSE

HALEY BANKS DIES SHOOTING UP HEROIN

Wait… Heroin overdose?

"Did your mom call?"

I nod. "Yeah. Mom will already be dining out on the funeral plans. Gaudy show of her most obnoxious friends, dressed to the nines, all competing to make the most dramatic show of grief."

Harry is one of the few people who I've told about my fucked-up family, since he has an even more fucked-up family himself.

"Jesus." Harry hops aside as Tequila slinks in and aims a swipe at his legs.

She jumps onto the bed, eyeing him murderously. I stroke her matted fur. Tequila is loyal. She knows when something's wrong.

"Meg," Harry says, eyeing Tequila nervously. "If there's anything I can do…"

"There is," I tell him. There's a core of clarity swirling in the boiling mess of it all. "Do you still have connections to the NYPD?"

Harry shrugs, confused. "Sure. Still got a lot of friends back there. We keep in touch."

For some reason I don't like the idea of Harry having friends I don't know about. I shelve the feeling under "makes no sense."

"Good enough friends to look something up for you?"

"Yeah. maybe. Why?"

"Because Haley didn't kill herself," I tell him. "She was murdered."

CHAPTER ELEVEN

MEG

Harry has insisted I eat something. Which means I reluctantly have to let him witness my motel buffet meals. Breakfast is twenty-four hours.

"Haley would never have injected heroin," I tell Harry as we board the shaking little elevator. Tequila flits in quickly behind, winding herself around my legs. There's a weird smell as the doors close, and I realize someone has spilled something sweet and sticky. I catch myself reflected in the doors. I look awful. My green eyes are completely bloodshot and my dark hair is limp. I'm wearing a large T-shirt I don't recognize that makes my boxing-honed arms look too skinny.

"That's quite a leap to get murder from," Harry points out. "Haley was an addict, Meg," he adds in that voice people use when they think you're acting crazy. He puts a hand on my shoulder. "You're in shock. I know you didn't have the greatest relationship with your sister, but…"

The elevator doors jerk open. "We would have patched things up," I say, picking up Tequila and heading into the restaurant. "We always did. Eventually."

"Whoa." Harry is taking in the selection of food laid out on the hot station.

"I know, right?" I locate the server. "Hey! Dwayne? I'm bringing my buddy, OK?" I hold up a twenty and slip it into his tip jar.

"Whatever you say, Meg."

"This is…quite something," Harry says, slowly taking a plate as I clutch Tequila under one arm and heap potatoes and crispy bacon. "Kind of full-on and basic at the same time." He's looking at a tray of suspiciously pink baloney. "I was going to ask how you got them to let your cat in here, but seeing the food kind of answers that question."

I'm heading for the Bloody Mary and mimosa station.

Harry loads a few spoons of egg and arrives behind me.

"Really, Meg? Vodka, for breakfast?"

"My sister just died." I add more juice since he's watching.

We take a seat and I put my plate down fast before Harry notices my early-morning shakes. I put meat on a saucer for Tequila, and she gobbles it. Take a slug of my drink and wish I'd added more vodka. A few more gulps and the shakes subside.

The burn in my stomach feels good for about ten seconds. Then my body reacts.

"You OK, Meg?" Harry leans forward.

"Yeah. Give me a second." I wait for the nausea to pass. "I'm good. Nausea. That sometimes happens with the first one."

"The first one? Meg, since when did you start chugging vodka with your morning eggs?"

"Could you give me a small break? It's basically tomato juice. Everyone here does it."

"These people are on vacation."

"Not all of them." I swallow. The vodka is helping me think. "The place Haley checked into is a luxury rehab. They trade on their reputation. Haley rubs everyone up the wrong way. She had about three celebrity feuds going on. What if someone got mad enough to kill her and they covered it up?"

"I guess it's possible. Wouldn't be the first time something got covered up in a drug rehab facility. They're a law to themselves, lots of them. Question is, does it matter? You're not going to bring your sister back."

One of the things I like most about Harry is he tells the truth. But today I'm not so sure about that quality.

"Something about Haley's death stinks, Harry."

"Why don't you go to her rehab and investigate? Take some time off from the booze and pills. Turn over all that crazy stuff you got going on up here." He taps his head.

"I'm serious, Harry. Do you think Saint-Clair could have sent someone in to get to my sister?"

Harry shakes his head. "You're being paranoid. Saint-Clair was arrested half a year ago."

"Am I? He still has influence. Said he'd come after my family, remember?"

Harry shrugs. "It's what gangsters say. At my old cop precinct, every time some guy threatened your family, you dropped a dollar in the office jar. It used to pay for our Christmas party." He sighs. "Meg, when someone dies suddenly, it's a shock. You hadn't spoken to your sister in a long time..."

I shake my head "It's more complicated than that. I just... I *know* she wouldn't leave me like that. Without even saying goodbye."

Like she did the first time.

"Verdict of suicide was already issued," says Harry. "If anything fishy was going on, the pathologist would likely have found it."

"Likely." I seize on the word. "Could we take a look at the autopsy report?" I feel animated by the thought.

"Generally, they only issue the cause of death. If you want the full pathology report, you got to apply to the coroner's office. Takes a few days to…" Harry notices how I'm looking at him and stops talking. "Let me make a few calls."

"Thanks," I breathe out. "Thanks, Harry."

"I can't promise anything." He raises a warning finger, then takes out his phone and presses buttons. A few seconds pass while his call connects. My hand slides to the pills in my pocket.

"Hey, Zack?" Harry is talking into his phone. "I got a favor to ask, buddy." Pause. "For a friend of mine." Harry's eyes slide to me. "Yeah. That girl." He smiles at me, then stands, still talking, walking out of the restaurant.

I push a couple of oxy in my mouth and walk over to top up my vodka. My head hurts. My body hurts. I have the worst feeling in my brain. Like an aching mental nausea.

My phone rings, and I kill the call when I see Mommy Dearest flash up. Seconds later comes the beep of a voicemail landing. Guess I'd better listen. Without enthusiasm, I tap through to my mailbox.

Ten messages. I really should get around to disabling my voicemail.

I prop myself on my elbows, one hand holding my phone, the other on my painful head. The strange robot voicemail voice announces my first message, received two days ago. Nine to go.

"Hey, Meggy." I nearly drop my phone when I hear the familiar voice in my saved messages.

Haley. It's Haley.

"How's it going?" she continues.

Haley *never* leaves messages. She sounds a lot cleaner when we last spoke. But something else too. Excited. Manic, even.

Slowly, I put the phone on the table, breathing hard and holding my injured shoulder. The sound of Haley's voice…alive. My brain won't accept she's dead.

When she next speaks, it comes all breathy. "Listen, Meggy. I think I've messed up this time. Oh God." Her voice chokes in a sob. "I've messed up *really, really badly*."

My skin breaks out in goose bumps. I'm used to hearing Haley screaming, shouting, crying. But this… This sounds different. This time I actually believe her.

"You're the only one who can help me, Meggy," she whispers. "Please. Call me. I need to tell you something about when we were kids. I need to tell you before it's too late."

CHAPTER TWELVE

MEG

When Harry returns from his phone call, he has a thoughtful look on his face.

"What's up?" My Bloody Mary is now mostly vodka and Haley feels more distant. Manageable. Tequila is in my lap. She hisses as Harry nears.

"They're not investigating it as suspicious," he says, eyeballing her. "My guy says it all checks out. Impartial pathologist. Local coroner. Everything was done properly and the verdict was death by misadventure. Heroin overdose. Suspected suicide, but they couldn't be sure."

"They couldn't be sure?" I leap on it.

"That's standard," Harry says. "Scientists almost never give you a straight answer. The cops are sure. And the owner of the place, Dr. Lutz, sounds like a real piece of work. Getting some kind of injunction against police so they can't talk to his celebrity addicts. I tried for a list of current patients to see if anyone has a record, but the confidentiality is bound up like Fort Knox."

"Like the Clinic is hiding something?"

"Or they don't want their rich clients disturbed or publicized." I log this. "OK. What else?"

"Not much. The only people on the floor that night were patients," he says. "No one else came in or out. Police confirmed it."

I'm thinking this rules out Haley's crazy, controlling, cokehead manager, Frank. Last I heard he had somehow became her boyfriend. *Ew.*

I take a breath. "What if I go to that rehab? Check it out?"

"You're joking, right?"

"I actually think you had something. Earlier. I know you weren't serious, but…"

Harry frowns. "OK… What did I miss?"

"I had a voicemail. From Haley."

"Oh, Meg. I'm so sorry, kid."

"It's OK. She left a weird message though. Listen." I play it, watching his face.

"Weird," Harry says as it finishes.

"Yeah… I basically remember nothing from my childhood."

"Did you ever see a therapist for this stuff, Meg?"

"Just stick with me, Harry. I need you as a detective."

Harry hesitates. "OK. Your sister is in rehab. Quitting drugs. Having therapy. It all jogs up some sad memories she wants to share with you right away. Coincidence is all."

"Two coincidences." I hold up my fingers. "Number one, Haley would never inject herself with heroin. Number two, Haley calls me saying she's in trouble. Two coincidences start to look like evidence, right? Isn't that cop logic?"

Harry gives this some thought.

"I *know* Haley didn't kill herself," I press. "You said yourself, cops aren't getting anywhere near the other patients. I could. And I can tell when people are lying. Better than most cops, right?"

"True," concedes Harry. "But it's still the worst undercover I ever heard. You've got no suspects, no motive. Know what I think? I think you want to run away. Your sister called you before she died, and you feel guilty because you never called her back. You're a fighter. It's what I…" He clears his throat. "It's understandable. You want to take action, right? This isn't the way."

"C'mon. This would be good for me, right? I could cut down to prescribed levels."

"Do you even know where the rehab is?"

"Sure. Someplace in the Pacific Northwest with plenty of rain and cold so they can all feel good and miserable, paying megabucks for the privilege while some shaman channels their auras or something. All very Haley." I'm already searching on my phone. "Here."

I hold up the screen.

"Jeez." Harry stares. "It looks like a haunted house or something."

"Not all of it." I scroll through pictures. Spa. Swimming pools. Polished glass and luxury furnishings looking out on to the blue-gray sky.

"Salt cave?" says Harry, reading. "Guess they've got to justify their price." He takes the phone. "'Most prestigious new clinic to hit America.' 'Groundbreaking treatment.' 'Highest success rates of any rehabilitation'…" He looks up at me. "They've been open less than a year," he says. "How could they claim that?"

"That's the cop talking."

"I think I've heard of this place," Harry says. "I'm pretty sure…" He taps on my phone. "It's the new big thing for celebs. Sierra Johnson checked in a few weeks back."

"Should I know who that is?"

"You really don't read the news. Sierra Johnson is the singer who won the TV competition. Major-league girl band. American sweetheart. Professional nice girl. You know the type."

He scrolls on his phone and holds up a news article.

The headline reads: "Sierra's Rehab Shame: Sweet Sierra becomes a MONSTER after two drinks, bandmates reveal."

Sierra stands with two other leggy girl band members. She smiles demurely, chestnut hair caught in a bouncy ponytail, famously thick brows perfectly made up.

"Oh yeah. I know her," I say. "Big voice, big eyebrows. Haley would have hated her," I say, noticing how Sierra stands shyly left of center. "She can actually sing. Plus, I think she's half Puerto Rican. Grew up in a bad neighborhood in LA."

"I don't think you measure people's heritage that way nowadays, Meg."

"What I'm saying is Haley would have killed for that kind of backstory. That whole humble-girl-did-good stuff that Haley's team were always trying to sell, Sierra actually has it."

"You're missing my point," says Harry. "If a famous pop princess is in this clinic right now, how would you even get in?"

"Sol gets us good insurance, right?"

"Meg, you need to quit drinking vodka at breakfast time. This place might accept insurance but it will require a supplemental fee. Probably more than you earn in a year." He relents, seeing my face. "If you want to go to rehab, there are a boatload of great places right here in LA."

I shake my head firmly. "There must be a way into the Clinic," I tell Harry. "It's like a poker game, right?"

"How? How is it like a poker game?"

"There's always a way to get in on a game if you know the right people." The vodka is kicking in for real now. I take another slug.

Harry lets out a puff of air, and I can tell he's holding something back. He's smart. I'll bet he can get me in somehow.

"How about I agree to come off the oxy? Will you help me then?"

He hesitates. "You'll actually give this a try? Do the work?"

I nod.

"All right," he says. "All right, Meg. Here's the thing. Sol would pay your bills to keep you on the team."

"Really?" I had no idea I was worth that much to him.

"Yeah. Just ask."

I take a long, quavering breath. Maybe. Just maybe I'll actually do this.

"Will you feed my cat?" I ask Harry. Doubts are already setting in. How am I going to get to the truth of what happened to my sister without my oxy?

CHAPTER THIRTEEN

CARA

My alarm goes off, and my feet hit the deep pile of the gray carpet. Outside, a fat line of mist sits low on the horizon. Like someone took an eraser and rubbed a cloudy section of white through the center. Pastel-green coast grass at the bottom and a dark line of fir trees at the top.

Since the police left, I've been waking up with the strangest sense that I'm being held prisoner. Completely dumb, I know. I can leave at any time. I have the master code, and I know all the door lock codes. The fact that I *haven't* left the compound in the months since I arrived is only because there's nowhere to go.

When Dr. Lutz first outlined the benefits package and salary, it was dreamlike, really. I had never heard so much money mentioned so casually. The only bad part was vacation leave, which was basically nonexistent. But honestly, what did I need with vacation? I had no relationship, no dependents. It wasn't like I was going to go touring the Oregon coast alone on my downtime. Really, vacation would mean being stuck out here with nothing to do.

I open the wardrobe doors, which are built invisibly into the wall, and slide my rack of clothing. Structured dresses and shining high heels. Splashes of color among the neutral furnishings of my apartment-room-style personal quarters.

Showered and dressed, I head for the catering kitchen. My watch shows 5:15 a.m. No one else will be up for hours.

I enter the kitchen, unclip the heavy door of the large catering fridge, and start rifling for food that's due to go out of date. I start work, loading up a large bag labeled "Soup Kitchen."

There's a basket of raspberries at the back, and I drag it forward.

"Hello, Cara." The familiar voice makes me tilt the container in my hand. Fruit falls to the floor with a red scattergun effect.

Dr. Max. What is Max doing in the kitchen?

Even after several months, I still haven't gotten used to Dr. Max. When we first met, I couldn't figure out why a man in his late thirties dressed like he was in a wartime soap opera. He wore a tweed jacket and trousers that didn't suit his broad shoulders and handsome face. Exacerbated by the neatest clean shave and haircut I'd seen outside a razor commercial. Like a catalog model wearing clothes for regular people. Or a sporty guy trying to look like a nerd. The moment he opened his mouth, it all made sense. He was British.

Even now, the accent gets me. It's so preposterously aristocratic that I never quite know how to respond.

"Let me get that." He takes the empty container from my unresisting hand and stoops to pick up pieces of fruit. "Are you OK?"

"Yes. Thank you, Doctor," I shoot back, defensive. "Why wouldn't I be?"

He rises, basket of bruised fruit in his hand. "Maybe because I said 'hello,' and you leaped about three feet in the air?"

"I wasn't expecting you, is all," I mutter, looking at the floor.

His constant sardonic expression is bothering me. Yes, I'm a klutz. No, I'm not a PhD graduate or whatever he is. But I've got a right to work here, same as him.

"Couldn't sleep?" he suggests.

"I get up at 5:00 a.m.," I explain. "Gives me enough time to do everything that needs to be done."

His eyes settle on the food I've laid out on the counter.

"I wondered who was donating to the soup kitchen. Isn't that logistically tricky? With the distances?"

"I time it to match the weekly delivery truck from Seattle. I used to work with elderly addicts," I add. "Can't stand to see food thrown away that could be doing good."

"I thought you used to work in a hotel in LA."

"Hotel in name only. We had a…colorful cohort of long-term guests." I'm trying to choose my words to describe the drug addicts, dealers, petty criminals, prostitutes, and mentally ill people.

Max's mouth twitches. "How come you ended up there?"

I look up at him. "I think you've probably seen the memes. They went viral." I don't believe that Max is quite as backwater as Hanson and Meyers.

He looks away. "Social media can be very cruel," he says. "Sexist too."

"It was a great weight-loss tool for me," I say, twisting my mouth ironically. I'm trying not to call to mind the characterization of myself as a chubby, plain-faced man-eater. "I didn't know he was married," I blurt out. "And I wasn't… It didn't matter to me that he owned a hotel group."

Max colors. "Your past is in the past," he adds, looking awkward.

"You couldn't sleep?" I ask, to change the subject.

"No." He shakes his head. "Thoughts keep going 'round.

Haley." Max heaves up a long sigh. "I really felt we were making progress. It was…uncomfortable for her. But we were getting to the heart of her trauma. Things happened to Haley that she had blacked out. They were coming to the surface."

I'd like to ask what kind of things, but that doesn't seem professional.

"Maybe…that trauma was too much for her to bear?" I suggest gently.

Max frowns deeply. "The last time I worked with Haley, she was adamant she wanted to reconnect with her sister. Tell some big secret from their childhood. She wouldn't tell me what. But it felt like growth."

"She wouldn't tell you what? That sounds like Haley. A big childhood secret, dangled in front of a therapist."

"You think…Haley was being manipulative?"

"Never mind." I all but roll my eyes. I'm the only person in the entire clinic who was immune to Haley's charms.

Max swirls the mop with practiced strokes. I find myself staring.

"Am I doing it wrong?" He looks up.

"No. I…" I force myself to speak coherently. "You strike me as the kind of guy who was raised in a stately home with servants or something. Not mopping floors."

What is it about Max that makes stupid things come out of my mouth?

His face changes, and for a moment I think I've crossed the line. Then he smiles.

"I suppose I was," he says. "Medical school was a steep learning curve."

Abruptly his face shuts down. It's always this way with Max. As though he can't stand for me to get ideas above my station about relating to medical staff.

"Did you know there's a new patient admitted today?" His voice is coldly professional.

"Megan. Yes."

There's a long pause.

I'm not about to say what we're both thinking. That neither of us is completely convinced that Haley's death was a suicide. If it wasn't, any new arrivals would be at risk.

"Max, you see the guests for therapy. Did anyone…"

"Are you suggesting that one of our guests confessed to me that they murdered Haley Banks?"

"No, of course not." I'm thinking of how Dr. Lutz refused to let the police see the medication room. Could he be covering for someone? All our patients are extremely wealthy and powerful people.

"If you're asking if the guests are distressed," says Max, "yes, they are. And in my opinion, it probably isn't smart to throw another guest into such a potentially volatile situation."

CHAPTER FOURTEEN

MEG

Harry was right. Sol was happy enough I was going to rehab to pay the premium. He didn't even question my choice of clinic. It was so fast that the flight and bed were booked the next day—right after Harry and I came up with a convincing cover story. I was committing to rehab as a high-roller poker player. Using the family surname I didn't share with Haley, since she's had a stage name since kindergarten.

Which is why now I'm in the back of the Clinic's private transfer car, winding through boggy pine forest after a short flight I don't remember too well.

Harry did warn me not to drink on the plane, but the cart was too much temptation. I also packed some oxy for emergencies. I don't want to break my promise to Harry, but I also need to find out what happened to Haley. Can't do that when I'm crying with pain and shaking.

We pass cute fishing towns, which I privately dub "Boring Pines," and the driver mentions something about it being a shorter trip on account of low tide and a particular road not being flooded. But it still takes long enough that I find myself dozing off.

I wake to my phone blaring. When I lift my wrist to check

my pocket, a cold sensation slices across my leg. I notice that a half-drunk beer bottle is clamped in my hand and I just tipped the contents over myself.

"Megan?" It's my mom's slightly nasal voice, less strident with her own self-importance than usual. "The funeral will be in three days." She delivers the news in a whisper, like she's fighting tears.

"*What?*" I feel the phone start to slip from my hand and grip it tightly. I hold it out to check the date and realize it's on video call. My mom's angelic features, maintained by fillers and zero body fat, is a distance from the screen. She wears a designer scarf tied artfully at her neck and a button-fronted pink Gucci sweater. Her tastefully styled pixie-cut blond hair is streaked with careful highlights that complement the violet eyes she and Haley are famous for. She's holding a cocktail.

"I can't believe it." Mom rests a hand on her forehead, tears falling. "How could she do this? How *could* she?"

"Mom. The funeral…"

"I know three days feels like a *lifetime*," she continues. "We need it done. They need to go through…something for suicides…" Her voice breaks and she sobs. "Then they'll repatriate the ashes."

Haley's ashes. I tune out as my mother continues talking.

"Thank God for Petey," Mom is saying. "He's arranging it for us." Petey is the last hanger-on Mom has left after a lifetime of unreasonable behavior. God knows what he gets out of putting up with her. Drama, I guess.

"Can Haley's dad make it?"

Her face contorts. "Oh. Kurt is making problems about the timescale. Something about Granny not being able to come. When I'm burying my own daughter!" Her voice rises, then she puts two manicured fingers to her temples and draws an audible suck of breath.

"I think you should make sure Dad can come," I tell her.

"Why should you care, Meg?" she says sharply. "He's not *your* father. *Your* father ran back to Italy the moment…"

"The moment the crib got delivered. I know, Mom."

She shakes her head. Pauses.

"Petey is running contingencies. He's concerned the press might get hold of Haley's therapy notes somehow. Cause me even more grief."

"You worried they'll find out how bad you treated her, Mom?" I say sarcastically.

Mom's face does something weird. "Don't be silly, Megan. You and Haley had a charmed childhood. But you remember how difficult Haley was. I've already had one round of publicity after she sued me for her child-acting fees. I don't want another."

Mom lowers her voice, glances behind her.

"Haley said a lot of spiteful things to me, before she went into rehab," she says. "Made out I was too hard on her as a child. But I *had* to be hard on her, didn't I, Megan? You remember how she was."

"Sure, Mom."

She talks on about the showy funeral arrangements, and I feel myself zoning in and out. I must have fallen asleep again because my feet are wet with beer and Mom's face has vanished from the screen.

The car is coming to a halt, I blink groggily.

"Here we are," announces the driver. "The Clinic."

CHAPTER FIFTEEN

MEG

We've stopped outside a mansion house. Kind of fairy-tale, like one of those big, old Victorian stick houses you see in tourist shots of San Francisco, only a lot bigger. As if someone had taken a duplicating ray and kept on zapping.

Wraparound balconies. *Zap.*

Fish-scale siding. *Zap.*

Turrets. *Zap. Zap. Zap.*

There's a very high fence, like you see at maximum security prisons.

I must have fallen back to sleep because the next thing I know, I'm being partially carried out of the car, and there's a needle sinking into my arm.

"Hey!" I shove at the arm injecting me. It's a bored-looking man in nurse's scrubs. "All done." He announces to someone else.

A woman's voice is at my ear. She has a Maine accent that I bet she thinks she's shaken off, with a schoolmistress edge to it.

"This way, please."

I'm cold suddenly. Didn't think to dress for the Northwest weather. Sweat pants and a short-sleeved shirt and bare feet. Must have taken my sneakers off. I rub at the spot where I was injected.

"Did you take anything other than alcohol?" I focus on the woman, whose bossy tone annoys me. She has the neatest makeup I've ever seen. Slick brows, contoured shades, and symmetrically drawn nude lips beneath immaculate blond curled hair.

"Who are you?" I ask her, not bothering to ask politely.

"My name is Cara. I'm the manager here at the Clinic," she says smoothly. "I'll be handling your admissions, and I need to know if you've taken anything other than alcohol."

For the first time I notice her outfit. All exaggerated shoulder pads and black pencil skirt. It suits her overbearing manner perfectly.

"Give me a break, lady," I tell her. "Everyone has a couple of beers on the airplane."

"Couple of beers, huh? And here was me thinking I could smell Jack Daniel's."

I kind of hate Cara.

We've passed the fence now and moved across a courtyard. Now I'm walking, I realize I got a little drunker than I intended on the airplane.

We pass through a carved-wood lobby, then under a lot of glass ceiling, finally into a snaking warren of perfect corridors that seem to have been hand built from polished stone.

The low light gives way to a giant glass-walled lounge area with a panoramic view out over the cliff edge out on to stormy ocean and moody sky.

There's a luxury cabin feel made large, with an artful mix of striped linen and vintage leather armchairs. Handwoven rugs dot the smoked-wood floor. The ceiling is wooden too. Narrow planks of soft green, hung with a huge woven-seagrass pendant light shade and accented at intervals with chunky ropes dangling brass lamps.

Everything is soft, tasteful, and impeccably finished. A therapeutic hug in decor.

"Dramatic," I say, taking in the expansive sea view. "When do I meet the other patients?"

"You might meet Jade and maybe Madeline right now."

"*Jade?* Like the fairy princess cartoon?"

A wash of memories sweep in. Haley would play that game with me. She'd be the magical princess, making our family perfect with her golden wand.

"I'm not familiar with that one," says Cara. "Jade and Madeline are your roommates."

"Wasn't that famous singer here? Haley Banks?"

Cara's lips purse. "I would ask you to keep your voice down," she says in a low hiss, glancing to a door at our left. "There are group therapy sessions taking place and guests can hear you."

Sensitive subject. Through the fug of my airplane whiskey intake, I log it.

"Your room is this way." Cara leads me into a large room of midnight-hued walls. The designer cabin theme is continued. Silver-wood floors, rope-hanging lighting, and four king-sized beds, plump with high pillows and patchwork comforters. Pin-sharp images of coast and forest stud the walls.

A sudden realization hits me. Is this where Haley's body was found? The idea of that unexpectedly knocks my thoughts out of alignment.

"Don't I get any privacy?" I blurt out, wondering how I'm going to keep my oxy levels comfortable in a room full of junkies.

"Shared rooms are normal for rehab. We don't offer private rooms," says Cara. "Not since…" She stops herself. "We don't offer private rooms."

I take a look around. Each bed has a small unvarnished oak nightstand and a metal gold-shaded light with a drooping head, like it's bowing. Each has various personal objects arranged on top.

I stride over and lift a heart-framed photo of a baby girl and a smiling blond woman on the nightstand, acting a bravado that I predict is going to push Cara's buttons.

"Whose is the kid?" I ask, watching her body language.

"That's Jade's nightstand."

"So this is Princess Jade, huh? She famous?"

"Jade is doing very well with us. I'd ask you don't touch other guests' belongings," says Cara stiffly.

"She's English?" I'm looking at the background to her picture. Big Ben. "Flew all the way here for rehab?" I replace the picture.

"We don't discuss who people were before they came to us."

"OK, what's she like now?" I eye the stuff on her little table. Neatly arranged cosmetics and nail polishes. I can tell my proximity to Jade's personal items is driving Cara crazy, but she can hardly tell me where to put my eyes. She'd obviously like to though.

"Jade gets along well with everyone." Cara sounds guarded. Like she doesn't expect the same from me.

"What about this chick?" I move to a nightstand overflowing with junk. There's a teetering, untidy stack of books, with titles like *The Democratic Conspiracy* in angular letters. Used tissues are balled in a heap, along with candy wrappers and a beat-up two-liter Evian bottle.

"That belongs to Madeline." I guess from the way she says it that Madeline is not well liked.

I move to an empty bed and sit on it.

"That's Sierra's bed," says Cara.

I get up, rolling my eyes.

"*This* is your bed," Cara says, pointing. "Someone will bring up your belongings."

I head to where she's standing and throw myself backward onto the fresh linen, head sinking into the chubby pillows. Cara's mouth twists in disapproval.

"So this is the female dorm," I say, thinking out loud. "Who are the male patients?"

Haley would have had a relationship with at least one man in rehab. It was how she dealt with life.

"You'll meet them later," Cara says tightly.

Fairly certain I've pegged her now. Uptight, rule oriented. My eyes shift to my nightstand.

"There's no lock," I say, sitting up, pulling open a drawer, and thinking of the oxy sewn into my bra.

"No locks anywhere. This is rehab."

I bounce a little on my hands and notice the room doesn't stop bouncing when I do.

"I'm supposed to trust total strangers?"

"I wouldn't trust anyone here," says Cara. "They're all drug addicts. Just like you."

A pager at her hip beeps, and she checks it for a few seconds too long.

"Bad news?" I suggest.

"Wait right there, please," she says. "I'll be right back."

Her pursed lips tell me I got the read right. Something's off at the Clinic. And I'm going to find out what.

CHAPTER SIXTEEN

CARA

Security is paging. Hanson and Meyers have somehow managed to come back with a warrant to search the medication room.

Dr. Lutz arrives flushed and barefoot in the lobby, in a waft of tiger balm. His T-shirt announces: "Today Is a Gift. That's Why They Call It the Present."

There's something comically mismatched about his teddy-bear physique, profusely bearded face, and dark enragement.

"They've already investigated the scene, and Haley's death was filed as routine with the proper channels," he says, woven bracelets waving wilding as he gestures with his hands. "These backwoods police are desperate to glimpse celebrities. Make sure they don't get *anywhere* near the guests."

"I'll reschedule the group session to another room," I say, tapping keys quickly. "The police will be nowhere near them."

"That's why I hired you, Cara." Dr. Lutz beams. He makes a hasty prayer sign, then exits, padding barefoot over the hardwood floor.

I let Hanson and Meyers in. The medication room route means I lead them past the free-time area, with its various treatments. Meyers slows as we pass a bank of purple-lit glass with gym equipment behind.

"Addicts like to work out with nightclub lighting?" she quips.

"That's a hypoxic gym," I explain. "It creates conditions with lower oxygen so that training is more efficient. There are running machines inside."

Meyers grimaces like this is her worse nightmare. We walk on.

"That's our cryotherapy chamber," I explain, as Meyers stares with undisguised curiosity through the glass panel of a door. Inside is a large white chamber with more than a passing resemblance to a rocket ship. "It's a kind of ice therapy. Patients are exposed for short periods at minus 100°C."

"Minus *one hundred*?" Hanson replies, his mustache jumping.

I'm about to tell him that we haven't killed anyone yet, then realize it would hardly be appropriate under the circumstances.

"For a few minutes it's completely safe," I say, trying not to sound defensive and walking determinedly past. "Cryotherapy helps boost immunity and improve mental health. Well proven in many clinical studies," I add.

Hanson glances back. "Meyers and I were wondering. Is it possible someone could have followed Haley to the medication room?"

"We have a strict curfew and everyone was in bed. It is unlikely, but I suppose…not impossible," I concede.

"Let's see now." Hanson licks a finger. Flips a page. "Everyone claimed to be asleep the whole night. Shared dormitories, but none of them can rule out the possibility that another patient woke and slipped out without them knowing. This would be on account of the heavy sedatives you issue at nighttime. Am I right so far?"

"Addicts struggle to sleep. We help them."

Hanson returns to his notepad. "In your statement you were very certain only patients were on this floor. No medics."

"Our security systems use fingerprint access, time-stamped.

Staff sleep in their own quarters. No staff entered the guest area that night. Not until the alarm was raised in the early hours."

As we reach the medication room, Dr. Lutz is waiting for us, eyes closed in silent meditation. He opens them slowly and gives Meyers and Hanson a slow, beatific smile.

"Good to see you again, Dr. Lutz," Hanson says tonelessly. "This is your medication room?"

"As you can see," Dr. Lutz says, nodding, "our medication storage is extremely well hidden and secure."

"One coded lock and a flimsy door?" Hanson asks. He's eyeing how the room is disguised by a portion of wood cladding in the wall. There's an electronic number pad, and Dr Lutz enters a code.

"Medications are kept so close to drug addicts?" Meyers tilts her head at Dr. Lutz in polite confusion.

Dr. Lutz's jaw tightens. "We are still trying to discover how Miss Banks found the code."

The door of the medication room opens. Meyers and Hanson walk inside. Despite the clandestine access, it's a boring place. A concrete bunker of a room that also houses much of the building's power supply. Thick black cables run up the walls and exit the floors in a mazelike pattern. The hum of electricity fills the air.

Against the walls are white shelves, holding rows of neatly ordered boxes and bottles. Everything in its right place.

"You use injectable medications here," Hanson asks.

"Not usually," I say, walking to where boxes of opiates are stored. "The heroin Haley used was taken from here. Medical grade. For extreme pain relief. She took about 50 mg in vial form."

Hanson is shaking his head. "Still can't get my head around why a rehab would keep heroin."

"It is perfectly standard for a medical facility," says Dr. Lutz, his accent thickening. "We keep a federally approved pharmaceutical supply of licensed drugs. As do all professional rehab facilities."

Hanson walks toward the shelves, peers deeper, and frowns. "Diamorphine?"

"It's the medical term for heroin," I confirm. "It's used for pain relief in certain circumstances."

"Miss Banks knew the medical terminology?" Hanson lets the observation hang, stroking his mustache.

"I–I guess so." I glance at Dr. Lutz.

Hanson is scanning the shelves. "You've got injectable vials. But I don't see any needles."

"Those boxes hold preloaded syringes of diamorphine," says Dr. Lutz.

Hanson nods slowly, turning to Meyers. "Preloaded syringes. You ever heard of those?"

Meyers shakes her head. "No, sir. Never heard of them."

"Yet Haley Banks did." His gray eyes land on Dr. Lutz. "What drugs did Miss Banks use?"

Dr. Lutz looks at me. "She came to us for help with cocaine addiction," I confirm. "Cocaine and alcohol." I clear my throat.

"Nothing intravenous?" Hanson asks.

"Correct." I glance desperately at Dr. Lutz.

"Yet Haley Banks knew the medical name for heroin. And where to find packs with preloaded syringes inside. One smart girl, wouldn't you say, Meyers?"

Meyers nods. "One smart girl."

There's a pause.

"We'd like to visit your morgue now," says Hanson.

There's a moment between the two men when both stand

perfectly still. Like a game of chess before the final piece is about to be played.

"Do you have a warrant for that?" Dr. Lutz's voice is pure, carefully nuanced ice.

Hanson's mustache makes a small, unhurried rotation. "Sir," he says. "I don't know how things are done in Switzerland. But in this state, a mortuary is regulated public property. Police and other officials may access without a warrant."

Dr. Lutz takes in a long breath that causes his nostrils to flare.

"I'm afraid there would be nothing for you to see," he says. "Haley's body has already been cremated."

Meyers actually jerks in alarm. If Hanson is shocked, he doesn't show it.

"You cremated Haley Banks four days after her death?" Hanson says.

"The *crematorium* local to here processed Haley's remains, with all the correct permissions," says Dr. Lutz. "We supplied documents to expedite the process. Her mother was anxious for a rapid funeral."

"You have the paperwork you supplied, sir?"

"Naturally," says Dr. Lutz in the tone of a man announcing "checkmate."

Hanson's mustache rises and falls. "We'd like to see Haley Banks's full file. Everything you have on her."

"Some of that information requires medical permissions," says Dr. Lutz. "We'll see what we can do. Miss Morse can take contact details on your way out."

CHAPTER SEVENTEEN

MEG

Cara comes back with my luggage at least a half hour after she said she'd be a few minutes. She is thoughtful and on edge.

I need her to leave me with my luggage now. I can't think straight without oxycodone. I lie back on the bed and close my eyes, willing her to go.

Sadly, she has other ideas. Cara is pulling on a pair of surgical gloves and unzipping my bag.

"Hey!" I sit up in the bed.

"Standard for every patient," says Cara. "But now that I've got your attention, am I going to find anything in here?"

I shake my head. She pulls free a clutch of miniature bottles of spirits and holds them up.

"You want to try that answer again?"

I stare up at the ceiling. She dives back into the bag.

"Did you take all of these?" She's holding up a fan of spent pill foils and two white boxes.

"They're prescribed."

"Not in here they're not," she says. "In here you'll have what our doctor prescribes you. Nothing else." Cara continues her methodical search. I have to admit she's dedicated. She finds the blister packs hidden in my shoes and sewn into the lining of my bag.

She holds them up victoriously.

Joke's on you, lady. Those are the pills I wanted you to find. Little trick I learned at the poker tables. Let someone catch you cheating badly, and they won't suspect you of cheating well.

Cara submits me to a strip search whilst I pretend to be bummed about being caught out.

And because Cara already thinks she's found my stash, she doesn't pay close enough attention.

The pills sewn carefully into my bra stay hidden.

I watch as she passes right over the lockpicking tool I slid into the cord of my jogger pants.

"I'm disappointed," she says. "You're not the first to try. But it doesn't bode well for your intentions."

"I am so sorry to have disappointed you," I tell her with zero sincerity. Her mouth purses tight.

"I'll be informing Dr. Max," she says. "And we'll be keeping a close eye on you. We have a zero tolerance policy for drug use in here, and we test daily."

I planned for this too. Synthetic urine powder from the internet to provide clean samples. Insurance policy, in case it all gets to be too much. I try not to think about what Harry would say.

"Dr. Max will be along shortly." Cara's heels click away. I *think* she shoots back, "Take care around Madeline." But maybe I misheard. Because then she's gone, and I'm alone.

I pull out the emergency oxy, stashed in my bra. I hadn't been planning on taking the pills right away. But I need to be on alert for the first few hours at least. I slip two into my mouth and crunch.

"Won't be taking more for a while," I tell the pack, popping free two more.

Next I check the mobile phone on the hidden strap attached to my inner arm. From nowhere, my stomach roller-coaster lurches, and without warning, the entire room expands and contracts like a heartbeat. I put a shaking hand on my head and blink. OK.

I need a drink.

My mind desperately cycles through ways to make that happen. I wasn't expecting to be so far from anywhere behind a big electric fence.

I turn my focus back to my secret phone. With a few clicks, I'm into the Wi-Fi network, courtesy of whoever didn't change the admin settings on their router. I'm about to try calling Harry when there's a noise in the corridor. I quickly stash the phone.

"Hello?" calls an English-accented voice from the doorway. An unfamiliar young woman walks in. The first thing I notice is that she has two major black eyes. Full-on purple and green. "Came to check on the new recruit."

She sashays into the room in bare feet, workout shorts, and a tan T-shirt announcing "I Can't Adult Today" stretched over the lacy white outline of a bulging padded bra. Everything about her is honey toned. From her caramel-colored hair to her luscious golden skin. Pancake stack, I think. That's what she reminds me of. All honey hues and buttery voice and sweet brown eyes.

While I'm taking it in, the world does a gentle belly flop, like reality has decided to sit down for a moment. I lean against the wall and manage to focus.

"Are you OK, chick?" She's at my side, arm around my waist, supporting me. I can smell her perfume. Something fruity.

"Yeah."

"You're heavier than you look for a skinny girl," she puffs. "You feel solid."

She helps me sit on the bed, looking at me with open concern. "I'm Jade. And before you ask, yes, I was named after the fairy princess cartoon. Try living *that* down as an English girl on a council estate."

I fit the pieces together, trying to imagine her without the facial injuries. She's the girl with the baby picture on her nightstand. Her voice is warm, with a soft burr. There is something so familiar about Jade. I feel like I've met her before.

"Where are you from?" I ask, staring at her busted-up face.

"England," she says. "Common England. Not posh like Max. You met Max?"

I shake my head, slotting her accent into place. Northern British maybe.

"I'm Meg. Are you famous?" I ask her.

She laughs. "I was proper starstruck as well, coming in here," she says. "I'm an actress. Done some UK stuff you won't have seen. Some people thought I was good, so"—she shrugs—"I got headhunted for a big part in Hollywood. Flew out here six months ago."

"Cool." I'm still trying to place her. Maybe we met at a club.

"Would have been. I fucked it all up. *Nearly* fucked it up." She grins wryly, correcting herself. "The production company is paying for me to get clean. One last chance."

"What did you do to your face?"

"This?" She touches the deep bruising like she forgot. "Got wasted right before I checked in. Fell flat on my nose in the parking lot, like a fucking idiot. Would have been embarrassing if I could remember it, Meggy."

"It's Meg." I say it a little too sharply. But only Haley calls me Meggy.

Her eyes glide distractedly around the room, not noticing my blunt tone. "You met Cara?" She asks.

"Nurse Ratched?" I rub my head. "Yeah, we met."

Jade laughs. "Cara's all right." She says something else, but the words are distorted, underwater. There were more details, but I can't hold on to them. My head is still doing something strange. I blink, righting my whirling vision with effort.

Without warning, the walls turn to pixels and they begin falling like rain. I fix my eyes on the bed. Jade helps me to sit.

"Fuck." I put my head in my hands. When I look up, Jade's round features are stretched in concern.

"Did they inject you?" she asks. "When you came in?"

"I… Yeah, I think so."

Her mouth turns down. "Fuck." She's shaking her head. "Max *promised* us they'd stop doing it."

"Doing what?" Soft clouds of darkness are knocking at my awareness of the room, bouncing me deeper back into my body. When I try to claw back into light and color, I keep losing my grip.

Jade takes a breath and glances at the door. "They'll be coming soon." She puts her mouth right by my ear. "You need to get out," she whispers. "Don't sign anything. Get out while you still can."

I just have time to absorb that when my vision gives out completely and I tumble into a crocodile roll of watery darkness.

CHAPTER EIGHTEEN

CARA

Max arrives at the reception desk right after I finish checking Meg in. He looks devastated.

"The housekeeper bagged up Haley's personal effects." He holds up a clear plastic bag. "More emotional than I thought it would be. I really thought we had a chance with Haley."

He looks much older for a moment, though I know he can't be very old. The young psychiatrist award he won could only have been given to a man under forty.

I take the bag. Addicts are allowed a small number of personal belongings, and these are Haley's. There's a gold-lidded mascara I happen to know costs more than my entire makeup collection. A perfume from Haley's own branded Cowgirl line. Some shining cheap costume jewelry that would have looked expensive on Haley. A journal with a brown and gold leather Versace cover.

"Max, you could have let me collect those from housekeeping," I say.

"You have a work addiction. I'm trying to save you from yourself." He smiles like he's joking, but I suspect he means it.

"Takes one to know one," I tell him.

He doesn't answer. My eyes settle again on the bag.

"No key?" I ask, shaking it.

"Key?" Max frowns, confused.

"Haley had a key to her private room. Had a fancy little gold key ring. C for 'Clinic'"

"It wasn't with her things," says Max. "Did you check with housekeeping?"

"No. Actually, they asked me for the key. I don't seem to have a spare. Haley's room had been left locked and they needed to get in."

We exchange looks. "I'm sure it will show up," says Max uneasily. He pauses. "What did you make of the new guest, Meg?"

I consider. "She's rude. And to be honest, I'm not sure she'll last here."

"No?"

"She tried to smuggle in three miniature bottles of JD and blister packs of oxycodone."

"Anything else?" Max asks. His even features are serious, eyes studying me a little too intently. I find myself wondering how that shade of blue can be real.

"Some guy named Harry who sounds like a New Jersey gangster called, demanding to speak with her. Maybe her dealer."

"Agreed," says Max. "Or it could also be an enmeshment situation. Boyfriend-girlfriend who depend on each other for their addiction."

He checks his watch. "We'll talk later. Oh, one last thing. The police contacted me. Requesting Haley's full medical file. They thought some tests were missing."

"The full file got sent," I say, confused. "Dr. Lutz took care of it. I was cc'd on the email."

Max nods as if he were expecting this answer.

"I can take a look," I add. "Make sure everything was included…"

"No," says Max a little too quickly. "I'll talk to Dr. Lutz myself. Thank you, Cara."

He makes this his parting shot, the English accent making it sound even more dismissive. Max always manages to cut the conversation short in a way that makes me feel dumb. I guess he's making the point that I'm not important enough to see any medical files.

The phone rings, making me jump. I answer.

"Cara?" It's Dr. Lutz. "Please secure the room for Megan."

"Right away."

I tap keys on my computer, pulling up a plan of the building. Then I zero in on various locks in the corridors. A red line zooms across the rooms where I tap, and all across the Clinic, doors seal themselves.

A soft glow lights up a panel on my electronic floor plan.

LOCKED

Job done, my eyes drop back to Haley's personal effects. I'm wondering how best to package them for collection in a way that reflects the Clinic brand.

As I take out the journal. I realize something is wrong. You can see from the spine that pages are missing. I open it. The first page is covered in Haley's signature looping scrawl.

My name is Haley Banks. I am an addict. The substance I use is human beings.

I am out of control.

And I don't care.

Quickly I shut the journal. But it doesn't stop the questions exploding in my mind. Who tore pages out? And why?

CHAPTER NINETEEN

MEG

When I wake up, I'm strapped to a hospital bed with a bunch of drips and wires coming out of me. I can't move.

My whole body hurts. And my mind… There's something weird back there. A tightly bound lump has been kicked around. Loosened. Like sludge in a sack. With this comes an image. Very clear and sharp. An old childhood nightmare I haven't thought about in years.

The man with playing-card eyes.

I stuff it back under the bed of my dark childhood and something else ripples out instead. There's a feeling… This man hurt me and Haley. A flash of him reaching out, trying to get us. I shudder and the image vanishes.

It's then that I notice a doctor by my bedside, looking at a chart. I jerk at my legs and find I'm restrained.

"Well, hello there," he says. "Glad you decided to join us."

He has an English accent, close-cut light-brown hair and very even features that are a little too perfect for him to be good-looking. He reminds me of a doctor from a 1950s poster. Not quite real. The effect is exacerbated by his tweed jacket and chinos combo. Never saw that look outside Harvard before.

His eyes move to my legs.

"Why am I tied down?" I demand.

"Standard procedure, nothing to worry about. Patients can jerk around. Here, I'll unclip you." He leans across, and the elastic restraints shoot free. I sit up, glaring. My head spins.

"Easy there." Leaning over me, he produces a medical light. "I'm going to take a look in your eyes," he says, gently easing up one lid and then the other. "Do you know where you are?" He clicks off the light and slips it in his pocket.

"Rehab."

He smiles, showing dimples. "Good. Good. Yes, that's right."

I shuffle to my last memory. *Jade. Bruised face.* It feels so surreal I wonder if I dreamed it. I need oxy. Badly.

"My name is Max. Doctor Max if you prefer." He turns and retrieves something from a nearby table. A tray of food. "I brought you some breakfast."

"Breakfast?" Wasn't it dinnertime?

He holds out the tray. There's creamy-looking oatmeal, a muffin that smells just baked, and a cup of fresh coffee. Max rests the tray on my bed.

"I'm allowed caffeine?"

"You're allowed caffeine."

I tip back the cup and drink gratefully. "How long was I out?"

"Two days."

I sit bolt upright and almost spit my coffee. "Two days?"

My oxy. Two days. Did they find it?

"Try to stay calm. Most people feel disoriented when they come to. Standard treatment for us is a sedative we give to all our patients," he explains. "Then we induce a medical coma. All perfectly safe, and you are monitored throughout.

And the good news is you're through it now. Two days clean. Congratulations."

Different feelings are landing from all directions in waves. Violation. Shock. Rage.

"You put me in a coma for two days?" I demand.

"In the beginning we used eight-day comas, but I'm of the opinion patients should experience a degree of physical withdrawal for their rehabilitation. Else it's too easy, and part of getting better is doing the work."

I'm taking it in, outraged.

"We don't claim to be orthodox, but we commit to do what's best for your recovery and we get the results," says Max mildly, noticing my expression. "It's all in the entry documents you signed. We only accept patients who are serious about treatment."

My shoulder hits me with a surge of pain.

"I need oxycodone," I tell Max. "It's prescribed."

He shakes his head briskly, and a chasm of rage opens up in my chest.

"It's *prescribed*, for my shoulder…" I begin. He holds a hand up.

"Oxycodone is addictive, Meg. You won't be on any addictive substances in here. You're in rehab. I will give you something to help you sleep and make you more comfortable, but it won't be oxycodone."

He has a firm but fair demeanor that is maddening. Like a textbook father figure. It makes me want to sock him right in the jaw.

"I imagine you're feeling extremely angry with me at this moment," he says, apparently reading my thoughts. "That's usual. I'm going to be completely honest and tell you the pills you were on aren't easy to come off. And you had one of the highest blood alcohol concentrations I've ever seen. Even with two days clean you're going to have shakes, cramps, pains, sickness. There's the strong possibility of hallucinations, paranoia. Maybe even convulsions. We're giving you meds and monitoring you closely. Doing our best to keep you as comfortable as we can." He gives me a smile that looks sincere but comes off as bland on his symmetrical face.

I turn over what he's telling me.

"So what happens now?" I ask, wondering how soon I can be alone to check my oxy.

"I'm here to conduct your guest admission," says Max. "Lots of personal questions you probably won't enjoy answering. Ready?"

CHAPTER TWENTY

MEG

I try to sit up slightly in the hospital-style bed in anticipation of Max's guest admission questions. *Just get it over with. Check my oxy is still there.*

My forehead breaks into a sweat, and a horribly familiar pain breaks out along my spine.

I need my oxy.

"Firstly, how are you feeling in general?" asks Max.

My face twists as I try to put thoughts together. "I don't know. Nothing."

"Nothing at all?" He looks mildly amused.

I shake my head. "That's regular for me. I'm just…flat most of the time."

He studies me for a moment. "As in depressed?"

I shrug. "I don't think so. There are times when I get high energy."

"I see. Times when you do things that might be considered impulsive?"

"Probably. Sometimes." I'm guarded now.

Max takes notes. "Have you ever been in therapy before?"

"Um. Yeah. As a kid." He doesn't reply, so I keep talking. "My mom made me go after I got expelled the third time."

I reach for the muffin and take a cautious bite. It's probably delicious, but my stomach recoils.

"OK." He's scribbling furiously. "So trouble at school. What kind of trouble?"

"Just…fighting. Breaking things. Stuff like that. I was kind of crazy."

"Did the therapist offer any diagnosis at that time? Bipolar, ADHD, anything like that?"

"It was some weird old guy who wanted to talk about nightmares."

"You were having nightmares as a child?"

"Yeah. Drove my mom nuts. Used to scream in my sleep about a man with playing cards for eyes."

"Sounds scary. You're a professional poker player, right?"

"Right."

"How did you learn to play poker?"

"I don't remember."

He looks at me for a little too long.

"We'll come back to that," he says. "Let's move on. What was it that brought you into rehab at this point in your life?"

I wasn't prepared for this kind of direct question.

A bubble of paranoia rises up. Did Sol tell him about the Saint-Clair thing?

"The reason I ask," Max says, "is in my experience, addicts always have had trauma. Usually childhood trauma that reemerges in some significant way right before they come to me."

"Always?" I twist my face to suggest the unlikelihood of this but Max nods.

"I've never met one who didn't."

"Well. I'm not an addict. I just need a little break from life."

"The amount of drugs in your system would suggest otherwise. But we can ditch that term if it makes you uncomfortable. Wait there a moment," he adds. "I have another form to fetch."

He exits, and the first thing I do is check my bra.

Thank Jesus fucking Christ and all the stars in the sky. It's there. The fucking oxy is there.

I debate not taking one. But the weird waking nightmare feeling I woke up with is still there. I quickly pop three and wait for memories of playing-card eyes to sink back where they belong.

But as I push the tablets back in their hiding place, something strange happens. There's a crackling sensation by my collarbone. I lift an exploratory hand.

It's a note. Someone tucked a note under my blanket. While I was unconscious.

Max is striding back into the room as I read it. His eyes land on the paper, then widen.

"What the…?" He snatches it from my hand but not before I read the message.

Stop asking about me, or something will happen to you. Haley.

CHAPTER TWENTY-ONE

CARA

The last few days have been completely crazy. All the guests are unsettled. It's been my job to reassure them, but I don't know if I can keep it up. The mystery of Haley's missing journal pages is bubbling away at me. Housekeeping does the final cleaning of her room today, but I don't hold much hope the pages will turn up.

When I asked Max, he suggested he try to bring the issue up tactfully during therapy sessions. See if someone might return them.

I didn't agree, but it wasn't my place to say. It even crossed my mind to call the police. But imagining Dr. Lutz's reaction was enough to stop me. *The verdict was suicide*, I told myself. *Don't be dramatic.*

Glancing around, I pull out Haley's journal, and reread the first and only page.

I am bored out of my tiny little brain. No drugs. No drinks. No parties. No fun.

15 more days.

Since I got admitted, Frank hasn't called once.

*** came to my room last night. We got into a fight, since he's the kind of guy who needs drama. Definitely more of a taker, but that doesn't bother me, sometimes.

I've thought a lot about what this means. Three stars instead of a name. Was Haley having an affair with a patient? They both would have been kicked out if they were caught. If Haley threatened to expose them...

Footsteps in the lobby jolt me out of my dark thoughts.

I look up to see Dex, and my feelings take an anxious twist. Dex is the famous front man of an infamous rock band. But in real life, he's nice as pie.

We all love Dex. He is too cute, dark hair woven into dread-locks that bounce around his engaging features. He has soulful brown eyes and tattoos everywhere skin is visible. One moment he's bounding around full of energy, another, low and quiet. But it all has a puppyish, little boy quality.

One of his addictions is sex. But he's never been anything but very polite with me. Maybe I should be offended.

"Hey, Nurse Cara?"

"I'm not a nurse."

"Oh. Yeah. Sorry." He gives me that cute grin that I bet has groupies falling into bed with him. He puts a finger in his mouth and gnaws at it. "You read our therapy sessions, right?" He gestures to my computer where all the therapy sessions are held. "Stuff we talk about with Max and Dr. Lutz?"

"I type up the notes." I don't know if I should be admitting this. Dex had an extremely messed-up relationship with his stepmother, and the thought processes of his sex addiction are disturbing to say the least.

He takes a breath. "I need to tell you something. About me and Haley."

I blink at Dex. "Are you sure you wouldn't prefer to talk with Max?"

"I just…" His teeth dig further into the nail bed. "When she died…" He stops talking suddenly, freezing midsentence.

"Dex?" I'm on my feet. "Are you OK?"

Dex is standing stock-still. His mouth half-open. As if someone has put him on pause.

I'm at his side when he comes to, blinking in confusion. He sees my face. Puts a hand to his forehead. Like he's woken up somewhere he didn't expect.

"Oh man." He frowns. "Sorry, what was I saying?"

"Dex?" A voice sounds loud across the tiled lobby. Max is approaching with a black look on his face. *Whoa. He actually looks pretty scary.*

Dex straightens up, rubbing the back of his neck. "Oh. Hey, Doc," he says, looking anywhere but at Max. "I was asking Nurse Cara…"

"It's Miss Morse to you," Max says sharply. "And I think you have somewhere you need to be."

"Sure." Dex looks at the floor grumpily, like a kid caught with his hand in the cookie jar.

"I don't think you should be alone with Dex," Max says as Dex scoots off.

"What?"

"It's too much temptation for him."

I'm shaking my head because, really, it's funny.

"I don't think I'm too much temptation for Dex," I say, trying to keep the smile from my face. "He's the front man of a *rock band*." I'm actually laughing now. "He dates *models*. Actresses. The world's most beautiful women. I'm *pret-ty* sure Dex can resist me." I smile.

"And I'm his therapist telling you he can't," Max snaps back. He sighs. "Just…keep away from Dex. For your safety as well as his."

"My *safety*?" This should be hilarious. But Max looks deadly serious.

There's something else too. I dismiss it right away, but it pops back up. A tiny part of me thinks Max might be jealous. He catches my disdain and his expression changes.

"I apologize," he says. "I may have overreacted. The truth is, I'm concerned about Dex. With Meg checked in, there is another attractive woman in rehab. I don't know how that could affect Dex's recovery. When I found him talking to you, I felt out of control."

He sounds every bit the measured, introspective therapist.

"Thank you for your honesty," I say, overly formal now because I can't help but think there's something else Max isn't admitting to. The way his eyes are searching mine is confusing.

"It's not...the only thing I'm concerned about," he says finally.

I wait for him to go on.

"Someone left a note for Meg to find," he says.

"A note?"

"Signed 'Haley.'"

My eyes widen in shock.

"Someone is clearly disturbed by Haley's death. Messing with the new girl." Max lets this percolate.

"From what I've seen of Meg, she isn't particularly tactful," I say. "She mentioned Haley Banks loudly as she passed the therapy rooms when I admitted her. Maybe someone heard and took an instant dislike."

"Could a patient have slipped in unnoticed?"

"I... Well...yes," I admit. "It's not like we lock the doors on patients in medical comas. There's never been a reason to."

"Until now," Max says grimly.

CHAPTER TWENTY-TWO

MEG

A few hours after I finish the session with Max, Cara arrives in yet another power dress to set me up with a scheduling watch. She seems to have a lot on her mind.

"This will tell you where you're supposed to be at all times." She fits a sleek silver device to my wrist. "You have group therapy next."

"Sure." I can tell she doesn't like my offhand reaction, but I don't care.

"You might feel anxious or alone now," she adds, "but all our guests checked in alone, and they've become good friends. Most of them."

"Most of them?"

Cara doesn't answer, leading the way in awkward silence. We pass a bank of doors with looping copper words on each.

"Tranquil, energized, reflective, productive," I read. "Spa rooms are scented with mood-enhancing aromatics."

"We use principles of ancient Ayurvedic energy," says Cara. "You were assessed and allocated your own health route. Oh." She pauses. "I nearly forgot. Your phone call."

We switch back. This is very out of character for Cara. She's the kind of person who color codes her towels.

She brings me to a wall of exaggerated silver curves and stops. They are numbered. One to ten.

"These are phones?"

"Yours is number five."

"Who am I calling?"

But Cara is tapping into her phone, looking upset and distracted.

I approach the curve labeled "five" and lift the receiver from its discreet fixing to the wall. There's a single white button. I press it, expecting to connect with a therapist or nurse or something. So I almost drop the slick shape when I hear Harry's voice.

"*Harry?*"

"Meg? Thank Christ. You OK?" He sounds groggy, and I realize it's probably early for him since he's on shift. "I called you a hundred times. Why didn't you call back?"

"They knocked me out for two days," I glance back at Cara, who is standing a tactful distance away. "Induced a medical coma."

"What?"

"I know." I lower my voice. "Messed up, right?" I can't tell how much the nurse can hear, and I don't much care. It's so good to hear his voice that I feel tears bubble up.

"Did you feed the cat?" My voice comes out weird.

"Yeah, I fed your crazy aggressive fleabag. You OK, Meg? You sound terrible."

"Yeah." I take a breath. "Yeah, I'm OK. My thoughts and stuff are all jumbled. Words too. Some words…go." There's a long pause. I picture his horrified expression.

I glance around to check that Cara is fully out of earshot.

"This girl called Jade with a beat-up face tried to warn me away," I tell Harry. "It's…surreal in here. And Harry. Something else happened." I take a breath. "Someone slipped me a warning note. Signed by Haley."

"OK. Wow," says Harry thoughtfully. "That's…weird."

"I know." I grip the receiver tighter. "But I'm definitely onto something, right? Why would someone try to warn me away if they weren't hiding something?"

"Or it's from this Jade person? She already tried to warn you away, right?"

"Right." I hesitate. "It was a good attempt at Haley's handwriting."

"You still got the note?"

"The psychologist took it away."

There's a long pause.

"You sure you're OK? Only…you seem paranoid."

"What the fuck, Harry?"

"Don't get mad. It's… You're telling me they put you in a coma. A girl tried to warn you. You're getting notes signed by your dead sister. It sounds a little insane."

"You're saying I'm nuts?"

"No… OK. You don't sound good."

I hesitate. "Haley was trying to tell me something about our childhood before she died," I say. "And since the coma I'm getting these memories. Old nightmares. I can't shake this sense that something bad happened. To me and Haley. Maybe even something she was killed to cover up."

Harry pauses for a long moment. "When you stop drinking a bottle of JD a day, you're probably going to remember stuff," he says uneasily. "Listen. Meg. I think you should come home. Today."

His voice is wrong.

"Is there something you're not telling me?" I demand.

"Um. OK. So. My buddy on the inside says local police are pushing for an investigation. Into Haley's death."

"What kind of investigation?"

"Murder."

Everything is very still all of a sudden.

"Meg? You still there?"

"I'm still here. This doesn't change anything for me," I tell him numbly. "I knew it all along. Haley didn't commit suicide."

Get the group therapy session done. Find out who has something to hide.

"Maybe you should come home, OK? OK, Meg?"

"Is it public knowledge?" I ask. "That it's become a murder investigation?"

"Not yet," says Harry. "I'd guess you got a day maybe before police start showing up asking awkward questions."

"That gives me the advantage," I say. "It's group therapy next. If I can get them all together in a room, it's just another poker game, right?"

"Meg," Harry says slowly. "You understand this means you could be trapped in there with a killer?"

I think of Haley. Back when we were kids, she was my entire world. We would have gotten to be friends again. It took time with us.

"I'm not trapped in here with a killer, Harry," I tell him. "They're trapped in here with me."

CHAPTER TWENTY-THREE

MEG

Cara walks me at a ridiculous pace along the aromatic corridors, her shiny heels clicking.

"You always move this fast?" I huff, struggling to keep up. I'm already losing track of where I am.

We pass a corridor cordoned off by police tape, and I notice her slowing.

"What's down there?" I ask. Cara's shoulders move together and up by a half inch under her pin-striped dress. Aha.

What's Cara trying to hide...

"Wait there, please," Cara switches back and vanishes down the cordoned corridor, moving the tape aside to pass.

She's seen something. I creep behind at a safe distance.

I hear Cara's sharp voice. Sounds like she's giving someone a reprimand.

Craning my head I see...Dex Adamos. Wow. It's a weird double take, seeing him in real life.

Dex is the front man for a band whose name escapes me, since their reputation is mostly based on his bad temper and string of model-actress girlfriends.

He is also jaw-droppingly sexy. Even more so in real life. Artistic tattoos on his finely muscled forearms, glowing black skin, and the brown eyes I assumed he kohl-lines for performance are actually framed by very thick black lashes. A pretty guy trying to look manly in his "My Life Rocks" ripped shirt.

Haley would *definitely* have been interested in Dex. And if Haley was interested in someone, that meant trouble.

I move closer. Catch pieces of conversation.

Dex's tone is low. Apologetic. Cara's low and serious.

"No one…" Cara is saying. "Haley Banks's room… Police… Locked."

OK. Dex was trying to get into Haley's bedroom?

That seems significant. Cara turns, and I drop back fast before she can see me.

When she arrives back, she is flustered and deep in thought. Immaculate brows drawn in.

Dex Adamos isn't with her, I notice.

"This way," she says. "Group therapy is in the moon room."

Several corridors later, we're outside an oak door.

Cara checks her scheduler. "Right on time," she says, pleased. I notice she waits for me to enter the room before she departs.

Inside, it's noticeably warm, with no hard surface in sight. I walk in slowly, taking in the room, wondering if Dex is going to be joining the session or if Cara has sent him off elsewhere.

The floor is padded and dotted with a circle of outsized velvet cushions in various deep shades with high backs. A humidifier pumps a steady stream of lavender-scented mist into the warm air. I look up to see that the ceiling is made of pillowy midnight-blue silk, with lights dotted behind in star constellations.

Jade is already here. She treats me to a warm smile and welcoming wave. There's a chair, presumably reserved for Max.

My poker instincts are kicking in, strategizing which seat is the most advantageous. I want to be last in line for any questions so I can see how the others act before I pitch in. But as I walk across the room, the walls pixelate and stay that way, and I end up collapsing into the nearest place. As my vision rights itself, I can see I've picked the worst position. *Damn.*

"Hey, Sierra!" Jade waves at a figure behind me.

I turn. Sierra Johnson. The eyebrows make her instantly recognizable. Smaller in real life than on TV, dressed like she's ready to watch polo. Dazzling white pleated shorts and a designer cream turtleneck that subtly highlights her caramel skin. Her eyebrows are just as thick without makeup, a half inch deep over her cat-shaped brown eyes.

She has an anxious energy that fills the whole room.

"This is Meg," says Jade, "the new girl."

"Hi, pleased to meet you," says Sierra, glancing at me distractedly. Her petite frame is twitchy, bristling with nerves like a taut bow. Her accent sounds deliberately educated and I wonder if she had a Latino accent that she ditched, or isn't telling the truth about her humble origins.

Sierra seats herself very carefully. Adjusts her pleated shorts beneath her. Then adjusts them again. She can't sit still. Her body language is neurotic.

Bad hand. My poker instincts have fired up. *Sierra has a bad hand.*

Then something strange happens. She lowers her famous eyebrows and stares me right in the face. "Do I know you?" she asks.

And that's when it suddenly hits home.

Oh fuck. She does.

CHAPTER TWENTY-FOUR

MEG

The group therapy room feels smaller suddenly. Sierra is looking intently into my face, blinking in an agitated way.

"Haven't we met?" she adds, twisting at a strand of dark hair.

I have a sudden image. A party. Maybe...five years ago, before Sierra got famous. A VIP area with Haley. Sierra was there for a short while, I think.

I was wasted. Hard to remember.

"Sorry. Don't think so," I say casually, desperately trying to pull the memory together.

I think...it was late. Sierra was wasted too.

She looks at me for a final puzzled few moments.

"Must have been someone else," she says finally. Her eyes skid about my face, unconvinced. Then lift to the patient coming in the door.

"Hey, Tom," she calls with a nervy little smile.

I turn. The shock of recognition takes my breath away.

That's Tom Abrams.

He's an old Hollywood legend. The housewife's favorite. Rose to fame in a slew of cowboy movies, then caught a prime-time TV series as a cop, which ran for a decade, spawning several box-office smashes.

I can't imagine Tom Abrams being an *addict*.

He's still in good shape, with broad shoulders and rugged features. Close-cut dark-brown hair and tanned smooth skin. But tired-looking, with a puffiness to his cheeks.

Walking in behind him is Dex, in his rock-star uniform of tight black jeans and ripped shirt, with Dr. Max behind him.

My mind skids over why those two people would be together.

"That's everyone," says Max. "We're all here."

Get it together, Meg, I tell my fuzzy thoughts. *If something did happen to Haley, it was because of someone in this room.*

The idea makes me calmer. I start with Tom. There's a guarded edge to him, like life has given him a hard time and he's used to being defensive. I've seen that look when people start betting big right after a big loss.

Dex has already sat down. He looks like he doesn't want to be here at all, arms crossed, glowering, legs extended out in front of him on the padded floor, dreads flopping over his eyes. If this were a poker game, this guy tried out at the wrong league and lived to regret it.

My eyes skid back to Sierra. She is the biggest bundle of nerves I ever saw. Literally cannot sit still. Every part of her is curated, like she's making a statement on how serious and intelligent she is. But she won't quit adjusting and straightening clothing. Arranging strands of hair, rubbing imaginary lipstick from her teeth. Someone who got hustled into playing.

Finally there's Jade. An easy read, I decide. Heart-on-her-sleeve type with zero capacity to hide her feelings. People like her will only ever win a game by luck, but somehow everyone feels happy when they do.

I make a mental calculation.

Four patients.

Jade. The up-and-coming English actress.

Sierra Johnson, famous girl band singer.

Tom Abrams, legendary Hollywood actor.

Dex Adamos, tattooed, outrageous rock star.

Who's the fifth?

"Shall we start?" Max asks. "Madeline is in treatment again. She won't be joining us."

Is it me, or does a ripple of relief go around the group?

Who is Madeline? No one seems to like her much.

"How's everyone feeling today?" asks Max. There are muted smiles.

"Best thing about recovery is you get your feelings back," says Dex. "Worst thing about recovery is you get your feelings back."

They all nod and smile. I have the sense of being left out of some group catchphrase.

Max's eyes land on me. "We'll start with our newest arrival. Meg, could you state your name, your addiction, how long you've been clean, and how you're feeling today?"

I stumble out the answers, concluding with "I feel like shit." Jade smiles. Dex is watching me again.

Max looks at me. "I'm afraid you've joined the group at a strange time," he says. "Very tragically, there was a death last week."

"Yeah, I heard about that," I say, paying close attention to everyone's body language. "A girl was killed, right?"

I chose my words deliberately to gauge if anyone reacts. They do. Rock star Dex. His face gives away nothing. But his foot. He's a foot jiggler. Was he doing that already, or is it a stress response?

"It was a suicide," says Max.

I catch a movement. Jade has opened her mouth like she wants to say something. I watch as emotions play out on her face, and she thinks better of it.

Tom looks up at me and smiles. "Hey, congratulations for being here, Meg. We all know how hard it is, your first group session."

I flash a small smile, momentarily overcome. I was prepared for just about everything but people being nice to me.

Dex sits bolt upright on his cushion, hands flat on the floor. "How can you do that, man?" he demands, glaring at Tom. "How can you be playing all Mr. Nice after what you did?"

Tom swallows and looks at Max. "What is he talking about?"

"Because you tore into Haley in her last group session is what," Sierra's eyes are firmly down, hands playing with the hem of her shirt, but her voice is clear.

I can't get a fix on Sierra. She's so goddamn twitchy.

Anxiety? Or something more. Impossible to tell yet.

Tom's face sets in an innocent, palms-splayed gesture. Not fast enough to hide a flash of lip-curled anger. There's a mean streak there, and he's practiced at covering it.

"You *both* ripped into Haley," says Sierra quietly, looking at Dex. All her features seem to be twitching at once.

Dex looks furiously at Sierra. "I wanted her to be straight with me for once."

Good luck with that.

"And I was trying to protect her," continues Dex, pointing, "from *him*."

Tom leaps to his feet, furious.

"Tom, sit down," says Max.

There's too much going on. Too many different reactions to get a fix. I pick one person.

"It was *you* Haley needed protecting from," hisses Tom, ignoring Max, fists balled.

"Me?" demands Dex, outraged. Everything about his face shows blank disdain. You'd never think he was lying.

But he is.

This time, I've got it for sure. Foot jiggling. It's his tell.

OK. Interesting. Dex thinks Haley needed protecting. From him.

Max stands. "Everyone calm down," he says, a muscle in his jaw twitching. "Tom. Sit."

Slowly Tom folds his large body back on his cushion, eyeballing Dex, who glares right back.

I watch them all, trying to figure it out.

What was going on between Tom, Dex, and Haley?

CHAPTER TWENTY-FIVE

MEG

I'm heading back to the dormitory with Jade.

Everything hurts, even with the oxy. My head, big time. But the rest of me too. My joints hurt. I feel cold. My stomach is shut off, like it's trying out the idea of nausea but can't commit.

OK. Focus.

Dex accused Tom Abrams of ripping into Haley. *The* Tom Abrams. Hollywood legend. Whose aging handsome features appear in TV reruns across the globe. And Dex Adamos, who I last saw snarling and ripping his shirt on the front of *Time* magazine.

I pause for a moment to consider this. The rock star and the Hollywood actor.

Haley would have loved that attention. Or would she?

Dex was also outside Haley's room, and Cara was evidently worried about this.

I'm trying to figure out best next steps, but my brain isn't working. Get Dex alone? Try to see what he lets slip?

I need to speak with Harry, I decide. First chance I get to use my secret cell phone.

"I need a shower," I tell Jade. "There's a bathroom in the room, right?"

"Yeah. They're fancy," says Jade. "But cold. You've got to get in early, before Sierra takes all the hot water. She showers about fifteen times a day."

Jade picks at the flaking orange paint on one of her short fingernails. "Um, I wanted to tell you I'm sorry. For warning you away." Her eyes are at the floor. "I didn't mean to freak you out. It's part of the detox. I get paranoid and stuff."

I don't believe her.

Jade walks to her bed and sits. Picks up the photo of the kid on her nightstand and twists it back and forth in her hands. "You know I lose her?" she says sadly. "If I relapse."

Suddenly she sobs. Whole body-racking judders.

"Sorry," she gasps. "It's just that rehab is really, really fucking hard. You remember all this stuff you thought you forgot." Then, apparently with great effort, she takes a great shuddering breath and wipes tears.

I put an arm on her shoulder, uncertain how to deal with the wave of emotion.

She heaves up a breath like she's physically dismissing the sadness. "How you feeling?"

I hesitate. "I feel like shit, but I guess that's standard."

"Yeah." She nods. "I felt like clawing my own skin off for the first two days."

"Opioids?" I guess.

"Heroin. But really, with me, everything. Absolutely everything. Coke. Booze. But heroin was what tipped me over. I thought I was in control because I never did speedballs. How fucked up is that? Thought that meant I wasn't a dirty junky." She beams. I smile back. Jade is hard not to like. "What's your poison?" She asks.

"Alcohol. Prescription pills."

She nods. "It will get easier," she says, hopping from her bed and making for the door. "Take it one day at a time. We'll all take care of you. It's a nice bunch. We all look out for each other. Most of us."

Jade leaves. I walk back across the room, noticing my feet don't seem to keep step with where I'm putting them.

I stretch out on my bed.

This is maybe the first time since I can remember that I've put my attention where my body is, and I don't like it. I need to make sure they don't give me any more drugs, and I am figuring out how to do it when a paperback book hits me in the stomach.

"Get up, fucker!" roars a familiar voice.

I pop up, adrenaline hitting me like a jet of ice water. The first thing I illogically think is: *it's happening again*. It isn't. I'm not in a warehouse. There are no loan sharks here. But somehow my body responds the exact same way as if I was.

"Get the fuck out of my bed!" I make out an angry face across the room, mouth contorted in ugly rage. It's so surreal because I know this person. I just can't place them.

My instincts kick in, and I roll sideways. My body isn't complying though. I crash to the floor and lever myself up in time, fists raised.

I try to focus. Two large, exotic-looking eyes narrowed in fury, about a foot in front of me. She's taller than me, which means she's very tall. Unnaturally thin. Probably fifty, but cosmetic enhancements have held her at a weird-looking forty. Long, glossy dark hair.

"Oh, you're gonna *fight* me?" she shouts in a growl. "New girl's gonna fight me. Betcha think you're a real badass with all those muscles. Only wait." I feel pressure on my chest and stagger back. "You got out of the med ward and you can't even fucking stand, Rocky."

I feel a wall behind me, and confusing images slice past. There's one clear shot, and I take it, sending my fist forward. I hit air and stumble. There's laughter. My second punch connects and the figure falls out of view. I always did have a good left. No one ever sees it coming.

Suddenly, I'm grabbed from behind.

"What the fuck is going on?" I manage, as two people pin my arms behind my back.

"Try to keep calm." It's a male nurse.

"She was in my fucking *bed*," someone is shouting. The voice. Facts converge.

"That's Madeline Murphy," I tell no one in particular. "The Diet Coke girl."

"Yes, that's Madeline Murphy," says a nurse's voice. "But I don't think she's going to be giving you her autograph anytime soon."

CHAPTER TWENTY-SIX

CARA

Hanson is reopening the investigation. Dr. Lutz is dismissive. Thinks it's an excuse for Hanson and Meyers to gawk at our celebrity clientele.

Meyers has called a few times, asking for Haley's drug test results. I've forwarded messages to Dr. Lutz. I'm beginning to wonder if there's more to it.

Drumming my fingers on the desk, I hesitate before clicking to open Haley's file. The therapy notes are all here. Medical information is password protected. Confidential. I'm not authorized to see Haley's actual results. But…

There's nothing to stop me checking the *type* of files against what was emailed to Police Chief Hanson.

It takes me only a few seconds of cross-referencing to realize Hanson is right. None of these files were emailed to him. I breathe out.

Obviously, there's a reasonable explanation. These are medical files.

Max is handling it, in any case.

Nodding at the logic of this, I move to shut the folder. And that's when a test title leaps out at me.

Pregnancy Tests.

For a full ten seconds, my world drops away. Why would Haley have needed pregnancy tests in rehab? Romantic relationships are strictly prohibited.

But Haley has a set of... I count. Twenty pregnancy tests. One for every day she was in rehab.

"Must be a mistake," I say out loud. "Someone mistitled the file."

But it doesn't sound true, even to my own ears.

A blaring alarm sounds, interrupting my thoughts. I look to see one of the red lights on my panel flashing. Female dorm. I inwardly sigh. I *knew* it was a stupid idea to put the new girl in with Madeline.

I head out in time to see two nurses dragging semiconscious Meg from the female dorm. My heart skips a beat. Max arrives from the opposite direction, breathless like he ran here, face stricken.

"What happened?" Max asks the nurses.

"She flipped," says the larger of the two. "Started throwing punches."

"You sedated her?" Max asks. The question doesn't need asking.

"With 3 ml of benzodiazepine," confirms the nurse.

I wince. Even I know that's a heavy dose.

Max looks at me. "Cara, would you be kind enough to help me carry her to my office?"

My eyes widen. "Isn't it better if the nurses help you?" I suggest, taking in their expressions.

"If that was the case, I wouldn't have asked you," he says curtly.

"OK. Sure. Sorry."

"Don't be sorry. Just take her arms."

We escort Meg, half walking, half dragging her toward Max's office. Max is struggling for breath, pausing every few seconds.

"Are you all right?" I ask.

"Fine," he gasps as we reach his office. "Lung…condition. Had it since childhood."

As soon as we're inside and Max catches his breath, his tone changes.

"I'm sorry to get you into this, Cara," he says quietly. "The truth is, I didn't want those nurses around."

We're lying Meg gently in a chair. She's out cold. Max watches her face for a long moment, his mouth turning down.

"I don't like how Dr. Lutz's staff uses sedation," he says finally. "They use it like a punishment. Sometimes I question…" He looks troubled, then examines my face to reassure himself. "Sometimes I question if they are even real nurses," he concludes. "They seem like… I don't know."

He runs a hand through his hair.

"Henchmen?" I suggest. Something about how I say it breaks the tension. The idea of bare-footed Dr. Lutz as a cartoon villain is too funny.

We both laugh. Did I imagine it? Was there a look between us?

Meg stirs in her sedated state, and the moment is gone. When I look back at Max, his face is tight with concern. "Looks like the new girl isn't making any friends," he says.

We share a meaningful glance.

"Madeline is under a lot of stress," says Max. "They all are. It's a very strange situation."

"Max?"

"Yes."

"Did you get to talk to Dr. Lutz? About sending the extra files for Haley?"

Max hesitates for much too long before replying.

"Yes," he says finally. "He's…looking into it."

It wasn't what I expecting him to say at all. For a moment I'm caught off guard.

"So the police were right?" I press. "Those files were omitted?" I know the answer, but I want to hear it from him.

"Managing patient privacy is a very complicated matter," Max says. He looks tired. "It's something you'll learn in time."

I nod uncertainly, feeling confused and dismissed at the same time.

Should I ask about the pregnancy tests? I'm out of my depth, I decide. Of course Max and Dr. Lutz know best. Like Max said, there are complex issues at hand.

But as I turn to go, I have a strong feeling Max wanted to tell me something important and decided against it.

"Cara. Wait." Max is calling after me. I stop and turn. "Could you alter Meg's prescription?" he asks, walking back toward me and handing me the paper. "She'll come around quite shortly, and I'd like something to temper the heavy sedation."

"OK. Yes. Sure." I glance down at the paper. Two drugs are listed. And something else. A note in his looping hand.

Meet me in the library. 3pm.

"That will be all, Cara," he says severely, ignoring the question on my face. "I hope to see you later."

CHAPTER TWENTY-SEVEN

MEG

I'm sitting on a deep leather chair with no recollection of how I got here. Last thing I remember was being dragged out of the bedroom and a needle in my arm.

Opposite me is a chair. And sitting in the chair is the dead-eyed man of my nightmares. He wears a forties-style suit and a fedora hat.

The man with playing-card eyes.

I jerk to my feet. But as I do, the room comes into better focus.

There's no one sitting in the chair across from me. It's empty. I blink a few times to be sure.

A weird flash of an old nightmare, I guess. Haley's voicemail floats back.

I need to tell you something, about when we were kids…

I take a steadying breath, my heart still beating fast. The man with playing-card eyes. He's more like a memory now. I want him to go away again.

I take in where I am. It's a Charles-Dickens-novel kind of room. Wooden floorboards, antique Persian rugs, deep velvet drapes framing big, rectangular-paned windows. A cheery fire crackles in a grand fireplace. But as more details come into focus, the old world is overlaid with modern elements. Bright-colored spines of well-thumbed psychology books are stacked haphazardly on polished teak shelves. There's a grand fat-legged table with a computer and paper files. A little coffee table with a kettle and mismatched cups. The whole effect is homey, comfortable, and welcoming. It doesn't fit with the interior design of the Clinic at all. Maybe I've been kicked out.

I notice that an official framed doctorate on the wall bears the name Max Reynolds.

Standing to take a better look, I steady myself. Take one step after another. On the deep mantelpiece of the big fireplace are a bunch of framed cards. Thank-yous from former patients. My eyes glide over them. One reads, "I never ever thought I'd make it to twenty years of age. I never thought I'd have a family. Here I am, ten years later, clean and sober. I owe it all to you."

I look at that card for a long time.

"I keep the cards to remind me what it's all about," says a voice behind me.

I start at the voice and turn around to see Max in the doorway.

"You've helped a lot of people," I say. I get the strangest sensation looking at those cards. Like my body is having a feeling it doesn't want to tell me about.

"I've had a lot of failures too, I'm afraid to say. But it's good to remember why I do this. Please..." He gestures back to the deep leather chair I recently vacated. "Won't you have a seat?"

Max moves to another chair facing mine. His clean-cut professionalism makes me edgy. Everything about him is so *tidy*.

"I was planning on conducting your first therapy session tomorrow morning," he explains, clearing his throat and reaching for a notepad. "But given the circumstances, we thought best to move it forward." His eyebrows arch. "So you met Madeline. Our former supermodel."

"Yup." I feel my mouth turning up to meet his slightly sardonic smile. Maybe he's not as serious as I thought. "I remember Madeline from the Coke campaigns ten years ago," I add. "Before she went downhill."

"And you decided to take a nap in her bed?"

"It was an accident. I'm out of it on whatever you're giving me. You have to lower the dose."

"We're not giving you any drugs, Meg. Any sensations you're experiencing are the physiological effect of withdrawal."

"Bullshit! I'm seeing people who aren't even there!"

He opens his hands out. "The amount you were drinking was seriously sedating your brain. Now you've stopped, that returned function won't be comfortable for a while."

I don't answer, since it's obviously untrue. I'm still taking oxy, and it's not like I was an alcoholic. Whatever they're pumping me with is spacing me out.

"How are you feeling?" asks Max.

It's not a question I've ever asked myself.

"Jittery," I say after a moment. "Like I need something and it's not there. My head hurts. And I'm shaking all the time. My hands."

"That's standard alcohol withdrawal," he says. "What about severe pain?"

"Not so much," I say warily, moving a hand to my shoulder.

He frowns. "Well you lucked out so far. But I would say it's on its way. Opioid withdrawal almost always comes with physical pain, I'm afraid. When that happens, let me know. We can give you drugs to help. Mostly, however, withdrawal is psychological. Breaking the habit."

"Is that why I'd kill for a JD right now?"

"That's more insightful than you might realize, Meg. Habits are hardwired into the subconscious, which is far more powerful than your rational mind. The logical mind knows you won't die without your cigarette, but the subconscious thinks it's a matter of life or death. Currently you have a lump of meat in your head that thinks you'll die if you don't drink and pop pills."

"Seriously?"

He nods. "In time, that clump of neurons will rewire. But they will keep attempting to execute the habit for several weeks. And to a lesser extent for a year or more."

"Great."

"We're going to help you. Severe addiction like yours is also linked with trauma. Fears deep in the subconscious that keep you in a highly agitated state. So long as those memories remain unprocessed, you will almost always relapse. It's important we address both. Remove the habit. Process the trauma."

He looks down at his pad.

"Let's start at the beginning. With your permission, I'd like to ask some questions, take some notes."

I shrug.

"I'll take that as a yes." Max nods some more. "Let's take some history, starting with your childhood."

CHAPTER TWENTY-EIGHT

MEG

Max readies his pen. I lean back in the leather chair.

"I don't remember much of being a kid," I tell Max. Best to close this down nice and fast. It's unlikely Haley would have told a therapist anything detailed about her childhood, but best not to take the risk.

He writes notes.

"Can you tell me what you do remember?"

I frown, feeling irritable. Turning over what I can tell him, without giving away my connection to Haley. "It was your typical crazy Hollywood childhood. We were shipped around a lot. There was plenty of money. We got sent to lots of good schools."

"How many good schools?"

"Oh. A ton of them. Like, maybe fourteen schools before I even got to high school."

His eyebrows shoot up and he makes rapid notes.

"What about caregiving figures. Your mom, your dad?"

"Mom wasn't what you'd call a caring type."

"No?"

"When I got arrested as a teenager, she sent the nanny to pick me up from jail."

"Anyone else in the family you were close to? Siblings? Grandparents?"

"A sister," I say guardedly. "We were close. Then she got into the acting scene. Left home at fourteen."

"I get the impression that must have been very upsetting for you."

"I guess. Yeah. My sister would defend me sometimes. From my mom. When she left, it was me taking it all."

"Your mom was abusive?"

"Not...abusive."

Mom, watching through the window. Haley locked outside, shivering. Snow under her bare feet.

Please let her in, Mom. She'll die.

"Just...angry," I continue. "Like, we basically ruined her life. I don't think she intended to have one kid, let alone two."

Max's eyebrows rise sharply. "OK." He looks me in the eye. "Did anything else happen to you as a child that felt traumatic to you?"

Something about how he phrases it unexpectedly levers up a memory. Not fully formed but shapeless and untethered. With it comes a craving for alcohol so intense, I feel my fingernails dig into my palms.

"No." My face is sweating.

"You look as though you remembered something," says Max.

The man with the playing-card eyes. In my dream, he had a name. Mr. Priest.

"Just the nightmares. Like I said before," I say carefully.

He leans back in his chair slightly, tapping his pen on his lip like he knows I'm lying.

"Maybe we'll come back to that when you're more settled," he decides. "How about trauma in your adult life?"

"Not that I can recall."

"You seem very together for someone who is detoxing from oxycodone," he says finally. There's a note of suspicion in his voice.

"It comes in waves," I say quickly. "Right now I feel fine."

He looks unconvinced. "Your doctor's notes mention a serious shoulder injury that you're medicated for. May I ask how that came about?"

"It was a thing that happened at work," I explain.

There's a silence like he expects me to say more. I wait it out. Finally his eyes go down to his pad and loop back up again. "How does a poker player end up with a displaced shoulder?"

This is easier to answer. "I made a poor judgment call. Ended up in a warehouse with a bunch of gangsters, tied to a chair and soaked in gasoline. The usual bad day." I smile to include him in the joke, but his eyes widen, then seem to retreat back into his head. This is why I don't tell regular people, I remind myself with an inward sigh. They never understand this part. Harry would have laughed.

"I managed to get loose from the chair, but I hurt my shoulder in the process," I conclude. "Never liked duct tape since."

"You're using humor to divert. But what you're describing is an unspeakable trauma."

"It didn't bother me."

I really want him to move on.

"Being tied to a chair by gangsters didn't bother you?"

"Obviously it bothered me at the time. But not after. The duct tape remark was a joke," I add. "I have no issue with duct tape. It's not so bad when you're in it. You're running on adrenaline."

He leaves a long silence. I glare at him.

"I know that makes me a weirdo, OK? I'm aware I'm *supposed* to have deep feelings about this stuff. But I don't. End of story."

He considers. "I think you do have feelings about it," he says finally. "You've gotten very good at avoiding them."

I shake my head crossly. "I don't," I tell him. "Not since I was a kid. I basically look for cues of how to act normal, you know? Because, honestly, I've no idea. My childhood was so weird, I have no frame of reference for normal."

"And you imagine other people do?" He's smiling slightly.

"Well. Most of 'em. Yeah."

His brow crinkles a little. "Would it surprise you to know that a great number of people struggle to understand normal behavior? With knowing how they feel?" He smiles. "When did you last have strong feelings about something? I don't mean anger. Things like sadness. Joy."

I shake my head. "Those feelings... In poker, we call that 'tilt.'"

"I'm not familiar with the term."

"Emotions that cloud your judgment. Getting sad when you lose, happy when you win. Hating another player. Liking another player. It's all tilt. When you play poker, you aim for zero tilt."

"As in zero emotions?"

"Yep."

"This is in poker, or life in general?"

"Easier to avoid tilt in general, I guess."

Max smiles a little. "You're very clear that you don't have feelings for people, but that isn't what I see. I see an emotionally sensitive woman who has learned to play tough to protect herself."

I try this on for size. Parts of it fit, I guess. Not that I'm going to let him know that.

Max checks his watch. "OK. We're going to have to wind it up for today. I'm going to send the nurse to show you the dining hall." He checks his watch. "Lunch is in ten minutes."

"I'm not hungry."

"Doctor's orders. All our guests have to attend the meals. I'd advise you to eat. After that you'll be writing your honesty reading."

"What's that?"

"It's an exercise where you read aloud your worst mistakes on drugs to the group."

There's no way I'll be doing that.

"Sure," I say aloud. "Honesty reading. Sounds great."

I stand up too fast and the room spins. And as it does, a sliver of light from the depths of my mind whirls free in the dark.

Haley's words drift back: "I need to tell you something. About when we were kids."

The two things wheel around faster and faster like a spinning picture reel, one overlaying the other.

Something hits me, like a clunk of memory sliding back.

The man with the playing-card eyes. Mr. Priest.

Matthew Priest.

He wasn't a nightmare. He was a real person.

Or maybe…he was both.

CHAPTER TWENTY-NINE

CARA

I don't like the library so much. It's like being inside the snowy, white rib cage of some futuristic picked-clean dinosaur. And I'm nervous about why Max has invited me here.

"Hello, Cara." Max raises a hand in greeting. "Any update from Police Chief Hanson?"

I shake my head. "Dr. Lutz has been trying to keep them away from patients. They seem to have quieted down," I say. "Gone back to Beaver Creek for a slice of apple pie and a pot of mustache wax."

Max smiles. "That's a relief."

"Is that why you asked me for a secret rendezvous? To ask about the investigation." I meant it as a joke, but it comes out wrong.

Max gives me a half smile. His eyes drift upward, and I notice there aren't any cameras in this part.

"You wanted to know," he says. "Why Dr. Lutz didn't supply Haley's drug tests to Hanson and Meyers?"

OK. So Max is admitting it. Dr. Lutz is keeping information from the police.

"I..." I pull myself up a little straighter. "Yes," I tell him.

"There's nothing about Haley's test results that need concern you," says Max. "But there are aspects of the accountancy of the tests that Dr. Lutz would prefer remain confidential."

"The accountancy?" I ask, completely confused by his nonanswer. "As in, who is responsible for the tests?"

Something about how Max is delivering this information… Is there a subtext I'm missing?

"Dr. Lutz is completely dedicated to helping people," continues Max. "His background is a lot like mine. He's been at the frontline of rehabilitation. Sometimes this makes him too driven. Too willing to bend rules."

"Is Dr. Lutz breaking the law?" I ask.

Max looks disappointed. Whatever thin thread of trust was growing between us has snapped. He shakes his head, a quick, irritated twitch. "Of course not. I'm telling you the exact opposite."

Questions flow through my mind. Can I ask him about the pregnancy tests that were being carried out on Haley? He's made it clear this is all above my pay grade.

"Cara," says Max. "You managed Haley's schedule for the day she died."

I feel my stomach tighten. Is he switching subjects? Or trying to tell me something?

"Yes," I agree.

"It was…a regular day for her?"

"Um." My eyes are searching his face. "It was a regular day," I agree. "She had a massage scheduled. Some spa time. I think she visited the gym and the anger rooms. Then a group session."

Max nods. "Haley was…very animated in that last group session. Pushing everyone's buttons."

"Haley always pushed people's buttons."

Max's blue eyes look thoughtful. "Yes," he said. "But that last day... Did you notice anything? About how she behaved?"

"She was demanding," I say finally. "Acting like a diva. But that wasn't new."

"Are you familiar with current theories on trauma and addiction?" His tone is brusque.

I don't usually showboat my knowledge, but something about Max's supercilious manner goads me.

"The latest thinking is that trauma is a memory, trapped in a primitive part of the brain," I say. "These unprocessed memories trigger physical emotions. Anxiety, despair, panic. Addicts try to deaden them with drugs."

Max's eyebrows rise like he's impressed.

"I've been reading your books," I admit.

He hesitates. "What do you make of current trauma treatment?"

Is he...testing me? "There have been promising studies using relaxation and hypnosis," I say. "The patient has to calm the body, while calling to mind very stressful events. But...many experts believe childhood trauma is irreversible. The brain is damaged beyond repair."

"Do you think Haley Banks had trauma?" asks Max.

I feel my eyes widen. Where did that come from?

"I...um. From her notes..." I'm struggling to recall. "Haley claims her mother did some terrible things to her. Growing up."

I remember Haley's file. Haley's mom clawed her face for some minor infraction, then covered the open wound with makeup so Haley could attend a child-acting casting. The resulting infection needed surgery. She had a scar.

"Claimed?" Inquires Max. "You don't believe those things happened to Haley?"

"I think they happened," I say. "But you could never be quite sure of anything with Haley. The way she told all those dreadful stories of childhood neglect… She didn't *sound* like they even bothered her."

I'm remembering the account of Haley's frostbitten toes. When she was eight, the family briefly lived in Connecticut. Her mom would lock her out in the snow. But Haley seemed ambivalent on her session recording.

Max stands to leave. "I'd better get back to work."

I nod miserably, unable to shake the feeling that Max was testing me in some way, and I've failed.

"Max, can I ask you a question?" I blurt out as he nears the door.

He turns slowly. "Sure."

"Is there anything… The treatment Dr. Lutz carries out. Could that…do anything to a patient? Make them act out of character?"

I'm thinking of Dex. How Max warned me away. And the strange incidents I've seen of Dex freezing midsentence.

Max is silent for a little too long before replying.

"No," he says finally. "Treatment is tough. Emotionally. We're bringing up traumatic incidents. But, how a person responds to processing those memories… That's always within their character."

I nod.

Maybe it is.

My mind floats back to Haley's information. Her therapy notes. Her drug test results.

Dr. Lutz wants to keep the accountancy of the tests confidential.

Which makes me wonder. Who *is* accountable for the test results?

That would be in the administrator files.

I have the strangest feeling Max wants me to take a look.

CHAPTER THIRTY

MEG

Max asks Jade to show me the dining room where we eat. She shows up with her wide grin and a lot of inexplicable enthusiasm.

"Service to others," she told me in her cute British accent, navigating the shining corridors. "Means Max trusts me with the next step. Don't worry, you don't have to eat anything if you don't want to. You can watch me eat." She grins. "Honestly, the food isn't bad. I'm going to leave this place three sizes bigger."

My mind is so stuffed with questions I'm only half listening. Mr. Priest and the lipsticked lady standing next to him. I'm certain they *got* me and Haley somehow.

Jade links arms with me and pulls me in the direction of savory cooking smells. "This way."

"Whoa." I blink as we walk into the hall, momentary distracted. "This place is incredible."

Twinkling chandeliers hang from sky-high steel rafters. Like a quasifuturistic villain's lair. Everything is white. Tables, chairs. The only color is the food, which explodes from the white table-cloth like something out of Versailles. I'm staring at piled-up bowls of deep-hued fruits.

"Told you." Jade smiles as if she built it herself. "It's like one of those old paintings, isn't it?"

I wonder if Jade was friends with Haley. She is so trusting and open that Haley would have sunk her claws in right away.

You were either Haley's friend or her enemy. Friends were expected to give her everything. And it wasn't a good idea to be her enemy.

We approach the table, and more food comes into view. Whole chickens and joints of meat. Plates of cheeses set on vine leaves. It's grander than the mammoth buffets laid out in the casino. I'm trying to imagine what Haley would make of all this. Last time we spoke, she was on a strict clean-foods vegan diet.

"It's paleo plan or something," explains Jade disinterestedly. "I don't follow mad diets. Just eat." She smiles again and begins loading two plates.

"Don't worry," she adds, handing me the plate. "I'll eat anything you don't want. This way."

"How long have you been here?" I ask, since she seems to know so much.

"Oh, I'm kind of a newbie. At least compared to the others. Dex has nearly finished his thirty days. Speak of the devil," she mutters, looking over my shoulder and raising a hand. "Hi, Dex," says Jade. "How's it going?"

I switch around to see Dex's lean, tattooed form approaching our table. His long-lashed brown eyes are downcast, and his dreads are tied back.

Dex dumps a loaded plate onto the table.

"You met Meg already," Jade explains, sounding nervous.

"Did you tell her not to enter rehab, Jade?" Dex asks. He begins eating with a vengeance.

"Yeah." Jade sits and begins pulling apart a roll.

"Did you ask Jade to warn me away?" I ask Dex.

"Doesn't matter," says Dex, loading a large portion onto his fork and stuffing it into his mouth "Let's just say none of us thought another patient was a good idea. Fuck." He slams his hand on the table, and tears prick his eyes.

Jade puts her hand on top of his. "It's OK, Dex. It's OK." She searches his face.

"Is this about the girl who was here?" I ask. "Haley. The one who killed herself?"

Dex's fork crashes down onto the plate.

"What the fuck kind of question is that?" he demands. "You didn't know Haley. You don't know anything about it. You only know what you heard on the TV. Which was bullshit."

I stand up so fast my water tips over. "You think *you knew* Haley Banks 'cause you were in rehab with her for five minutes?"

Shut up, Meg. Shut up.

"Hey, Meg, it's OK." Jade's hand is at my elbow. "Dex is being a twat. Sit down."

I yank my arm away and sit down, trying to get ahold of myself. It's only then that I see something strange has happened to Dex.

He is frozen, fork lifted, glassy-eyed.

"Dex?" Jade snaps her fingers in front of his face.

He comes back to reality, looking sad. Then his eyes fall on me.

"Know what? I think I lost my appetite." Dex stands up and stalks away, his long body hunched.

"Sorry about that," says Jade. "Dex is a good guy, really."

"What was with the...freezing thing?"

"Oh, it's something that happens once you start treatment with Dr. Lutz. No big deal. You'll end up liking Dex. It's the weird thing about rehab. We all spend so much time together. They become like your family."

We finish lunch in silence, and as we head back to the dormitory, I hang back.

Out of habit I reach for the pack of oxy in my pocket, forgetting they're in my bra. Instead, there's an unexpected crinkle of paper.

Strange. I don't remember putting anything in my pocket.

Confused, I pull it out. It's another note. This time, folded over, with my name on the front in capitals.

I look at it for a moment, every muscle in my body completely still. The way my name is written is so familiar.

Slowly, I open it. Every part of my body turns to ice.

Haley's handwriting. Or a good imitation of it.

I read, the letters swimming.

"*Leave now, Meggy. Before it's too late. Love Haley.*"

CHAPTER THIRTY-ONE

CARA

Hanson and Meyers have arrived unexpectedly to ask more questions. I've paged Dr. Lutz urgently, wondering if I'm even allowed to talk to them.

"Miss Morse." Hanson is his usual low-key self. "Quite the trip we had down here. When the fog lies over that forest, you can barely see a hand in front of your face."

I nod politely.

"I suppose your boss prefers this place to be inaccessible?" suggests Meyers, with her usual sunny grin. "Keeps your celebrities under wraps?"

"We've been having some seasonal fall mist," I say politely. Although "mist" hardly covers the soupy fog that can descend without warning on the forest.

"Maine has the same weather, right?" suggests Hanson. "Fog and such."

My recollections of Maine were paint-pot-hued—bright-blue waters and colorful wooden houses under a jolly sun, a child's drawing of a summer day. Compared to tidy little Maine, this landscape feels wildly Jurassic.

"Just be sure you get back on the road before dark," I say. "Cars have gotten stuck in the swamp during poor visibility."

Hanson flips a pad, choosing words in that slow way he has. Like a glacier moving through a valley. No hurry, since there's no question he'll get there.

"How much do you know about your boss, Dr. Lutz, Cara?" he asks.

"I know he can seem a little unorthodox," I say, glancing nervously at my pager. "But he has twenty years' experience rehabilitating addicts and is truly committed to saving lives."

"Dr. Lutz tell you much about his specific treatment for addiction?"

"We treat childhood trauma as the cause of addiction." I hedge. "Using cutting-edge techniques."

Hanson nods. There's a silence. "How do you treat the trauma?" he asks finally.

"I'm not at liberty to discuss treatment," I say, vaguely aware I'm blindly protecting Dr. Lutz.

In reply, he holds up his phone. "I apologize, ma'am," he says. "What I'm showing you is not really fit for ladies. But if you wouldn't mind taking a look."

It takes me several seconds to realize what he's showing me, and I recoil. White, mottled limbs.

It's Haley's body.

"We investigated the coroner who allowed Haley's body to be cremated," he says. "All aboveboard. Everything by the book." He pauses unhappily. "Photos of the body taken properly." He holds up the phone. "Hard to see. But by my account these red marks here..." He swipes pictures clumsily with a large finger until a single arm is in focus. "Those look like ligature marks," he says.

"Like she had been restrained. And you see here? This is the part of her arm where the lethal dose was injected."

I look closer despite myself. "I can't see anything." I frown. My eyes fall on a little tattoo on Haley's pale hip, which reads, "Heartbreaker." I have an image of her in life, flashing that tattoo above her velour tracksuit bottoms, and feel suddenly, incredibly sad for her.

"Isn't that interesting?" opines Hanson. "Neither could we. Until we blew it up big." He flips to another photo, and this time a small pinprick mark can be made out on the vein of the inner arm.

"Small and neat, wouldn't you say?" continues Hanson. "For a girl who didn't regularly inject heroin?"

"Haley didn't," I say, confused. "She was here for cocaine, alcohol, and pills."

"I was confused too," says Hanson. "Lucky for me, Meyers here is smarter than I am." Meyers gives a small gracious nod at this. "Pointed out that there's another way Haley Banks could have got this tidy little injection mark. If someone else had done it for her."

We're interrupted by the slap of flip-flops on the tiled spa floor. Dr. Lutz is walking briskly toward us, bearded face like thunder. Beaten silver bracelets clanking at his wrists.

"Chief Hanson. Might I ask why you are interviewing my manager?"

"Not an interview, sir. Just an informal chat."

"No charges are being brought? No arrests made?"

"Not at this point."

"Not at any point," says Dr. Lutz. "To do so would be too ridiculous." He raises a sun-freckled, bronze-ringed finger. "The closest town to here has a population of twenty thousand. Last year there were almost one hundred drug overdoses admitted to the hospital, fourteen of them fatal. Not a single one of those overdoses were investigated by the police." He looks at Hanson. "And so. Would you mind telling me why the death of a celebrity would attract your attention when an ordinary civilian could not?"

"Hmmm," says Hanson. "Well, sir. That's what we call a good question. When a young lady dies under suspicious circumstances, it doesn't matter a whole lot to me, or Officer Meyers here, how rich or famous that person is."

"I'm afraid our lawyers don't agree," says Dr. Lutz. "I have been in contact with your superiors. You are no longer permitted on the premises without a warrant. Any further unscheduled visits will be filed as harassment. Cara, please show the officers out."

"Yes, Dr. Lutz."

It's hard to know what to feel as I lead Hanson and Meyers back through the lobby. Hanson stops, right before leaving through the main gate.

"Miss Morse," he announces. "You seem to me like a good person. A person who wouldn't like to be inadvertently complicit in any lawbreaking."

I stare back, wondering what he's getting at.

"Might be an idea to find out for yourself, what this cutting-edge trauma treatment involves."

I frown.

"Almost forgot," says Hanson. "The routine drug tests are still missing from the files we received."

Max's words come back to me.

There are aspects of the accountancy of the tests that Dr. Lutz would prefer remain confidential.

"I'm sure that's an oversight," I assure him. "I can look into that for you."

"Thank you kindly," says Hanson. He hesitates.

"Lots of famous people in your facility, Miss Morse, and in my experience, fame and wealth mean power. If someone in your clinic is covering up for a patient, we'll find out. And I would hate for a nice girl like you to be in a position of not knowing who she was defending." He glances at Meyers. "We'll be going now," he says. "Think about what I said."

I agree politely, with no intention of breaking the rules.

As I let the officers out of the facility, my pager beeps. It's a message from Dr. Lutz.

"Please meet me for lunch tomorrow. I wish to discuss your future at the Clinic."

CHAPTER THIRTY-TWO

MEG

The rest of the day passes in a blur. We have a meditation class and something called "sound healing," which is lying on your back while someone hits a gong. I get through dinner and to nighttime, when the reality of sharing a room with three strangers is only starting to dawn.

When it's time for our nightly urine sample, I take the excuse to call Harry from the bathroom stall with my plastic cup and sample-faking kit.

"Hey. Meg," He sounds relieved to hear from me. "You OK? Did you meet Sierra Johnson yet?"

"Yep."

"No way!"

"For real. Apart from the giant eyebrows, she's tiny and kind of boring. Like one of those California yoga chicks. But kind of nervy. Always on edge."

"You find anything out?"

I sigh, thinking back to the group therapy. "It's...*way* harder than I thought. Like a poker game on speed."

"They're addicts," Harry points out. "Best liars on the planet."

"Guess so." I rip open a package labeled "synthetic urine" and tip the powder into my cup. "Tom Abrams is here too, by the way. You're a fan, right?" I remember logging this, since Harry barely likes anyone.

"I watched his cowboy movies as a kid," he admits begrudgingly. "I liked Tom before he shaved the mustache and started playing maverick cop. I wonder how your famous sister would have reacted to an aging sex symbol," he adds meaningfully.

"If Haley was bored, she might have tried to sleep with him," I say, taking the cue. "But...I can picture him as one of the few who'd turn her down. Tom's here for alcohol and drugs. So weird, right? I can imagine Tom Abrams drinking. But drugs?"

"Anyone can surprise you," says Harry grimly. "Trust an ex-cop. I used to handle domestics. Tom's twice divorced. No kids. Wives got uglier and settlements got larger every time. Tells you something's happening behind closed doors."

"You can take a cop out of New York, but you can't take him to the movies," I observe dryly.

"Right." Harry pauses. "Did you work out who Haley was sleeping with yet?"

I consider this. "She would have gone for the most vulnerable person," I say. "Someone with plenty of soft plushy feelings to push at." I think some more. "My guess is Dex. But. Relationships didn't *have* to involve sex with Haley. Someone like Jade would have been perfect."

"How about you?" Harry asks softly. "You remembering anything you'd rather forget?"

"A name," I say slowly. "For the nightmare guy. Matthew Priest. We always called him Mr. Priest as kids."

"I can check out the name," says Harry.

I sigh. "I don't know, Harry. I feel like something happened with this guy when Haley and I were kids. What if Haley remembered too? Hurt someone because if it?"

"Why would Haley hurt someone at the Clinic because of a childhood memory?"

I sigh. "It's what she did when she was hurting. Hurt someone, or messed with someone. Or both. You had to know her really well not to blame her for it."

I tip water from my bottle onto the sample powder, swirl it, and tip a little more. Done. Fake pee.

"Someone put another warning note into my pocket. Signed by Haley. It was even in her handwriting."

"OK. Wow," says Harry thoughtfully. "You not keeping a good eye on your pockets, Meg?"

"I haven't exactly been at my most alert," I admit.

"Most likely person leaving them is Jade, right? She warned you away."

"Maybe…Dex. He doesn't want me here. If I could get him alone, I think I could maybe get a good read."

I hear a chair jerk. "Jeez, Meg, I just spilled my fucking coffee! Promise me, you will *not* get a fucking *murder suspect* alone and start asking him stressful questions."

"OK, OK, I promise. So how am I supposed to find out who's leaving me notes?"

"Did you manage to keep the note this time?" He sounds wary.

"Of course." It's hard not to be insulted by the obvious suggestion I imagined it to be.

"Can you get access to any fine dark powder? Eye shadow. Something like that. And a fine brush?"

"Yeah. Maybe." Madeline piles on makeup. Not sure she'd be happy to lend it though. "Why?"

"If you can, you might be able to fingerprint the note. It's a long shot. But if you get anything legible, take a photo. Send it. I'll analyze it against anyone we have on file."

"My prints are on the note too," I point out.

"I can adjust for them," says Harry. "You've got a record too."

I breathe out. "Thanks. There is another explanation for the note. You said the autopsy was done fast, right? What if Haley's still alive?"

There's a weird silence.

"You think your famous sister persuaded five rich and famous people to misidentify her corpse, along with a registered coroner?"

"It wasn't my theory, but it's a good one."

"No it isn't." Harry sounds completely exasperated. "It's a terrible theory. It's the kind of theory someone who never actually *stopped* using oxy would have."

There's a loaded silence.

"I know you, Meg," says Harry. "I know you're smart enough to smuggle drugs in if you want to. But that wasn't our deal." He sighs heavily.

"If my theory is so bad, what's yours?"

"I already told you. My theory is you're avoiding grieving your sister. You need to get out of there. It's not healthy."

For a moment I think Harry is going to try to insist I leave.

He sighs. "Just. Try to actually engage with the treatment, would ya?"

"Sure thing." I hear a door open. "I gotta go," I whisper.

"Good night, Meg."

There's a pounding on the door.

"Hey, what you doing in there?" growls Madeline.

"Fuck off and mind your own business," I say in a singsong

voice, scooping the phone up. "Not all of us can pee on command," I tell her.

"You need to come out. The nurse is here with the medication."

I leave the stall, thinking through how I can get hold of dark powder. And what it might tell me if I manage to fingerprint the note.

Theoretically, any patient could have gotten near enough if they were adept at sleight of hand. With my hourly shaking episodes and complete brain fog, it's not like I'm in any state to be vigilant.

It could have been anyone.

CHAPTER THIRTY-THREE

CARA

The patients have finished morning sessions and are headed to art therapy. Which means it's technically my lunch break. I am shaky with nerves as I head to Dr. Lutz's private luncheon room.

Why does Dr. Lutz want to speak with me? A lunch sounds... serious. Final, even. Memories of my humiliating hotel demotion rear up. The email ushering me out to the vagrant hotel. I can't get Police Chief Hanson's words out of my head. Why do the police seem concerned about our treatments here?

Dr. Lutz is waiting for me in the informal restaurant setting I remember from my interview. It's a private dining room for staff, bohemian style, with floor-cushion brightly colored seating and dream catchers hanging from the ceiling.

He stands to greet me, soft tummy encased in today's slogan shirt—"Clean and Sober"—and bows in greeting, hands in prayer. He hasn't bothered with flip-flops today and folds his legs, bare feet and all, cross-legged under the low table.

"Good to see you, Cara." He gestures, and I sit, awkwardly putting my high-heeled feet to the side.

"I wondered if you might be interested in taking a more clinical role. Learning more about our treatments here." He strokes his exuberant beard.

OK. Not what I expected.

"Ah!" Dr. Lutz fixes his eyes on the far end of the room and raises his hand. I resist turning, and moments later a nurse places a dish of food in front of us.

It's a plate of wafer-thin white sushi so far as I can make out. Arranged like a beautiful white flower with delicate translucent petals.

"Tell me," says Dr. Lutz, brown eyes looking intently into my face. "Have you heard of fugu?"

"Is it a type of sushi?" I guess, confused by the sudden switch in subjects. I'm hoping he's referring to the food and not some medical procedure I should know about.

"A very special type of sushi." Dr. Lutz picks up his chopsticks and takes a sliver. "Fugu is made from blowfish. Parts of which are highly toxic."

Right. The white slices take on a new meaning.

"In Japan, a chef must hold a special license to prepare fugu," adds Dr. Lutz, holding the sliver aloft. "He trains for many years. In Europe, the serving of blowfish is strictly prohibited." He smiles happily, then angles the chopsticks past his beard, dropping a small piece into his mouth. His lips make exaggerated chewing movements.

"Correctly prepared, it gives enough poison to make the lips and tongue tingle." He taps his lips. "The slightest mistake on the part of the chef, and it is deadly. There is no antidote; people die of fugu poisoning every year."

Dr. Lutz pauses for effect.

"The most terrible death, Cara. They are conscious but

completely paralyzed. Unable to move a muscle or communicate their distress. Death usually occurs in an hour but can take much longer. Can you imagine? Fully conscious, knowing you are dying, unable to move a single muscle?"

I shake my head slowly.

"In Japan, fugu victims have been mistakenly buried alive."

A flash of Haley's body pops into my mind. The brutal T-shaped autopsy cuts. I realize my breathing has quickened and deliberately slow it down.

"That sounds awful," I say, eyeing the fish.

"Please." Dr. Lutz moves the dish toward me. "Won't you try some? It has a unique flavor."

"I'd rather not. Thank you."

"But I insist." He waves a hand. "Call it an act of faith. Part of your training."

Good etiquette was part of my upbringing. "OK." I try to act natural. My chopsticks are shaking a little as I reach across the table and take a piece of fish. I drop it into my mouth. The flavor is like nothing at all. Cold white fish. But after a few seconds there's an unmistakable buzzing sensation. My tongue feels itchy and my lips are aglow.

"How is it, Cara?"

"Very good," I say politely.

"The sensation you are feeling is the tetrodotoxin killing neurotransmitters in your mouth." Inadvertently I put a hand to my tingling lips.

"You have been speaking with the police," Dr. Lutz observes, leaning over to take more fish from the plate. Bushy eyebrows lowered suggestively.

It's not a question.

"Yes." It comes out croaky. Like I'm guilty of something.

"I hope you were helpful to them." He leans back slightly, beaming. "You must forgive my little games, Cara. I am, at heart, a showman. I have a good reason for serving you this particular luncheon. I wanted to explain to you the treatment we do here."

He gestures to the plated fish.

"Did you know the neurotoxins in fugu fish have shown great promise in treating addiction?"

"They have?" My mind is trying to keep up with what he's telling me.

"Absolutely. Blowfish is already used to treat cramps in heroin withdrawal." He pauses for effect. "But it can also be used to treat trauma."

"How?"

"You're aware the main challenge to trauma processing is relaxation?"

"Yes." I call to mind my earlier conversation with Max. The conundrum of helping a traumatized person to relax their body during horrific memories.

"Fugu can put the body into a kind of trance," explains Dr. Lutz. "Where repressed memories can surface freely." He mimes with his hands, a bubbling up.

The theory makes sense, I guess. But it seems…unethical somehow. Forcing a relaxed state. Not to mention risky.

"Surely that would be extremely dangerous?"

Dr. Lutz looks delighted at the question. He waves a finger.

"I can see I chose correctly with you, Cara," he says. "You have intelligence. You are willing to learn."

"Thank you." It's hard not to feel flattered.

"Danger is a question of degrees." He looks thoughtful, holding his knife aloft. "Neurotoxins have a long history of safe use in clinical practice. Morphine. Botox. Initially they too raised great concerns. Now both medications enjoy some of the highest-growth financial shares in the world."

"We are already carrying out this treatment?" I know the answer.

"Absolutely. With extremely promising results. Max is developing the drug itself. I administer and monitor the effects." Dr. Lutz pauses. "Be a little careful with Max. He feels things very deeply and is not always logical. Excessive empathy isn't always a good thing in medicine."

He doesn't elaborate, and I fit it with what I've seen of Max. Stern, serious, aloof. Astonishingly committed to his patients. I never saw that as a negative.

"Do the police know we're conducting this treatment?" I'm thinking this could explain Hanson's insistence on seeing the drug tests.

"Everything we are doing is medically approved," says Dr. Lutz. "But now that I have told you all our secrets, perhaps you understand why we can't share our procedures with the police. We are currently seeking a patent. If another company discovered our secrets, we could stand to lose billions."

"I'll be sure to keep our work confidential," I tell him, thinking it explains the missing drug test results. Maybe fugu would show up in the urine samples.

Doesn't explain the pregnancy tests. I resolve to ask Max about that, first chance I get.

Dr. Lutz beams from behind his teddy-bear beard.

"You are a hard worker, Cara," he says. "We shall do great things together."

CHAPTER THIRTY-FOUR

MEG

When I wake up the next morning, I feel as bad as when I went to sleep. Worse. The headache is a sickly throb, my shoulder aches, and my whole body routinely erupts in head-to-toe shaking. I tell myself it's low blood sugar, but it doesn't go. Not even after I pop some oxy from my stash and eat breakfast.

My thoughts won't get in order either.

The note, I decide. That's my biggest clue. I need to get some dark powder. Luckily, the first session of the day is art therapy.

We all troop along together.

Fat beams of curved oak mark corridor intersections, as though you're walking beneath the skeletal keel of a half-built Nordic long boat.

By the time we arrive at art therapy, my mind is boiling over.

The room is the complete opposite of where we took group therapy. A tall vaulted ceiling is clad in sunny pine planks, with a giant floor-to-ceiling window looking out away from the coast toward the wild pine forest. Easels and materials have been set up on different tables. Paintbrushes, paints, pencils, and small wheeled carts holding various scrap supplies.

I enter to loud voices.

"Why don't you tell her the rest of it?" Dex demands.

He's talking to Madeline. She glares. "What does it matter?" she tells Dex. "It doesn't affect her."

"Haley's dead, Madeline," says Dex, his voice pitching into emotion. "She's dead and they're telling lies about it…"

Suddenly, he freezes. As if someone has delivered him an electric shock.

I stare. Dex suddenly comes to, with no apparent realization of what happened.

He stares at the picture in front of him, then at the pen in his hand. I walk into the room, taking in the strained atmosphere, looking around for anything to use for fingerprint powder.

The other patients are already at work. There's no art therapist, just a large notice with the day of the week and an instruction to "VISUALIZE YOUR ADDICT." Huh.

I return my mind to the issue at hand. *OK. What can I use for fingerprint dust. Paint powder? Charcoal?*

The cart nearest to Madeline has pastel chalks. *Perfect.*

But as I go to stand near her, Madeline moves the cart away.

"Hey, can I use those?" I try for a winning smile.

"Nope." Madeline's filler-bloated lips stretch up in a smug smile. She flips her long black hair. "Wait your turn."

I swallow my frustration. Twist my easel to face away from Madeline and pick up an ink pen and turn to Sierra, who is cutting and pasting some collage work next to me.

"What is treatment anyway?" I ask, deliberately picking a question I'm fairly certain will distract Sierra.

Nervous glances run around the group. "We're not supposed to talk about it with patients who aren't having it," says Sierra apologetically. "It's kind of like a memory processing thing," she adds, but she doesn't take her eyes away from the sight line of the brush I need.

"He gives you this drug so you can't move," says Dex, glaring at his easel.

"*Dex*," hisses Madeline. "You'll get into trouble."

I try to imagine how Haley would respond to that and find I can't. I only know that being paralyzed, unable to distract myself from my own terrible thoughts, is about my worst nightmare.

"Don't worry if you're not into art, Meg," Jade tells me, clearly trying to change the subject. "But when you get started, it's surprising what comes out."

I trail my pen distractedly. At school I was good at drawing. Don't remember the last time I sketched anything.

Visualize my inner addict.

I guess…she would be female. I start with that, trying to look busy while sneaking glances at Sierra's easel.

It's stuck with scrap newspaper stories, collaged to make a face. *Her* face, I realize, taking in the cupid mouth and signature brows. The eyes are lowered so only thick stubby lashes can be seen. Conceptually, it's a lot deeper than I'd expect from Sierra, who is famous for sugary pop songs with two vacant-looking girls.

There's a stack of printed news articles that she's working to cut up. The headlines pop out.

COKED-UP SIERRA, SIERRA TRASHES BAR.

Sierra looks up at me.

"They're all bullshit," she says with surprising venom. "Most of them, anyway." She tilts her head to look at the board, then tears off another piece and sticks it.

My eyes drop to the latest headline reveal on her table.

"SIERRA AND HALEY: THE FEUD CONTINUES."

I watch her paste. "I didn't realize there was a feud between you and Haley Banks."

CHAPTER THIRTY-FIVE

CARA

I'm working in the library, checking off a delivery of books, when Max finds me.

"Working in your free time?" he asks. "Thought I was the only one."

I smile. "Nope."

"Couple of work addicts," says Max. "That's why he hires us. We both know who 'he' is."

"You talk about it like a real addiction," I laugh.

"It is a real addiction," says Max. "We're fortunate it's socially acceptable. But you, me, our patients. We all have something in common."

Is it me, or is there a warning in Max's tone? Like he's trying to tell me something. About Dr. Lutz.

"Max," I say. "Did you know we were conducting pregnancy tests? On Haley Banks."

I leave it open-ended. Max takes the cue.

"We carry out pregnancy tests on all women patients. Your average rehab has a better hook-up rate than an online dating site. It's only sensible to take precautions when we're issuing medication. You ever heard of rehab romance syndrome?" he adds.

I shake my head.

"People are about five times more likely to become infatuated with one another in rehab," he says. "All that group camaraderie has its downside."

Relief washes through me. This makes total sense.

Max sighs. "You're doing a great job, Cara," he says. This should be a compliment, but oddly, he sounds sad about it. "Keeping everything running smoothly," he says. "Making sure everything looks pristine."

"Ever since I first set foot in a hotel, I've always loved them," I tell him. "That little bubble. Away from the chaos and dirt of the regular world."

"Shame about the guests," he says, deadpan.

Is he... Was that a joke?

"Addicts are hard to manage," I agree. "You need eyes everywhere. But...creating a perfect place for recovery means even more."

Max frowns at the word *perfect*.

"Do you feel like if things look perfect, anything bad will go away?" he suggests.

I open my mouth but no words come out.

"Sorry," adds Max. "I just got out of a therapy session. I'm still in psychologist mode."

He's good, I think to myself. Though I'm not sure I like how he's analyzed me so accurately.

"It's OK," I say, recovering myself. "You're probably right. My whole childhood felt like it was tidying up and covering up for my brother. Keeping the family reputation safe. And...maybe...there's a link between the two."

"Your brother was an addict?" Max guesses.

I hesitate. "Methamphetamine," I say. "He died of an overdose when he was twenty-one."

"I'm sorry to hear that. Addiction can be cruelest to relatives."

"Yes," I say with feeling. "Although…" I pause. "His death was a difficult thing to accept."

"I feel the same way about Haley Banks," says Max. "I really thought she was going to make it."

"She was doing well in therapy?"

"I thought so." Max looks defeated. "When we started treatment, Haley struggled with her value to men, besides sexual value. The day she died, she talked about a painful secret. A man from her childhood she wanted to connect with. It felt like growth to me."

I look at Max for a long moment. "You…don't think she killed herself, do you?"

Max puts his fingers to his temples. "It doesn't make sense," he says finally. "Dr. Lutz was helping her access her repressed memories. We were working through them. She was doing well." He looks thoughtful. "The only thing Haley was struggling with was ditching her old coping mechanisms."

"But if her coping mechanisms were drugs…"

"Drugs were one of the ways Haley avoided painful feelings. She was also very adept at using people. My fear is she went too far." Max shakes his head slowly. "But…I've been wrong so many times," he says with a wry smile. "Addicts will always, always surprise you. You never know who will get better and who won't."

"I nearly forgot," he says. "There was someone coming to pick up Haley's effects. Childhood friend of the family." Max closes his eyes for a moment. "It was…" he clicks his fingers repeatedly. "Matthew Priest."

"Won't the police want Haley's belongings now?" I suggest.

"Probably," agrees Max.

"OK." I mentally note the task. "I'll tell Mr. Priest to delay his visit."

CHAPTER THIRTY-SIX

MEG

The atmosphere in the art therapy room drops by several degrees. I could swear I feel all eyes on me. I ignore the shift, concentrating on Sierra's inner addict art.

The last headline. About the feud between Sierra and Haley. Underneath is a montage of three pictures. A large one of Sierra looking angry, out of control, looming at the lens. Two smaller broken-out shots. One shows Sierra tussling with another woman, whose posture and frame is very familiar.

Haley. She's being led away, looking tiny next to two security men, a vulnerable, frightened look on her face. Only I know, of course, that Haley is never *actually* frightened and vulnerable. She's playing to the camera.

There's a pause. I look at my easel. A female form is taking shape.

"You wound up in rehab with your worst enemy, huh?" I say, keeping my tone far lighter than the sudden tension in the room deserves. I can feel Madeline's eyes boring into me.

Sierra looks pained. "Me and Haley were friends," she says. "*Good* friends. We put all that shit behind us in rehab."

Something about the way she says it hurts. Because Haley could be a good friend, if she decided she liked you. A *great* friend in actual fact. Haley wouldn't have taken a bullet for you exactly. But if you were in her inner circle, she sure as hell would have fired one on your behalf.

Can't easily picture Haley being friends with Sierra though. Unless my sister wanted something from her.

"New girl still asking about Haley?" Madeline demands suddenly in a loud voice. "Someone should learn to keep their mouth shut about touchy subjects."

I'm about to tell Madeline to go fuck herself when there's a clatter from the other side of the room and Dex swears loudly.

His picture has fallen. I view it upside down. It actually shows extreme talent, like an inked illustration to a dark fairy tale. Naked women flow around a misshapen warty beast figure.

It's disturbing. The women are monstrous, like harpies or vampires.

His eyes raise to me. "Yes, in case you're wondering, I am fucked up."

"Dex," says Jade. "Chill out…"

I notice something about one of the women in Dex's picture.

"That's Haley Banks," I say, pointing. "Isn't it?"

It's actually a good likeness. Haley flies close to the dark central monster, sucking energy from it in a glowing vortex. Compared to the other hideous harpies, she's not so bad. But it's still far from flattering.

Madeline lowers her brush, brown eyes narrowed. "Did you not hear me the first time, dumbass? What the fuck is wrong with you?"

Irritation spikes me. "Why don't you mind your own damn business?" I fire back.

"Everyone here is my business," says Madeline. "We're all

supposed to be recovering together. And you're not nearly fucked up enough for someone three days off drugs."

"Leave her alone, Madeline," mutters Dex testily, as I summon my best neutral poker face.

"Oh, you want everyone asking about Haley?" Madeline demands. "'Cause we all know you *wanted* her dead."

Dex stares at Madeline. He looks haunted. Then his face twists and he hurls his pencil to the floor.

"Fuck you, Madeline," he whispers before turning and storming out.

"Go ahead; have you little hissy fit!" Madeline shouts in his wake, tossing her dark hair. "You know it's true," she voices to everyone else.

"What was *that* about?" I ask Jade in a whisper, trying to add the right amount of shock and casual to my tone.

Jade leans away from her easel to watch the direction Dex left in.

"Oh that," she says. "Just Madeline being a little bitch. She's fishing. No one knows for sure if there was anything going on with Dex and Haley."

"Wait. What? Why would that mean Dex would want Haley dead?"

"Dex is here by court order," says Jade, sticking another piece on her picture. "If Dex *had* gotten caught doing things he shouldn't with Haley…" She mimes throat cutting. "We're the do-or-die crew here," she adds. "All of us."

Something occurs to me. I've been waiting for the chance to question Dex alone. This could be the perfect opportunity. I need an excuse to leave the room.

I ponder this, turning back to my easel. And it's only in this moment that I take in what I've been sketching.

Oh *shit*.

The pen shakes in my hand.

Oh shit. Oh *shit*.

It's her. The lady.

I've drawn the woman who stands by Mr. Priest in my nightmares.

She wears vintage-style corsetry underwear. Deep panties with suspenders and stocking tops are visible on her half-sketched legs. And her face...

I've outlined the bee-stung lips. The heavy-lashed eyes. But the pixie nose. The angular cheeks.

They're Haley's.

The pen falls from my hand.

"Meg?" Jade twists to me, eyes wide with concern. "Are you OK, chick?"

"Um." My hand is at my mouth. "I just... I have to get out of here."

I'm not even lying. But if I learned anything growing up with Mom, it's to use any bad emotions to get what you want.

I fly out of the room before anyone can follow me. Heading after Dex.

CHAPTER THIRTY-SEVEN

CARA

Since the lunch with Dr. Lutz, I can't seem to sit still. It would seem to make sense that we can't share drug tests with the police if it risks a patent we're developing.

So why do I feel like there's more to it?

The results of the tests are on my system. Would it even be against the rules to look into them?

I must have opened and shut the folder with the sample results inside a dozen times.

Sighing, I close it down. I'm not the kind of person to break the rules. And I have plenty of work to do.

Writing up patient therapy sessions for one. Though if I'm being honest with myself, I deliberately put Dex's recordings on the top of the pile.

I click on Play and hear Max's voice issue from my computer.

"You think the sexual abuse from your stepmother messed up your feelings about women?" Max asks gently.

There's a pause. "Yeah. I guess. I mean. Like we talked about. I didn't see it as abuse at the time." Dex makes a noise that could be laughing or crying. "*Fuck*. I thought I was lucky. How messed up is that?"

Max hesitates. "Let's talk about your relationship with your father."

"Nothing to tell." Dex sounds sad. Reflective.

"You mentioned he worked away a lot," prompts Max.

"Yeah. He was a university lecturer," says Dex. "Once I hit thirteen, he'd leave me his credit card and the pizza delivery number."

Max is silent for a moment. "A university lecturer father doesn't fit with your stage image," he observes.

"Oh, the crazy, drug-fueled womanizer? No. My dad doesn't approve," Dex agrees.

"Do you think your stage persona might have been a way to attract your father's attention?" suggests Max.

My desktop phone rings loudly. I stop the recording.

Exterior call. Somehow I am not surprised to hear Meyers's chirpy voice at the end of the line.

"Cara? How are you?" There's a wail from somewhere in the background. "Sorry about that," she adds. "I'm not technically on shift yet. Just riding the baby around, trying to get him to sleep."

I can't help but smile. She has no decorum at all, but I'm minding less.

"Very well, thank you. How can I help?"

"We didn't get those tests sent through yet, wondered if you could help us out."

I'm already shaking my head. "I'm sorry," I say. "We have a very strict policy on any external sharing of data. It has to come from Dr. Lutz."

I hear a rumbling in the background that I assume to be Hanson.

Meyers clears her throat. "Hanson says we can formally subpoena them. That would be a lot of administrative pain for you all, so we'd rather avoid it."

"I'm completely torn. Technically, I am *able* to send the test files. It's against the rules. But the police are the ultimate rule makers, aren't they?" I realize I'm tapping my fingers distractedly.

"Give me five minutes to see what I can do," I say, stalling.

"All right," says Meyers cheerfully. "Guess we can wait five minutes. Right, Hanson?"

I don't hear his reply, but the tone sounds unhappy.

She hangs up. I chew at my lip, wondering what the best course of action is. Dr. Lutz is in treatment and can't be disturbed. Max is in a therapy session. I guess the most sensible thing to do is... send them myself.

Dr. Lutz is probably being overcautious. I can't imagine the police selling his medical secrets for millions.

I click on the folder. The password screen pops up, and it's enough to suck the bravery out of me. I know the system password, but I'd be full-on breaking the rules to enter it.

My finger hovers with the mouse for a second.

Then, very slowly, I push in the password, one letter at a time. My fingers hovers, and when I hit Enter, there's a thrill I haven't felt in a long time.

I check the company supplying the tests. The headers all appear legitimate, a Florida-based company. Pro Lab Florida.

My mind flicks briefly to an image of scientists in the Florida sun, packing up cassettes to send to the misty Northwest.

I click twice.

Inside the file are PDF copies of the test results for Haley. I open one at random. It's a basic list. Nothing that mentions fugu or any kind of specialized toxicology. I frown, confused. Nothing here that would risk any drug patents.

My eyes track down the list of what we test for.

AMPHETAMINES: NEGATIVE

THC: NEGATIVE

OPIOIDS: NEGATIVE

BARBITURATES: NEGATIVE

BENZODIAZEPINES: POSITIVE

Wait. Positive?

I take a second to absorb this. If Haley was testing positive, why was she still in rehab?

Shoot. I can't share this with the police. These test results show total negligence.

They could shut down the whole clinic.

CHAPTER THIRTY-EIGHT

MEG

Out of the art therapy room, I feel my heartbeat slow.

What the fuck was that? How could I have drawn the woman from my nightmare?

You're remembering things, says a dark little voice. *The alcohol has kept them locked up for seventeen years. Now they're coming back.*

The idea of that frightens me so much, I actually have closed my eyes for a moment. I pull free the oxy pack. Stare at the foil for all of two seconds before popping out five pills at once and swallowing them without water.

The effect shouldn't be instant, but it is. Muzzy relief, as one by one, the sharp-cornered thoughts sink back into the dark waters.

OK. Find Dex. I'm walking along the corridor, wondering which direction he might have gone, when I see him. Up ahead.

I freeze, stepping back so he doesn't hear my footsteps.

Dex is outside Haley's room. Behind the cordon tape.

His chest is rising and falling, like he's steeling himself. *How long has he been there?* Suddenly he lunges forward and grabs the handle. But when he twists it, nothing happens.

Guess the door must be locked. It's not what Dex is expecting, because he curses and slams a palm against the door.

OK.

Dex thrusts his hands deep in the pockets of his skinny jeans and strides away, head bowed low in defeat, belt chains jangling as he vanishes from sight.

I watch him go. Then my eyes slide to the door.

What was Dex hoping to find in there?

Something else flits into my mind. I've known Haley my whole life. Her secret hiding places. Drug stashes. If there's something hidden in that room, I've got a better chance than Dex of finding it.

And. I've got a lockpicking kit. My hand drops to its comforting presence, stitched into my waistband. Waiting to be sure Dex is out of sight, I slip under the tape barricade.

Haley's door. Haley's room.

Something horrible rises up. A gut-wrenching sensation. Like I have a cold hollow right in the center of me.

Sadness.

"Go away," I tell it, willing the oxy to work faster. "I don't have time for you."

I slip free my lockpicking kit. The door handle has a spring-bolt mechanism, which is so easy to hack that I have to wonder why people bother with them at all.

The lock pings. I walk into the room.

A few things stand out. The bed is neatly made, which suggests Haley didn't make it. The nightstand has a picture of Haley. I pick it up.

Another crippling wave of chest-squeezing thoughts grabs at me in the emotional equivalent of a headlock.

Haley's not here.

In the picture, she's onstage, microphone in hand, golden hair flicked back, and a wide smile on her pastel-pink mouth. Cutoff denim shorts and a little tight-fitting T-shirt. Every inch the sugar-sweet country girl. At this angle, the violet eyes that she and Mom are famous for appear deep midnight blue.

This was before the media found out that Haley was about as far from southern country girl as it was possible to get: educated at an LA stage school and mostly raised between Europe, New York, and Hollywood.

I begin to search the room, not sure what I'm looking for. My watch scheduler, which I would cheerfully fling out the window right now, begins its incessant reminder. Group therapy. I ignore it.

After ten minutes I find absolutely nothing. No point going to group. It will be half over by now. I'm sitting down on the bed, defeated, when I hear something. Footsteps? Am I imagining it, or is someone close by? I hear the sound outside too late. A key in the lock.

The handle turns and the door opens.

CHAPTER THIRTY-NINE

MEG

As the door to Haley's room opens, I have about half a second to dive into the small bathroom. I peer through the hinges to see Dex has walked in.

He must have come back with a key.

Dex sits on the bed and splays his palms, like he's feeling out the texture. Then, very slowly, he presses his head into the pillow and inhales deeply. There's a noise I can't work out. Sobbing. He's sobbing. His shoulders are shaking. I try to steady my own breathing. I don't want to see this.

This is how I should feel. I don't want to be reminded I'm a freak.

Then he slides a hand under the mattress—not a place Haley would ever hide anything, and searches.

I take a step closer for a better look, and my heel knocks an empty shower gel container. It spins across the tiles, sounding stupidly loud. Dex looks up sharply.

"Hey!" he snarls. "Is someone in here? If there's someone in here, I'm gonna kick your fucking ass." He stands, furious. "Come out."

I take a breath. No point hiding. I open the door.

Dex's eyes widen when he sees me. "Meg? What the fuck?" His shoulders sag. "Man. I thought you were paparazzi that, like, snuck

in here." His face crumples in relief. "Seriously. I thought I was going
back to jail for sure. Don't know what I would have done if I'd found
a reporter pawing over her stuff." He looks like a little kid suddenly.
Like he's out of control of himself and doesn't know why.

"Rehab not helping with your anger issues?" I say.

His eyes grow wide. "Is it helping you?"

"I don't have anger issues."

"You're kidding, right? You're the angriest person I've ever met."

"What are you doing in Haley's room?"

"I could ask you the same question." He sighs. "Group therapy
got to be too much, OK. I bailed. Everyone's pissed, by the way.
Max said you were supposed to read your honesty statement today."

"If I tell Max you came here, you'll get kicked out," I tell him.
"You'll go to jail."

"You'll get kicked out too."

"Doesn't bother me."

Dex's eyes narrow. "That's bull."

For a simple guy, I'm surprised at his insight. There's a loaded
pause. I glance at the door.

"Then I guess we'll just have to tell each other the truth," I say.
"You first. What were you looking for under the mattress?"

Dex takes a breath, and I fix my gaze, taking in as much as I
can at once.

Rigid body, curled fingers, lowered eyebrows…

Everything about him says he's about to fold.

"There were some pages, OK?" he admits. "From Haley's journal.
After she died…I snuck in here and ripped them out. I think Max
suspects," he adds miserably. "Keeps mentioning it in therapy."

"Why did you rip them out?" I ask.

His dark eyebrows lower, and he rubs his forehead. "I wanted to see what she'd written about me. Maybe even…to have a piece of her." His face collapses and he lets out a sob.

Sounds about right, I think gloomily. *Everyone wanted a piece of Haley.*

"We had something, all right? Me and Haley. I loved her. I think I loved her. They say in rehab, your feelings get fucked up… so…I needed to know if it was real. For Haley. If she felt the same."

Oh man. I suddenly feel very sorry for Dex. One thing you should never do with Haley is fall in love with her.

"Did she write about you?" I ask gently.

"Yeah. Well. I didn't read all the pages yet. Only just worked up the courage. And I'm too late. I guess one of the housekeepers must have cleaned the place out and locked the door." He manages a weak smile. "I know it's dumb, but…I imagined us having a life together. Outside rehab, you know? Like maybe we'd get a farm. Move away from all the LA crap. Or a house in England maybe. Have kids with English accents."

I sit next to him. I'd been planning to lie, but it doesn't seem right to let him suffer with his mad view of Haley. She had a gift for that. Letting people see what they wanted to see.

When Haley decided to turn it on, she was magnetic. Irresistible.

"From what I've heard, Haley was a complicated person," I tell him. "I'm sure she had feelings for you. But…she also liked to be the center. To string guys along."

His eyes flick to mine. "Wait. You knew her?"

"I moved in some of the same circles. Hollywood, all that stuff."

His body relaxes like I've given him good news. "You wouldn't say that if you met her," he says. "She was different in here than how she seemed on TV."

It hurts. Him talking about her like he knew her best.

"I had a friend who knew her really well," I tell him. "At least…

as well as anyone could know Haley. I don't think she would have given up her life in LA. She was too into the fame thing."

He's shaking his head. "She was for real." He frowns deeply. I think about this. Haley was unbelievably exciting to be around. I miss her. It's the first time I've let myself think it.

"She was kind of out there before she died," adds Dex sadly. "Treatments with Dr. Lutz hit her hard. Haley was talking about this guy in a fedora hat or whatever."

The fedora hat. Mr. Priest had a certain way of taking it off. I shudder without meaning to.

I need Dex to stop talking now. To stop talking about Haley.

His eyes settle on mine for a moment too long. Something flashes between us and suddenly we're kissing. I couldn't even tell you who started it. Only I'm pulling at his shirt, exposing his lean tattooed chest, when he breaks away, still holding my waist.

"Sorry," he says. "I'm sorry. This is… It's part of my addiction." He gives me a smile. His eyes are still on mine, and I can tell his resolve is basically nonexistent. One move from me, and it would be back on. My heart is pounding.

"Yeah," I say. "Don't know where that came from. Jeez." I scrunch my eyes shut, then open them and stand, thoughts racing. What's wrong with me?

Trying to score points off a dead girl, Meggy? asks an evil little Haley voice. *Lame.*

"It gets crazy in here," says Dex. "Emotions run wild. In a weird way, it's lonely. Completely natural to want to get close to someone. Least, that's what Max says."

There's a noise outside. Hammering on the door.

Dex and I exchange glances.

Fuck. Someone knows we're inside.

CHAPTER FORTY

CARA

I feel like I have been staring at my screen for ten minutes without blinking.

Haley's drug tests. I scroll through the results. She was testing positive the whole time she was at the Clinic.

A wall of positive results, and no one reported it.

Nothing gives any indication action was taken. There should have been a full meeting on Haley's suitability to stay in the Clinic. My thoughts fly to Max. He must be in on this somehow. He signed off on the papers.

I need to confront him, I decide. My scheduler shows him to be in therapy for another two hours.

Allowing myself a brief sigh of frustration, I check my emails.

I have a new email from housekeeping, titled:

Found in Room 5.

That's Haley's room. Or was. I open the email and scan the message.

OK. Looks like the missing journal pages showed up. Housekeeping found them under the mattress in Haley's room. There's a hasty photograph to accompany the message. Showing a clutch of the handwritten pages fanned loosely on her bed.

Dr. Lutz is cc'd and it looks like he's already replied. The pages have been added to Haley's confidential clinical file. Nothing more for me to do.

So why do I find myself looking more closely at the attached snap of the missing journal pages?

Zooming in, I can't read much from the way the papers are laid out. What appears to be a free-association-type scrawl. Song lyrics.

One page has two intertwined hearts drawn on it. I move my head closer to the screen. There is a name inside each heart. With a vicious pen mark etched over both, almost deep enough to rip the page.

I zoom in closer, trying to see. Just legible beneath the angry pen slashes. Make out one name: Tom.

That's all I can see. Looks like Haley might have written some more underneath, but a page lies over that entry.

As I draw back from the screen, a nasty feeling flushes through me. I missed it. It's my job to make sure patients stick to the rules. Was Haley sneaking around with Tom?

"Fucking *junkies*." My hands fly to my mouth. I actually said that out loud. I glance about the lobby.

In the last therapy session recordings for Tom, I remember him talking about divorcing his wife. He talks like he genuinely cares about her. But if there was something between him and Haley... Did I miss some subtext?

I search out the session, pull on my headphones, and click Play. Then fast-forward until I hear Tom talking about the tempestuous relationship with his third wife. Reading between the lines, she's a Hollywood bottom-feeder twenty years his junior who supplies his drugs.

Tom's famous voice comes loud and clear on the tape.

"I didn't do it," Tom is telling Max. "Didn't have the guts to break it off with her. Judge how you want."

Max's voice sounds. "Why would you think I would be judging you?"

There's another long silence. I recheck the recording, and it's still rolling.

"Well, you should," replies Tom. "When I was high, I put my hands around her throat. My own wife. If I'd have squeezed harder, I could be serving for life right now." His voice breaks. "I can't ever make that up to her," mumbles Tom. "I can't just ditch her."

Another pause.

"I know what you're thinking," Tom continues. "I've let you down. You were expecting good, old clean-cut Tom Abrams. Nice guy, right? Sorry to disappoint you, Dr. Max. I'm a dirtbag. Keeping that from the public is my agent's full-time job."

I blow out air. The clean-cut TV star is certainly *not* who he appears to be on-screen. Nothing on the recording to suggest he's cheating on his wife. But that doesn't necessarily mean he wasn't.

I take a short break, pausing the recording and neatening my blond hair where the headphones have pushed it out of shape.

It occurs to me I should probably alert Meyers to the missing journal pages. She left me her direct line. It picks up on the third ring.

"We found some missing journal pages for Haley Banks," I tell her. "Thought you might want them sent. I can email them when they get to me, if you let me know an address."

"Sure." I hear typing. "You can send them to 'soccer-mom-with-a-gun@hotmail.com.'"

"You're serious?"

"Fastest contact for me," says Meyers, with no indication she thinks her email grossly unprofessional. "Else it gets caught up in external servers and whatnot."

"While I have you on the phone," says Meyers. "Those drug tests show up yet?"

My eyes drift to my computer. Max's scheduler now shows "free time."

"Not quite yet," I tell her. "Let me speak with Dr. Max."

CHAPTER FORTY-ONE

MEG

Inside Haley's bedroom, the pounding on the door continues.

"Hide," whispers Dex. "I'll cover for you."

I shake my head slowly. "I can talk my way out of it better than you," I tell him. "You hide."

"No way," he hisses. "I done some bad stuff, but I never left a woman to take the blame for me."

We're glaring at each other.

More knocking. "I'm coming in," says a low woman's voice. "I know you're in there, Tom."

"Oh shit." Dex runs a hand through his dark hair. "It's Madeline."

"Why does Madeline think Tom's in here?"

"Hide in the bathroom, OK? I can talk her around."

I scoot out of sight as Dex opens the door.

Madeline glowers at Dex, matching his height, long dark hair tucked behind her ears.

"Christ, Madeline." Dex looks up and down the corridor. "You'll get us all kicked out."

"Where's Tom?" demands Madeline, peering behind Dex.

"Tom isn't here," says Dex.

In answer, Madeline strides toward the bathroom where I'm hiding.

I flatten myself behind the door.

"Tom? Are you in here?" I hear her voice call from the doorway.

What the fuck?

Madeline remerges.

"You want to tell me what's going on?" demands Dex.

Madeline glares at him for a moment, her famously exotic eyes now bloodshot and pinched. She lets out a sigh, her long body sagging slightly.

"Tom and Jade took off together, OK?" she says quietly. "I'm trying to find them before...I don't know...something happens."

Tom and *Jade*? I could never in a million years see that combination.

Dex absorbs this. From his expression, he couldn't either. "Probably not what you think," he tells her. "Tom told me he didn't divorce his wife yet."

"Because she's a junkie threatening to file assault charges," says Madeline. "There's no relationship there."

"I'm not so sure," says Dex. "And Jade would never take that risk. Not with her kid to lose."

"You're probably right," Madeline decides finally, her gravelly voice lowering in acceptance. "It's...after Haley. You get used to the feeling anything could happen."

Something twists on Dex's face. "Yeah," he says with feeling.

"Hey, Dex," Madeline winds a long strand of black hair around a red fingernail. "You don't think I'm a gross old lady now, right? We had fun once, remember?"

She puts a long finger on his chest and bats her eyelids. To my surprise, beads of sweat break out on Dex's face.

"That was before rehab, Madeline," he says. "I'm a different person now. You too."

Madeline's face does something strange. It drops. Like she's disappointed in herself. She swings her long black hair over one shoulder.

"I was messing with you," she says with an unconvincing grin. "I'm going to look for Tom. Don't be late for the next session." She stalks away.

Dex turns to me, sagging in relief.

"You and Madeline?" I say.

"Everybody and Madeline," says Dex, watching her leave. "Some messed-up party years ago. Thought I had that under control," he mutters. His eyes meet mine. "Lucky you were here. If you weren't..." Dex does some measured yoga breath thing.

"You would have fucked *Madeline*?"

"Maybe. Yeah. What kind of a piece of shit does that make me? I'm an addict, Meg." He looks deeply pained.

"Why was she so desperate to find Tom?" I ask.

"Madeline cares about people here. I know she doesn't show it in the best way. But she doesn't want people relapsing." He lets out a long huff of air. "You should go wherever you're supposed to be," he decides. "Before someone sees us together."

"Deal. Wait. Dex?"

"Yeah?" He moves a little closer to me. Enough to feel his body heat.

I focus on his eyes. "Have you, by any chance, been putting notes in my pocket?"

His expression says it all. He has absolutely no idea what I'm talking about.

"Don't worry," I frown. "Forget about it."

OK. I would bet every last chip that Dex has not been slipping me notes signed by Haley.

Dex gives me a lingering look. This time there's something very complicated mixed up in his expression. Anger, sadness. A fathomless black despair.

"Something about your eyes," he says in a low voice. His hand reaches to touch my cheek. "It's the same thing Haley had. Fucking irresistible. I couldn't get enough of that."

The tone of his voice is all wrong. We stare at each other for a moment. I think of Harry.

"This is fucked up," I mutter.

"Tell me about it," says Dex, moving in, hand still on my face so his body is closing mine against the wall. "Makes it more exciting, right?"

"See you later, Dex." I slip past him and head off at a fast walk. When I risk a glance back, Dex is still staring after me.

As I turn out of sight, I send a quick message to Harry. There are so many things I want to say to him. Harry is on shift tonight, so he'll be asleep.

I type out: I turned down a famous rock star because you're a better kisser.

I delete it.

I type, I wish you were in here with me.

I delete it.

I type. I fell in love with you and it scared the shit out of me.

I delete it.

There's a lot of words I want to say to Harry, and I know I can't put them in a text.

Breathing up a deep sigh, I look at the blank message.

Suddenly three little dots appear.

Is Harry awake? My chest squeezes. A message from him pops up on the screen.

I miss you too, kid.

I'm surprised by how that affects me. I want to reply, telling him I miss him too. I wish I'd never broken us up.

But how can I? I promised Harry I'd quit oxy. I wanted to get better, and I can't. If Harry truly knew what a loser I was, he wouldn't even be texting me right now.

I raise my finger and type a response.

Art room has charcoal. Going to try to get it for fingerprints.

CHAPTER FORTY-TWO

MEG

The art room is empty when I get back. The ring of easels stands in a semicircle. I step carefully to avoid looking at my own sketch. Can't handle seeing my insanity twice in one day.

Right now I need to concentrate on getting supplies to finger-print the mysterious note.

I steal a couple of pastel chalks and some charcoal. My eyes fall on a selection of fluffy brushes. I stuff one in my pocket, feeling optimistic. Charcoal. A lightweight brush. It's practically a finger-printing kit.

My pager beeps at me.

Inner-child workshop.

Inner-child workshop? Kill me now.

Better get there on time, I decide. I'm heading out the door when it occurs to me I might learn something from the other patients' art. My eyes land on the first. Tom Abrams.

I take an involuntary step back.

It's a portrait in oil paint. Black head and shoulders. Narrow demonic white eyes are the only features of the square head, and horn protrusions stick up from where hair should be. It's the kind of shadow-lurking monster horror movies are made of. If I were to name an emotion for this picture, it would be "rage." There's a venomous fury to the slitted eyes.

Behind the monster at the forefront is a shadowy figure. Like a ghost or a phantom.

His addiction. Maybe. Though what strikes me most is the raw anger that lunges out from the canvas.

Madeline's picture is a very simple black oil paint outline. A kind of naive style, like a sketch for a cartoon before it gets colored in. She's captured the shape of her own slightly feline eyes and shapely brows perfectly, adding a caricatured triangular pouting mouth. Her hair is piled on her head, movie-star style, and a fur stole is draped over her bare shoulders. A champagne glass is clutched in her hand. The background is scattered with the word "BITCH" in all different sizes, thickly scrawled.

A glimpse of Jade's picture reveals a surprisingly serious pencil sketch. It shows an evil female puppet master dangling a girl on strings.

"The girl on strings is me as a kid," says a voice. "My mom is the puppeteer."

I turn to see Jade. She's smiling guilelessly. No suspicion I could be up to no good.

"You didn't paint your addiction?" I ask.

Jade studies the picture closely. "Dr. Lutz is big on root causes. My mom basically farmed me out as a child model to earn her drug money. I was an income stream to her. Left me alone in the house while she binged. Day I was born, she let her dealer's kid name me after a cartoon princess in return for a bag of weed."

"Jeez. Sorry." I pause, searching for something to say. "If it makes you feel any better, I loved that cartoon princess," I tell her. "Me and my sister watched that show all the time."

"Yeah?" Jade manages a weak smile.

"It's one of my only good childhood memories," I tell her. "Jade makes the world right with her fairy wand. *Zap, zap, zap.* Only wish I'd have had a wand like that growing up."

Jade sighs. "Max actually thinks I should be less like that. Less about solving other people's problems." She loops her arm through mine. It's unexpected, and I feel a rush of good feeling toward her. Something else is there too. The idea that Jade is familiar to me somehow. Like I've known her from another life.

"Come on," she says. "I came looking for you. Need to make sure you make the next class. Even if I have to drag you kicking and screaming."

"What happens if I don't go?" The charcoal and brush are burning a hole in my pocket. If I can get a moment to myself, I can try for fingerprints on the mysterious note from Haley.

"You could get kicked out."

"For missing *one* class?"

"You missed group therapy," says Jade. "That's two classes. And they're pretty strict. They have to be with us. Don't look so shocked, chick," she adds. "We're all last chance saloon in here. I lose custody of my little girl. Dex goes to jail. Tom loses the only agent who'll work with him. Sierra gets kicked out of her band."

As Jade steers me away, she inadvertently takes me past my own easel. Only now… I freeze, staring at the picture.

There she is. The sketch of the creepy lady who stands next to Mr. Priest. Bee-stung lips. Long lashes.

But someone else has drawn on it.

Next to my scrappy picture, scrawled in hasty pencil, is an outline of a man. The artwork is bad. Childish. But the image is unmistakable. He wears a fedora hat.

"Jade." My voice comes out calmer than I feel. "Who drew on my picture?"

She glances distractedly. "What do you mean?"

"I mean," I say, "someone drew on it. After I left."

Jade frowns then shrugs. "I'm fairly certain you left it that way."

But I didn't.

A bubble of alcohol deprivation surges through me, shredding my thoughts.

And suddenly, I can't be sure it *wasn't* me who drew that extra picture.

I can't be sure of anything at all.

CHAPTER FORTY-THREE

CARA

My first chance to get Max alone he's in his research lab. I need to confront him about the positive drug tests I found in Haley Banks's file.

When I find him, he's completely absorbed, looking at colorful brain scans.

He holds one up as I enter.

"Look at this," he says. "Evidence that the cerebellum is actually rewiring." He beams.

"Did you sign off on a bunch of positive drug tests for Haley Banks?" I blurt out.

If he's surprised at the question, he hides it well.

"No," he says, lowering the scan. "And naturally, now I'm dying to know why you think so." Everything in his English accent sounds so damn serious, but his eyes... I can't work it out.

"Haley's urine tests," I say. "They were positive for drugs."

He takes this in for a moment. "Positive for benzodiazepines?"

"Yes."

"We prescribe benzodiazepines. They're heavy sedatives. Addicts often have problems sleeping when they're coming off drugs."

OK, that makes sense.

Now I feel like a prize idiot.

"Cara…" He hesitates. "Did you know that as staff, you're entitled to access any part of the facility? The anger rooms, for example."

"The *anger* rooms?" I'm hugely insulted but manage to keep my face calm. "Do I seem angry to you?"

"No. That's the point. I wondered if you ever did get angry. Scream and shout, that kind of thing."

"Scream and *shout*?" The idea of that makes me want to curl up and die. I am actually blushing at the mention of it. "I… No. No, I don't. It isn't something I do. I don't think that's necessary. Anger is a very ugly emotion," I add.

"A lot of women are brought up with that idea," says Max. "Just a thought."

My mind flips to my own upbringing. Anger certainly wasn't acceptable in my household. We kept unruly emotions firmly locked away.

Max pauses, then appears to make a decision. "While you're here, you might like to take a look at these scans of our patients' brains."

I blink, turning my attention to what he's indicating. MRI scans of human brains are pinned to the wall, lit with various colors in different areas.

Max lifts one off, pointing at the center. "This part is the limbic system. The center for very basic emotions. Anger. Fear. With trauma, we see excessive activity here."

I stare at the bright oranges and yellows flaring in that area.

"What does that mean in real life?" I ask.

"The owner of this brain is in a constant heightened state of fear or anxiety. Not hard to see why someone in that condition would abuse drugs, right?"

"Am I allowed to know which brain I'm looking at?" Compared to the others, the scan in Max's hand shows a huge amount of limbic activity.

"Of course," he nods. "That's Tom." Max pauses. "Lots of anger."

I think back to Tom's therapy notes. His admissions of violence toward his ex-partners. His current wife.

Max slides a pen from his pocket and points to a section of the scan. "See here? This green section? That's the area where emotion is processed. Drug addicts often have damage to this part, along with the reward centers."

"Can it recover?"

"Reward centers of the brain will recover naturally when addicts come off drugs."

"And the emotional areas?"

Max hesitates. "Emotional damage results from trauma, not drugs." His blue eyes land on mine. "The two are often a vicious cycle, of course."

"Would all addicts have unprocessed trauma?" I ask quietly, thinking of my brother.

"Keep in mind that trauma is personal to the individual," Max says. "One person's trauma is another person's bad day. But with that in mind, yes, I believe all addicts have unprocessed trauma. Including your brother," he concludes, making me blush at the childish transparency of my thoughts. "You too, Cara." He eyes me for a moment. "That wasn't a lucky guess. Dr. Lutz investigates everyone's families," Max adds. "As I said. That's why he hires us."

I'm unnerved by the idea that Dr. Lutz would have profiled me in that way.

"What about you?" I ask. "Did he find anything out about your family?" The directness of my question surprises me. But Max doesn't seem to mind.

"Nothing I hadn't told him already," says Max. "My mother left when I was a small child. By that I mean she left me completely alone. I developed pneumonia in the unheated house and nearly died."

I can't hide my shock. "I'm so sorry." I'm remembering his lung condition. Guessing those two things are linked.

"I've had a lot of therapy." Max sounds unconcerned. "You'll find almost all therapists have some dreadful trauma."

"Trauma always comes before drug addiction?"

"I believe so. Many experts believe trauma damage can't be reversed," says Max. "But look." He sounds excited. Childlike, almost. "The top rows show how the patients came to us," he explains. "This bottom row is after treatment."

I look carefully at the brain scan images.

"The bottom row is different," I say. "More activity."

He gives me a wide grin.

"Proof," he says. "This is completely groundbreaking, Cara. Our treatment is working."

My eyes wander across the scans. One stands out.

"What about *this* one?"

I point to a scan that shows almost no activity in the emotional processing part of the brain. It could almost be a different species.

"Oh that." Max sighs and pulls it down. "That scan was Haley's."

CHAPTER FORTY-FOUR

MEG

The shakes start again as Jade takes me out onto the manicured grounds to an external women's changing room. We don pink bathrobes.

"Inner-child workshop is held in the sweat lodge," she explains. "Helps people be more vulnerable with one another."

I don't like the sound of this.

"Size down your robe," warns Jade. "It's fucking hot inside. Less toweling is good. We're basically crawling inside a giant pizza oven."

I assume she's joking until we emerge to see the pizza oven. It's big as a yurt. Opposite is a giant chimney with a blazing fire. Behind is sheer cliff, the stormy ocean beyond.

"Oh shit," I say, eyeing the low igloo-style entrance. "We *crawl* in?"

"It's all about humility," says Sierra, arriving behind us. She lowers herself prostrate to the entrance and touches her forehead to the ground. Then crawls inside.

"We all have to do that?" I ask.

"Set your intention and ask permission before you enter," says a gravelly voice behind me. *Madeline. Oh great.*

"Move to your left. Never cross the center," she adds.

"Are you leading?" asks Jade.

Please say no.

"Yep," says Madeline, looking smug.

"Inner-child work can be useful," says Jade earnestly, her eyes growing large. "Really. I've learned a lot. With the mom I had, that isn't surprising."

"My mom wasn't the greatest either," I concede.

Jade looks happy about this. "That's great," she says. "I mean. It's not great. Obviously. But this will give you the chance to talk about it."

"I'm not sure I want…"

"Everybody in," says Madeline. I roll my eyes but follow Jade, bowing at the entrance and crawling inside. The others are already arranged on the circular seat that lines the inside of the sweat lodge. Faces shaded. I make out Tom Abrams opposite. The handsome features of his aging face look slack today. Haggard even. His square jaw is set with dark stubble. The famous steely-blue eyes are dull.

At the entrance, Madeline is levering a giant red-hot stone inside on what looks like a pitchfork.

"Isn't that a specialist job?" I whisper to Jade, as Madeline grunts under the weight of the burning stone. I wince as she tips it clumsily into the center. "What if she drops that on someone?"

"Everything is patient led," Sierra tells me. "It builds trust."

I'm already thinking I don't like this at all when Madeline shuts the door, plunging us all into darkness. There's a hissing sound, and a plume of herbal steam all but slaps me around the face.

Madeline begins talking.

"We're here to speak to our inner child," she says. "To tell our inner child they're worthy of love. That we'll keep them safe."

Kill me now.

There's no way I'm doing this. I stare up in the darkness.

Jade's hand touches my arm.

"I hated this stuff at first too," she whispers. "Just try."

"The biggest thing we're learning," continues Madeline, "is that rehab is about getting feelings back."

Murmurs of agreement. *Feelings.* The familiar sense of failure pools in my gut. I don't really have feelings.

"As children we didn't feel safe or loved," continues Madeline in a flat low tone. "We've come today to let our little kids feel their feelings. It's scary. It's hard. But we're here to be reborn."

Somewhere in the dark, someone is sobbing gently.

Sierra? Dex? I can't tell.

"I've been kind of talking to my inner child about my mom." It's Jade's voice. The English accent soft in the steamy dark. "Mom's in prison now. Drug-related stuff. We don't speak."

That is worse than my mom at least. It's also a strong motive.

"What about your mom, Meg?" asks Madeline.

Typical she would ask me. I didn't want to get drawn into all this shit. "It's getting really hot in here," I say. "Can I take a break?"

A cloud of burning steam erupts, splattering me with burning water. Madeline has tipped more water on the rocks.

"Ow! Watch it," I hiss.

"Sorry," says Madeline, sounding not sorry at all. "We start together; we finish together. Sweat lodge rules. If you're too hot, sit on the floor."

Jade puts her hand on my knee. "If it's too much, you can leave," she whispers. "But you should try to engage, Meg."

I sigh, my lungs burning. Guess I need to give them something.

"Well," I say, choosing my words in the unlikely event Haley spoke about our famous mother. "My mom made good money acting. We lived in fancy houses. But me and my sister, we kind of didn't exist to my mom. Like, there was no food in the house. Lots of parties with transient people from the Business who weren't necessarily nice to children." I'm getting into the story now. It's refreshing to be able to share with a bunch of mess-ups, at least. "We basically fed ourselves from catered buffets," I continue. "Our kitchen was just for mixing cocktails. I remember asking my mom one time, like, 'What are all these saucepans and stuff for?' And she was like, 'Oh honey, they came with the house.'"

A little ripple of laughter goes around. But it's *nice* laughter. Understanding.

I never told anyone that. The weird thing is, I do feel...better.

"I had some of that going on too," says Dex. His voice sounds reflective in the dark. The steam is hitting me now. My heart is pounding.

"My childhood was very fearful." Sierra is talking. "You could hear gunshots most nights. Things happened. To me. To my mom. Singing was the only thing that took me away from that."

"My dad was violent," says Tom. "Like really, really violent. I had to hide bruises... I would literally wet my pants when I heard him come home." Tom's voice catches. He sobs. I literally cannot imagine Tom Abrams being beat up as a kid. He is a dark-haired all-American hero. A cowboy with a chiseled jaw.

"It's OK, Tom," says Madeline. "Breathe." She hesitates. "You all know what happened to me," she says. "Parts of it."

The uneasy silence that follows suggests something very bad happened to Madeline.

"We're going to repeat together now," says Madeline. "Speaking to our inner child."

She begins intoning. "I'll keep you safe now."

Oh Jesus. Am I going to have to do this?

Everyone repeats. I mutter along.

"It wasn't your fault," says Madeline.

I open my mouth, but I can't do it. I literally can't make the words form.

It was my fault.

A horrible memory stirs. *If you'd been a better kid, Haley would never have left.* Mom blamed me. *Because it was my fault. Wasn't it?*

A bruise-colored memory stirs in my solar plexus. I need to get out of here. I need a drink.

Something else occurs to me. *This is an emotionally loaded situation.* Great chance to walk out and see if Harry's makeshift fingerprinting is going to work.

I stand quickly, just as everyone is chanting that no one is going to hurt their inner child anymore.

"I'm going to pass out," I mutter. It's not even all a lie. My shoulder has started throbbing along with my current headache that never goes away. "I need to leave."

In the dark, I can't see reactions. But I can guess. Jade will be sad for me. Sierra and Dex disappointed. Tom and Madeline angry.

Something unpleasant prods at me, and I instantly push it back.

I need to get those fingerprints. And I never was one for group love-ins.

Without waiting for an answer, I cross the circle of trust, open the sweat lodge door, and crawl out into the cool relief of the outside.

CHAPTER FORTY-FIVE

CARA

I can't stop staring at Haley's brain scan. Compared to the others, it has completely different activity. The front part is green and blue. Almost no activity at all.

Max regards the scan. He looks deeply sad. "Haley was starting to make progress. She was…incredibly brave. There was deep and persistent trauma in her childhood. Dr. Lutz was helping her remember."

"She'd forgotten?"

"Haley had worked up the courage to track down an old family friend."

"This is the person who's due to collect her belongings?" I guess. "Matthew Priest?"

Max nods. "It was a healthy step, if a tough one for Haley. There were a lot of complicated feelings there. She always struggled to separate sex from admiration. Haley carried an unbelievable amount of shame and pain. In adult life it manifested in manipulation, unreasonable demands, and so forth. But deep down, she was a frightened little girl who was overwhelmed by painful feelings."

I try to sync that with the Haley who would stalk into the lobby and complain about the temperature of the food. It's a tough sell.

"People run low on sympathy when the traumatized adults have coping strategies that make them unlikable," Max observes.

I don't reply.

"Not all addicts are as damaged as Haley Banks," adds Max. "That's Sierra scan. She's responded very well to therapy and meditation for her anxiety."

"This is two weeks later?" I point.

"Yup. Sierra's brain has begun to heal itself." Max sounds like a proud parent. "Hoffman said it couldn't be done. We're talking an 80 to 90 percent projected success rate. That's unprecedented."

"What's the usual success rate for addiction treatment?"

"Depends on treatment. Therapy. Drugs. These can all help. The gold standard is rehab. Success rate for completing the twelve steps in rehab is 50 percent."

"Is that all?"

"Oh. It can be even lower," says Max. "In no other field of medicine would we accept such a high fail rate without seriously revising our strategy. More patients relapse than recover. Yet most centers still use a plan for treating addicts devised in the 1920s."

I stare at the brain scan. "Meditation and therapy alone caused these changes?"

Max looks uneasy. "They were part of the package."

"Is fugu treatment part of the process?"

"It's a key aspect, yes. But it's experimental. And as you saw with Haley Banks, progress can be slow." He hesitates. "What I'm interested in is this latest."

He plucks a scan from the printer that hasn't made it to the rows. "Haley again?"

"No. This is our latest patient. Meg."

I do a double take. "They're so similar."

"Aren't they? We never got the chance to assess Haley. But I'm running a number of more complex assessments on Meg. I think… I'm missing something important."

He looks from Meg's scan to Haley's and back again.

Max shakes his head distractedly, as though dislodging a thought.

"With most people, as the drugs leave their system, feelings come up. For Meg there's nothing. During her entire time with me, Meg has only reported *remembering* feelings. She learned to turn them off. I'm thinking I'd like to schedule a bipolar assessment," he adds. "Dr. Lutz wants her in for treatment. I'm resisting signing her off. But he has his schedule."

Something about the way he says it sounds loaded with emotion.

My eyes settle back on Tom's scan. The flare of red and yellow.

All that irrational anger in one place. My mind drifts back to the altercations and dramas at my old hotel.

"Shame we can only treat rich people," I say sadly.

"You took the words right out of my mouth," says Max. "Treating a lifetime of trauma is expensive. Our drug innovations with fugu could help reduce those costs," he adds. "Fugu is also extremely robust. Blowfish venom can withstand mass transport and relatively high heat. Freezing is the only thing that damages it. *But*," Max looks back at the scans. "With great power comes great responsibility. We cannot put patients in treatment who are not mentally stable."

Something tells me he's thinking about Meg again.

"Max," I say carefully. "Dr. Lutz. Do you ever feel like he doesn't care as much about the patients as you do?"

"He doesn't," says Max unhesitatingly. "Not in the way that I do. But what I've come to realize is you need that balance in medicine. You need someone with a head for figures. Who can make unflinchingly logical decisions." The lack of conviction must show on my face, because he goes on talking. "The problem with Dr. Lutz is he can't communicate in a way that doesn't unnerve people. But I promise you he is aware of his shortcomings and is committed to working on them."

"Dr. Lutz undertakes therapy?"

Max nods. "He wouldn't mind you knowing that. In my opinion, his willingness to work on his shortcomings is worth ten of a highly empathetic person blind to their frailties."

I think about this. Dr. Lutz as the rational foil to Max's emotions.

I'm reassured. Hanson and Meyers don't know what we do here. Dr. Lutz is a groundbreaker. And he's hired Max to keep everything in balance.

"Dr. Lutz doesn't do everything by the book," he says finally. "But his time in Florida taught him a hard lesson. He's learned from it."

"Don't you mean India?" I say. "Dr. Lutz was in India. For ten years."

Max's face does a strange thing. "Dr. Lutz was in Florida briefly," he says. "He doesn't like to talk about his time there. Probably best not to go into it. I'd better get back to work," he adds.

His expression makes it clear the subject is closed.

As I walk back to the lobby, it occurs to me, the name of the drug-testing company we use. They're called Pro Lab Florida, aren't they?

Probably a coincidence. Right?

CHAPTER FORTY-SIX

MEG

The women's dormitories are the best place to attempt to finger-print the note unseen, I decide.

I make it to a bathroom stall in the bedroom without anyone seeing me. Take out the note and stare at it for a moment.

Leave now, Meggy. Before it's too late. Love Haley.

I could even swear it's her handwriting.

OK. Let's see if this works. Taking the pastel chalk from my pocket, I tap it to let the fine dust fall on the note. Then I work it carefully across the paper with the brush I stole.

Nothing.

I try with the charcoal.

That doesn't work either. In desperation, I turn the note over, powdering every last square inch. But despite my best efforts, there's nothing the powder is clinging to.

Oh well. Harry said it was a long shot.

My disappointment is interrupted by shouting outside. Is that *Tom*?

I creep carefully out of the bathroom trying to steady my breathing.

Isn't everyone in the inner-child workshop?

Must have taken me longer with my fingerprint attempts than I realized.

The voices are coming from the corridor outside the dormitory. I tiptoe to the doorway, flattening myself against the wall to listen.

Tom's voice. Angry.

There's another voice. Woman. Frightened.

Jade.

"People will see the bruises, Tom."

What?

From my vantage point, I snatch a quick look.

Jade is pulling down her top to show an ugly mark beneath her collarbone.

Tom's face is stricken. He puts both hands on her narrow shoulders, frowning. But at the sight of her exposed chest, his breathing visibly quickens.

"I'm sorry," he says. "I never wanted to hurt you. I lose control. Hurt the people I most care about. I don't even deserve to be alive."

"Don't say that." Jade's brown eyes are wide, sincere. "You've had a lot of bad stuff happen to you."

OK. What?

"I care about you, Jade."

Jade's round little mouth turns up at the corners. "What about Haley Banks?"

Tom's expression twists. Anger flares deep in his famous blue eyes.

"That's over. Just a stupid game. Why do you keep bringing it up?"

It's hard to compute that veteran megastar Tom is talking to Jade as if they're in an actual relationship. She's young enough to be his daughter.

Tom grasps the hair at his temples in a gesture of helpless frustration I'm sure I've seen in movies.

"What do you want from me?" he demands.

"I'm only trying to help you," says Jade. "If we can find a way to pay the people you owe…"

Tom's expression shifts into something nasty. "You think you're going to rescue me, is that it?"

Jade's round features show blank, open hurt. And something else. Acceptance. She's used to people hurting her.

Unexpectedly, Tom grabs her hard by the shoulders.

"You think I don't know what you're doing?" He slams her hard enough against the wall to make me wince. "You're looking for a backup plan, in case you don't make rehab and your studio ditches you. I'm a meal ticket for your goddamn kid. I can see it in your eyes every time we fuck, Jade!"

Tom's fist shoots out, hitting her in the ribs. Jade raises her arms to fend him off, and he grabs her wrist and twists. She jackknifes forward with a soft cry of pain.

I'm about to come running out, when Tom abruptly backs off, pushing Jade away so she staggers.

Jade straightens up, and I see something fierce in her expression. She might be nice, but Jade isn't a pushover. She has a core of steel under that nice exterior. I like her for it.

Jade opens her mouth to say something.

My schedule watch goes off. It beeps softly. Therapy with Max.

"Hey," snarls Tom, dropping his apologetic act with apparent ease. "Who's in here?"

Another sound comes from deeper in the corridor. The click of briskly moving high heels. OK. That could only be…

"*Excuse* me." A voice comes from farther back in the corridor. I have never been so grateful to hear Cara's sharp little voice.

"You know the rules," she says, putting both hands on the hips of her couture dress. "You shouldn't be hanging around in the corridors."

"I'm sorry, Cara," says Jade. "Tom was giving me some acting tips."

I look carefully at Jade's face, trying to work out if she's telling the truth. Cara seems to be doing the same thing.

"Jade, you are working on your codependent issues," Cara says. "Being alone with other patients is temptation. For both of you."

Codependent. Where did I hear that term before? I have a feeling it's where someone gets high from watching someone else do drugs.

There are retreating footsteps. Then silence.

I breathe out hard. *What did I overhear?*

Do Jade and Tom have an abusive relationship? Was Tom unfaithful with Haley?

Or…was Jade telling the truth? Tom was giving her tips. They were acting a scene.

Haley and Tom. Could she? Would she? Ugh. He is so old. But…maybe. If there was something to win.

Haley was the queen of game players, and she always, *always* won.

Queen of hearts.

I don't know why that came into my head. Thoughts on Haley, my eyes land on the note, still in my hand. Then I see it. My nervous breathing must have helped the pastel chalk stick.

Up in the top corner. Small. But unmistakable. Harry's hack worked.

Three little fingerprints.

CHAPTER FORTY-SEVEN

MEG

I stare at the fingerprints for way too long.

Fuck. I can't believe it. Moving carefully, so as not to disturb the delicate patterns, I take out my phone from its bathroom hiding place and take a close-up picture. Despite the cracked screen, the phone is still working. I text the picture. Then call Harry.

"Hey, Harry, I got the prints. Just sent them."

"Hello to you too."

"So can you run them?"

There's a pause. "I think so," he says finally. "Looks like you got good clear prints." I can picture him rubbing his forehead the way he does when he's sleepy.

"How long to get something back?" I ask.

"Couple of hours, maybe."

"Really? So fast?" I want to punch the air with victory.

"You're working with the best."

I smile. "They look too small to be a man's. And Madeline's supermodel size. Tall. Big hands. I think they're Jade's or Sierra's."

There's a pause. "You got a reason to suspect either of those people?"

"Jade," I say immediately. "She tried to warn me away from the start. I think there's something messed up with her and Tom, so maybe jealously there. And…" I struggle to pull to mind the word Cara used. "She's codependent. Maybe she got Haley high."

"Jade is the English one—the actress? From how you speak about her, she sounds nice."

"Yeah. She's nice. But I don't trust her. She's way too friendly."

"I think that says more about you than her."

"What's that supposed to mean?"

"Just… Maybe you've been hanging out with hustlers and loan sharks so long you forgot there are good people out there."

"It's not just that," I say. "I have this weird feeling I've met Jade before." I frown. "A long time ago. Maybe in my childhood or something."

We're both silent for a moment.

"Does anyone else have a motive?" Harry asks.

"Sierra had an ongoing feud with Haley."

"Yeah that was all over the news," Harry says. "You're not making detective of the year with that one."

"But…Sierra being here seems like a coincidence, right?"

Harry considers. "Anyone who knew your sister knew she had a beef with Sierra. And the celebrity rehab crowd is small, right?"

This is true. Haley could just have easily met Dex at a party. Or Tom.

"Madeline too," I add. "She seems kind of unhinged."

"What's Madeline's motive?"

"She's a grade A bitch."

"Measured, Meggy. Thought through. So, your suspects are basically everyone? I take it you don't have any friends on the inside yet?"

"Are you out of your mind? Someone here killed my sister."

"Which means four of them didn't," he points out reasonably. Harry sighs. "So you're four days into rehab, and you don't like or trust a single person."

"It must have been one of them. No doctors or staff were on the floor that night. Everyone here loses big if they get kicked out."

"Detective work is supposed to be about elimination," says Harry. "Not looking for evidence to fit your theory. Since you're in rehab, why don't you do the work on yourself? You might get more answers that way."

That's the last thing I want to do.

"Did you run the name Matthew Priest?" I ask him.

"Yeah. There's a lot of them," he says. "None I could fit to any connection with you or Haley. I'll keep trying… What's that noise?"

I look down distractedly to see my scheduling watch is beeping more urgently now. Screen flashing angrily.

"Shit, I'm late for therapy." I should have been with Max ten minutes ago.

"Try actually engaging with it, Meg."

"Ha-ha."

I hang up. I'm about to slide my phone back into its hiding place when I see the screen is flashing. Is Harry calling me back?

But when I focus on the screen I realize I got the name wrong. The person calling me isn't Harry.

It's Haley.

CHAPTER FORTY-EIGHT

MEG

I watch the screen of my cell as it flashes Haley's number.

How can Haley be calling my phone?

It's not her, of course. It can't be.

So who is it?

I'm strangely calm as I press to accept the call.

"Hello?" I say.

Nothing. A scratchy sound.

"Hello?" I try again. Tapping. Then nothing. I look at my screen. The call has cut out.

Fuck.

Frantically, I call Haley's number. The feelings I should have had when the phone first rang are loading up now. My hand holding the phone starts to shake. It's ringing. Once. Twice.

Pick up. Pick up. Pick up.

There's a click as the call connects on the third ring.

"Hi, this is Haley," says a breathless voice.

"Haley? Where are you—?"

She talks over me. "You can call my manager, Frank, or leave me a message."

Voicemail.

Grief hits me like a freight train. A stupid tiny part of me thought Haley had answered the phone. I take another breath. Get my thoughts in a better order.

The phone call was an accident, I reason. Haley's phone was probably shipped back to my mom. Someone called a last-dialed by mistake.

My sensible theory is blown out of the water by a message landing in my Recents. It's from Haley. *Haley's phone*, I remind myself. But the message blindsides me.

Quit while you're ahead, Sis. You'll get us both killed.

I call Haley's number, hand twitching with the effort to press buttons fast.

The call goes to voicemail. I try again.

Voicemail.

But this time before it connects, there's something else. I could swear... Do I hear a phone *ringing*? Somewhere inside the Clinic?

Frantically I call again. This time I'm sure. The faintest of sounds.

I head in the direction it seems to be coming from. This time when I call again, it's straight to voicemail. Did the phone run out of charge?

Fuck.

I make three more frustrated attempts before accepting defeat.

Another idea occurs. Cloud-tracking apps can show where a phone was last used. And they're internet based. Anyone can log on if they have the right email and password combination. Logging on to the cloud server, I open the tracking app and type Haley's email. The password screen pops up, empty.

OK. Password. Password.

I *did* know Haley's password, didn't I? Back when we were kids. Good chance it's the same.

What was it?

I rub the side of my face, trying to call it to mind.

Maybe…numbers? I shake my head, frustrated. Haley wasn't a numbers kind of girl.

My mind swirls. I punch in "Queenofhearts." For a few seconds I'm hopeful. Then the screen flashes. Wrong password. Less hopeful now, I type in her first album name, then her first platinum record. By the time I've entered her production company and manager's name, I'm clutching at straws.

I knew Haley's password once. Now I can't remember it.

Something about that feels like a very deep failure. The misery that seeps into my chest has a poisonous quality.

We would have made up in the end. But she's gone.

Defeated, I call Haley's phone number again.

Nothing. Not even voicemail.

I slam my hand against the nearest wall in frustration.

Someone turned the phone off.

CHAPTER FORTY-NINE

CARA

I'm back at my computer, trying to dismiss the idea that there's a link. Max let slip that Dr. Lutz had some kind of bad experience in Florida. The drug-testing company we use is based in Florida.

Just a coincidence, I tell myself for the tenth time. Everything about the drug tests and how they're carried out appears aboveboard.

I think some more. Then search "Florida Pro Lab" on the internet.

Their web page is that of a highly uninteresting and generic medical organization based in Florida.

Nothing there. Defeated, I punch the testing company name into the search bar again, not expecting to find anything besides more generic descriptions.

My hands are still on the keys.

I can't quite understand what I'm reading. It looks like the Florida testing company we use is associated with something called the "Florida shuffle."

Florida shuffle... I remember something about this from my LA hotel. I think it's when addicts are shuffled between rehabs and sober houses. Like a vicious-cycle kind of thing. Though I don't know why it happens in Florida more than anywhere else.

I click on a news report, where a TV personality stands on a white sand beach, a palm tree behind her. She wears a bikini, a sarong, and a sardonic smile.

"Sunny Florida," she announces, "where thousands of young people are lured annually by the promise of luxury drug rehab." She frowns. "Addicts are attracted with promises of world-class rehabilitation at luxury beach resorts," she explains. "In reality, they are kept hooked, while their insurers are billed for thousands."

On the video, the shot switches to a grim-faced police officer standing in what looks like a crack house. It pans to the woman, who has switched from her bikini to a suitably serious black-jacket-white-shirt combo and matching frowning expression.

"A so-called sober house," she announces, "where addicts who have detoxed transition back to the real world. They arrive expecting managed accommodation and, instead, are sent here." The camera makes an obliging sweep of a mattress with filthy sheets and mold climbing the walls. "A crack house," she says. "Complete with dealers ready and willing to help them use again."

I frown at the screen, trying to work out how the drug-testing company we use could be involved.

The reporter talks on. "For many women patients hustled into the so-called Florida shuffle, it gets much darker." She continues, "As Officer Michaels here knows only too well."

The police officer at her side nods on cue.

"Much of the Florida shuffle bleeds into human trafficking," he tells her. "Women addicts are kept addicted and prostituted."

I pause the video, considering this. Then look back to my screen.

It's a million miles away from the treatment we offer here. Our patients are kept in total luxury, their every need catered.

My pager beeps.

It's from front gate security.

"URGENT front gate. Police are here. They have a warrant to search the spa."

My first thought is how unhappy Dr. Lutz will be.

But as I race to let the police in, I can't help but feel strangely relieved to see Hanson's and Meyers's familiar faces. They walk after me, Meyers keeping her trooper hat on inside the building. Firmly wedged down on her perpendicular curly brown hair. Hanson's mustache hasn't gotten any smaller, and his huge boots are mud spattered.

Behind them is a small team of officers, taking in the vast lobby with awestruck expressions.

"Wondered if you could help us for a spell," Hanson says. "Little mystery Meyers and I are trying to solve here."

"Oh?" My eyes rest on the team of police behind them.

"Haley Banks's cell phone. Someone has been making calls from it. And the signal looks to be coming from inside your clinic."

CHAPTER FIFTY

CARA

I'm escorting the police to the spa, having sent several urgent pages to Dr. Lutz.

"There's no way Haley could have been using a phone in here," I tell them. "I searched her bag myself."

"Never underestimate human beings when it comes to contraband," advises Meyers. "Hanson and I are surprised daily."

"I don't even know when she would have gotten time to use it," I say.

"Whether she did or she didn't," adds Hanson evenly, "someone did."

"You're certain the call came from the spa?"

"We tracked a phone call from that part of the building, 3:00 a.m. on the morning Haley died," Meyers explained. "And this week, several more calls popped up."

I notice she has another dried-out milk stain. Front of her shirt this time.

"The spa was the last place Haley Banks went before she died, right?" Hanson asks.

I nod sadly. We walk on in silence.

"You know, I looked you up on the internet," chirps Meyers,

seemingly needing to fill the void with her total lack of tact. "Your thing with your old boss. They couldn't fire you. You refused to leave. So they shuffled you into a deadbeat hotel and hoped you'd quit of your own accord."

"Thanks for the summary." I give her my best icy smile. "Where I come from, people keep their internet stalking to themselves."

"Oh, I come from a big family of oversharers," Meyers says happily. "I also saw that you turned the hotel around," she beams, oblivious to my displeasure. "Made friends with the hobos. Started turning a profit. Good for you. That's woman power for you," she adds, directing this last remark at Hanson.

His mustache twitches in a noncommittal way. Suddenly, I don't mind Meyers prying so much.

We complete the journey wordlessly. Me wondering what Dr. Lutz would make of my negligence in letting a phone slip into the building.

The posse of officers gathers behind Hanson as I unlock the glass door of the spa and put out my hand to signal them to pass.

"This is the pool," I explain as we pass under the vast vaulted ceiling. "Spa is through here."

"No chlorine smell," said Meyers, sniffing the air in a way I know Dr. Lutz would hate.

"It's ozone filtered," I say. "Better for your skin and hair and fewer toxins, since our clients are detoxing already."

The officers exchange another loaded glance, and I feel strangely embarrassed. As is, they were judging how the other half lives, and I'd been thrown in.

Meyers's eyes opened wide. "You ever see a place like this in your whole life, Hanson?"

He shakes his head slowly. "Can't say I have."

"Dr. Lutz is from Switzerland, and the spa pool's design is based on the Junghorn mountain range near his hometown," I explain in a monotone. I'm in tour-guide mode again. "The network of water-filled ravines you find between mountains. Hence, high black walls." I nod to the looming quartzite walls that stretch double height. "And the tunnel-like effect."

"Where do they lead?" Meyers cranes her head as if that would help her see through stone.

"There's a sound cave and a scent cave," I explain. "Also an ice pool with ice chips. You need to float through the tunnels to find them. That's part of the fun."

It's the wrong choice of words. Meyers's face very much suggests she would not find this fun. For once her bright mouth is downturned.

Hanson is regarding the huge premises with stoicism. I guess he's thinking of all the hidden places to search.

"Why is the water that color?" asks Meyers.

"It's a special clay exported from Iceland," I explain.

"Think we're going to need to drain it?" Meyers glances at Hanson.

"We'd need a different warrant for that. Let's do our best."

The officers begin sweeping the scene like a flock of descending birds. I check my pager again, completely unsure of protocol. Should I stay? Nothing from Dr. Lutz.

The search begins methodically, but I can sense after an hour that the atmosphere is becoming desperate. They're not finding what they came for.

Dr. Lutz arrives, hipster beard beaded with steam. Today's shirt is tie-dye with "Keep On Coming Back" in waving psychedelic writing.

"Dr. Lutz." Hanson holds up a large hand in greeting. "How are you, sir?"

"Not so well for seeing you here," says Dr. Lutz, closing in. "Am I entitled to know how you got your warrant?"

Hanson's gray eyes slide to Meyers. She gives an imperceptible nod.

"When a suspicious death occurs, police look for criminal records of those close to the victim," says Hanson.

"Our guests have troubled backgrounds," says Dr. Lutz airily. "I'm afraid several have had problems with the law."

Hanson nods. "DUIs, assault charges. But we also found connections to organized crime"—he pauses for effect—"on every single one of your staff. With the exception of Dr. Max and Miss Morse here."

A smile plays on my lips. He's got it wrong. Of course he has.

"Your staff came with you from your other rehab. In Florida. That right?" asks Hanson. "The one that got shut down."

I hear myself draw in air. I notice that Meyers is eyeing me with open concern.

"You OK, Miss Morse?" she asks quietly. "Dr. Lutz didn't mention his other rehab to you?"

I negotiate a smile. "Yes, I'm fine."

Dr. Lutz balls his fists. Hanson turns to me.

"Ma'am, can I suppose that as manager, you're aware Dr. Lutz's nursing staff all have records for violent crime and worse?"

I am literally stunned into silence. Hanson's piercing eyes don't leave my face. It's obvious from my discomfort I had no idea.

I'm saved from replying by a grim-faced policeman. He approaches Hanson, tapping him on the shoulder. Talks into his ear.

I catch a few words. *Nothing* and *road before dark*.

For the first time, I see a small flare of some nameless

emotion in Hanson's eyes. Defeat, maybe. He rallies almost immediately.

"Thank you," he tells the officer. "Dr. Lutz, we'll be leaving you for the time being. We appreciate the chance to take a look in here."

Dr. Lutz beams victoriously. "We won't be seeing you again, Chief Hanson. Cara, please show the officers out."

"Yes, Dr. Lutz."

It's hard to know what to feel as I lead Hanson and his team back through the lobby. Everything I thought I knew about Dr. Lutz has imploded.

CHAPTER FIFTY-ONE

MEG

A whole day later, and I'm no closer to finding Haley's phone. It's not ringing when I try to call, and I haven't been able to get a spare second to search.

Between back-to-back holistic therapies and mealtimes, Madeline has made it her business to watch me like a hawk. I'm due in therapy with Max, and I trudge unenthusiastically. He keeps mentioning special tests and assessments that sound boring.

But when I open the door to Max's office, he isn't inside. Instead, there stand a nurse and a man. Aging, with a hipster beard and a slogan shirt that reads: "Keep On Coming Back." I've seen him around. He's the owner, I think.

"Forgive the interruption," he says. "You must be Meg. I am Dr. Lutz."

I haven't seen him close-up before. And the moment I look into his eyes, I feel that familiar jolt in my chest I've grown used to categorizing. The unblinking eyes, something about the pupils. He reminds me of the mob bosses we deal with in the casino. The bad ones.

"Max has been detained, so I've decided to move your treatment forward," says Dr. Lutz. "If you'd care to follow me."

"OK." I shrug, wondering what it's all about, and follow them along several winding corridors to a part of the building I've never been in before. This part looks a lot less luxurious. Like a regular hospital. I can't decide if this is reassuring or freaky.

The nurse opens a door and ushers me into one of the strangest rooms I've ever seen. At first glance it looks like the security room at the casino.

CCTV screens line the wall, flashing images of almost every room in the Clinic. But the rest of the room is like a hospital. Complete with a stretcher bed in the center with a lot of scary tubes and wires.

The bed has restraints attached, I notice.

"What the fuck is that?" I start backing out of the room, but the body of the nurse is surprisingly solid.

"Just a precaution." Dr. Lutz is behind me, putting a doctor's coat over his jeans and T-shirt combo. The coat looks ill-suited to his bushy beard and side-parted hair. "Please don't concern yourself. The treatment itself is a simple injection. Nothing more."

"Are you sure Max is OK with this?" I ask.

Dr. Lutz ignores the question. "I think you'll learn a lot about yourself in this session, Meg."

What is it about his eyes? There's something both very familiar and very wrong about them. As though I see myself mirrored back in a twisted-carnival-mirror way.

"And if I don't want to?"

Dr. Lutz blinks at me slowly. "We have a schedule," he says. "It's important we follow it. We're here to help you get better." He unfolds his hands. "If you don't want to get better, you can discharge yourself from the Clinic today."

Checkmate. There's no way I can leave when I'm so close to finding Haley's phone.

I get awkwardly onto the bed.

"Lie back and try to relax, please," says Dr. Lutz. "There's really nothing to be afraid of. Nurse, would you mind applying the EEG electrodes?"

The nurse steps forward and fits a stretchy cap with a chin strap over my head.

"This monitors electrical activity," explains Dr. Lutz. "Now..." He pats the plastic above my head. "The treatment is a simple injection." He moves behind me, and I feel a tiny pinprick in the back of my neck.

Adrenaline courses through me. I try to sit up, but the nurse holds me back. As she does, all the pain in my muscles suddenly drains away.

"I can't feel anything." I can hardly believe it.

"Yes." Dr. Lutz nods. "How is your speech?"

"OK, I guess." As soon as he says it, I'm finding it harder. My mouth won't open like I want it to. Words are too thick to form.

"The hardest part is always immobilizing the body sufficiently, while retaining speech," says Dr. Lutz casually.

That's when I realize my muscles are leaden. I can't move my legs. My arms, hands... Nothing. I can blink my eyes.

"I can't move," I say.

"This is the beauty of the procedure, Meg. We don't need your conscious mind to relax. Your body *thinks* it is relaxed. In this state, your subconscious is a great deal more amenable."

"I want it to stop."

"It won't be metabolized for around thirty minutes," says Dr. Lutz. "In the meantime, I'll be asking you some questions, and you will answer them truthfully."

A strange malaise is washing over me. Like nothing is worth the effort of struggle.

"When I click my fingers"—Dr. Lutz clicks—"you will return to the exact state you are in now." He moves closer. "But for now. You mentioned a dream to Max. A nightmare. Why don't we talk about that?"

Somehow, the sting of being pushed around is completely absent. Like it's all very logical and a slightly tedious thing to get through.

"I told Max," I say, and the *x* of Max comes out soft and partly formed, "I don't remember."

"Try," says Dr. Lutz. "I think you might surprise yourself. I would like you to go back to the place you were in your dream now."

I don't know how much time passes. There's a humming noise. Like a droning sound. Then something is circling right in front of my eyes. A ceiling fan. The old-fashioned plantation kind. I'm lying underneath it, watching the blades turn.

Whump, whump whump.

"Where are you, Meg?" Dr. Lutz's voice breaks through. "Can you describe your environment?"

I see textured wallpaper. A velvet couch.

"I'm in a big house," I say. "It's like a museum or something. Everything is from another time." It smells damp. Slightly moldy. Like a Goodwill. The wooden ceiling fan's whirl is the constant background noise.

Whump, whump whump.

"What do you see?" says Dr. Lutz.

"There's a telephone. A cream-colored one. Like I saw classic movie stars use. There are only old things here. No cell phones. No TV."

"Tell me more about the house."

"There's a bedroom. Upstairs."

There's a pause. "What happens in that room?"

"He's waiting for us," I whisper. "That's where he waits for us."
My voice sounds afraid, but my body doesn't feel it.

"Who is waiting there, Meg?"

"The man with the playing-card eyes."

"Can you go into that room. Can you take us in there?"

Something else detaches from the fog in my mind and floats
free. A hazy drift of memory.

"She's in there too."

"Who might she be?"

"The lady. There's a lady. She dresses in underwear."

"You are afraid of the lady?"

"Yes," I whisper. "She's the one who won't let us leave."

CHAPTER FIFTY-TWO

CARA

Since the police left, I've been in a daze. I can't really believe what Hanson told me was true. Dr. Lutz ran a rehab facility in Florida that was shut down? Our staff has records for violence? Connections to organized crime networks?

It's too ridiculous. Like something on the TV. The police are trying to make Dr. Lutz look bad.

I'm still trying to forget all about it when Max arrives at my desk, looking flustered.

"Do you know what happened to Meg?" he asks. "Her scheduled therapy location was altered."

"Not by me." I frown. Tap my scheduler. "Looks like... Oh. Well, Dr. Lutz changed the session," I say, confused. "Meg has treatment now."

Max's eyes show dark rage. "I *told* him," he mutters. "I told him it was too soon."

My mind pans back to our earlier conversation. Max's implication that Dr. Lutz wanted to rush Meg into treatment before she was ready. But surely Dr. Lutz wouldn't...rearrange without consulting his lead psychologist?

Before I can respond, Max sets off in the direction of the treatment rooms at a fast stride.

I watch him go, my previous suspicions of Dr. Lutz taking a lurch to their feet. Making a decision, I turn to my computer. I'll search online. Settle once and for all that there's no truth in what the police said about Dr. Lutz. I click on the search bar and my fingers hover.

For a moment, I have a horrible flashback. Searching the internet for my own name. Finding it.

Mystery blond and hotel mogul.

Married hotelier checks into own hotel for adulterous fun.

Plain Jane and Mr. Beaumont.

I shake away the memories with a shudder. Type "Dr. Lutz" and "Florida rehab" into the search.

Pages of information roll past. Nothing suspicious or strange. Just information on Dr. Lutz. His experience. Research projects he's funding.

I breathe out. *See?* Dr. Lutz is a good guy.

I open up a page at random. A mini bio confirms exactly what Dr. Lutz told me. He spent ten years in India, using holistic treatments for addiction.

There's a picture of him outside an Indian rehab facility, sitting cross-legged and barefoot, with all his smiling rehabilitated drug users behind him.

There's a smile on my face. How could anyone suspect gentle, bearded Dr. Lutz of anything untoward? I look a little closer, reading the caption.

"Abhaya Lutzheimer and his students."

Abhaya Lutzheimer?

I ponder this. Some kind of yoga name Dr. Lutz took maybe? In India?

Another possibility hits me. Could he have been using his alternative name in the Florida rehab the police spoke about?

Very slowly I repeat the earlier search. This time using "Abhaya Lutzheimer" and "Florida rehab."

Somehow I know what I'm going to see even before the pages and pages of news roll up.

Multiple headlines leap out, none of them good.

15 ARRESTED IN SOUTH FLORIDA PATIENT KICKBACK SCHEME

ADDICTS LURED TO RELAPSE AT SWISS-RUN CLINIC

SWISS DOCTOR CHARGED AT CORRUPT REHAB

There's a tight knot in my stomach.

It looks like Dr. Lutz was involved in some kind of corruption at a Florida rehab facility. He wasn't prosecuted, but there was strong evidence that he was involved in some version of the Florida shuffle.

My mind flashes back to the testing company. To Haley Banks's test results. Max has confirmed there was nothing untoward. So why do I still feel like these things are all connected?

CHAPTER FIFTY-THREE

MEG

I can't feel the hospital bed beneath me, and I'm only vaguely aware of Dr. Lutz and his nurse in the treatment room.

An urgent beeping sound starts up, somewhere far away.

Something by my ear is beeping wildly.

"Look at the EEG," whispers Dr. Lutz. "Have you ever seen anything like it?"

"She's at 100 beats per minute," says the nurse. "We have to stop. She'll go into shock. We could risk organ failure."

I see Haley. Young Haley. Putting a finger to her lips.

"It's a secret, Meggy," she whispers. "Promise not to tell?"

Dr. Lutz clicks his fingers.

The frantic memories drop away.

No! Take me back! Take me back to Haley!

"She's not responding to the wake-up signal," says the nurse's voice.

"Fascinating," says Dr. Lutz. His face is in front of my eyes suddenly. I must have opened them. With a huge amount of effort, I close them again.

"She's metabolizing it already," says the nurse.

I feel my body being tugged and my eyelids opened. Fingers clicking in front of my face.

I'm back on the bed. Motionless. It takes everything I have, but somehow I manage to move the tips of my toes. Then I'm making a fist.

"Fascinating," repeats Dr. Lutz.

My vision returns, and suddenly Max is in the room. I blink. It looks like he's...conversing in a highly agitated way with Dr. Lutz. I blink some more, trying to make sense of it. Catch the words. "Not ready" and "mentally stable."

"We've never seen anything like this brain activity," Max is saying as my hearing returns fully.

"Not the same, but similar," says Dr. Lutz. "Remember Haley Banks?" He hesitates. The nurse says something I don't hear.

"We're making progress," says Dr. Lutz. "Let's keep the momentum going. The sooner Meg relives her troubling memories, the sooner she can get better."

"Absolutely not," says Max. "Not until I sign her off."

"Max," Dr. Lutz is saying calmly, "unless she engages with regular treatment, I won't keep her place at the Clinic."

"Then she'll have to leave," says Max. "I won't risk more treatments until I know she can process her trauma."

I feel hands at my head.

A nurse is helping me stand, taking off the EEG cap, and rolling complicated equipment away.

"Meg?" Max's face is close. Stricken. "How are you feeling?"

I rub my forehead. "Fine, I guess."

"We were quite successful, I believe," says Dr. Lutz, "in beginning to unearth some memories."

My bare feet feel out the floor, marveling at the sensation.

"But the balance of treatment was not correct." Dr. Lutz considers. "It was not strong enough."

Something flickers on Max's face, then is gone before I can identify it. Fear, I think.

"You won't be undergoing another treatment for a while, Meg," he says firmly. "Not until we've gotten your other assessments back."

I get the feeling this is more directed at Dr. Lutz than it is at me. "Can I go now?"

Max hesitates. "After treatment, patients find themselves in a very heightened emotional state," he says. "The process turbo-charges memories and feelings that are locked very deeply. Much like drug withdrawal, you might feel negative effects before you get better." He hesitates. "Some clients experience waves of depression, crying. Perhaps a little separation of self or dissociation. This can be frightening. But these feelings are harmless and will pass."

"Disassociation?"

"It's where your mind offlines as a response to excess stimuli," he says. "You'll experience nothing at all, but those around you will notice you have blanked out and stopped talking. It only lasts a few seconds. Likewise with separation of self. You'll feel like you're not in your body for a few moments."

I'm putting it together. Dex. His strange lapses in speaking.

"Can I go to the spa?"

Max nods. "Certainly. Relaxation is advised."

Weird memories of the session peel away, combined with a deep, cold swirl of terror. The lady. Mr. Priest.

I push them back.

I'm thinking I'll make another attempt to hunt for Haley's phone.

CHAPTER FIFTY-FOUR

MEG

The spa tunnels are warm, dark, and high walled. Raw black quartz, cut in slim jagged rectangles, stretches up on either side of me. The gauzy blue-green water is ethereal, lit from beneath like a fairy grotto, as I wade through the semidarkness. Each tunnel looks the same. But different areas are discreetly placed. A low-ceilinged sound cave with gentle music playing. A scented area wafts steam.

After the treatment with Dr. Lutz, it's hard to know what's real and what isn't. The lady. It feels as though she could be lurking just around the corner. My mind feels strangely detached, as though it's bobbing a little way above my body.

I find the fire pool, edged with copper-hooped pipes raining a constant flow of blazing-hot water. The ice pool takes my breath away, as I search in vain at the frosted openings where ice chips steadily tumble free. In another tunnel, I duck low to swim through a narrow entrance, emerging in a six-foot square enclosed pool only large enough for one person.

I don't find anything. And once I admit defeat, I realize I've completely lost track of time. Missed group therapy.

Fuck.

I dress in the changing rooms, failure washing through me.

I'm remembering Max and Dr. Lutz's conversation. Unless Max signs me off for more treatment, Dr. Lutz will kick me out. I need to engage with therapy. But I have no idea *how* to do that.

Stop taking oxy, says a mean little voice that I instantly dismiss.

Heading out to the corridor, I hear my scheduler beep. Therapy with Max.

I pull out my phone and try a last-ditch attempt to ring Haley's number. I'm fully expecting it to go straight to voicemail.

It rings. I nearly drop the phone.

OK. Keep calm, Meg. Can you hear the ring?

I listen carefully. I can. I'm sure I can. One thing is for sure. It isn't coming from the spa.

It's coming from…the female dorm.

Do I follow the ring? Or head to therapy?

Obvious answer. I set off at a run toward the dorms. I'm rounding the corner when a familiar voice resounds along the corridor.

"What do you think you're doing?"

Oh *great*. Madeline. I turn slowly with a weary expression.

"And therapy is that way, Rocky."

"How do you know I've got therapy?"

"Service to others. I make it my business."

"Gee, thanks."

"There's something not right with you," accuses Madeline. "How come you're not sick like the rest of us were? Three days in, I could hardly walk for stomach cramps."

I'm suddenly so done with Madeline. "Why should you care anyway?" I fire back.

"I'm on my final steps," she says. "Making sure other people don't slip up and drag the rest of us down."

She closes right in on me, finger pointing accusingly, stopping short of poking me in the chest.

"I don't trust you," she says.

I roll my eyes. "I'm new here. I walked the wrong way. Big deal."

I'm so mad at Madeline for stopping me, I actually want to kill her.

She moves her face close enough that I can make out the uneven pores of her aging skin, stretched tight over her skull. Eyelashes curled in unnaturally.

It's hard not to rise to the bait of her proximity. The only thing that stops me from knocking her on her ass is I have a strange feeling that that's what she wants me to do. Her eyes narrow.

"The way you took me out before?" she announces. "That was a cop move. You got your weight down low. I've seen cops do that before. You're undercover, aren't you?"

I laugh. "You know I've got a criminal record, right? They giving you something for that paranoia, crazy lady?"

She scowls at my reaction. "There's something about you not on the level, and I'm gonna find it out."

"Knock yourself out." I move past her, using every ounce of self-control not to push her out of the way as I do. "Oh, wait. I already did that for you."

"I know people like you, Rocky," she says. "You're all puff when you're mad. You got no stomach when you're not. Me, I learned the hard way to take revenge when people least expect it. So watch your back. You know what happened to the last girl who pissed me off right?"

Her eyes have a malevolent shine.

Is she *confessing*? "You did something to Haley Banks?"

Her aggressive energy recedes. "I'm telling you not to mess with me, is all."

I stare into her face, trying to decide if she's bluffing. She is. I think.

"If you're trying to be a gangster, Madeline, trust me, I've had worse from better," I tell her. "Now leave me the fuck alone. I've got a headache."

"Not until I get you to the therapy session."

I'm mad. Much as I hate to admit it, she's won this round. I can't go search for Haley's phone without Madeline seeing me.

CHAPTER FIFTY-FIVE

MEG

I arrive at Max's therapy room to notice he's got a deck of cards and two stacks of chips on his huge leather-topped desk.

"How are you feeling after treatment?" he asks.

"OK, I guess. Little hazy."

"Anything come up you'd like to talk about?"

A memory of the lady rears up. I wrestle her back down. "Don't think so." I keep a cheery tone.

Max absorbs this. "It was too early for treatment in your case," he decides. "Dr. Lutz expects patients to follow a certain schedule. It's not correct in every case."

"I'm too messed up for treatment?" I'm not surprised. It's the story of my life.

"I think you would benefit very greatly from treatment, if only you would engage with the rehab process," says Max. "I notice you missed another group therapy," he adds. "I'm guessing the impact of that treatment was overwhelming, so I'm going to let you off this once. But you attend every session from now on, OK?"

"OK. Thanks."

"And write out your honesty statement."

"Every bad thing I ever did on drugs? Seriously?"

"Seriously." He looks at my face and seems to determine something. "I've booked in your assessment as a video conference," he says. "But first I thought we might try something different," he explains. "Would you like a game of poker?"

"*You* play poker?" I'm looking at Max quizzically. It's fair to say he doesn't seem the type.

He gives me a lopsided smile. "Not very well. But…we could have a game."

"For real?"

"You seem very happy with that idea."

"Sure." My mind is mostly on Haley's phone. But my fingers are itching to hold the cards.

"We can't gamble for money, obviously. And I have one condition."

"Shoot."

"We talk while we play."

"Fine with me." I cut the pack in seven fast riffle shuffles. "All the faster to pick up your tells."

Max is watching me shuffle and deal the cards incredulously. "So," he says, regarding his cards carefully. "Why poker?"

"It's the perfect blend of skill and chance," I tell him. "You have to control your reaction to the chance and play with skill. It's a hard thing to do. And if you can do it right, you've mastered yourself. Why are you smiling?"

"This is the most conversation I've got out of you since we met."

I look at my cards. A jack and a queen. Not bad.

Max matches the bet. I deal the flop and watch him carefully before recalculating my ratios.

"You look very at ease there," observes Max.

I nod. "It's…nice to be back in a game," I admit.

"You feel safe playing cards?"

I hesitate. "Cards are predictable," I agree.

"Unlike people?"

"Unlike people. Are you in?"

Max nods. Slides chips. "Last time we spoke, you mentioned something that happened to you at work."

Images of the abandoned warehouse flash through my mind. Men in ski masks.

I frown. "It was a very uncool moment for Hustler Francine."

"You joke when you're deflecting from trauma," he says.

Max taps his cards to his chin. Studies the flop. "When Madeline threw a book at you, did you experience sensations in your body that could be considered emotional?"

I consider this. "My body felt like ice water," I admit.

"Have you ever felt that way before? The ice-water feeling?"

I nod slowly. "The warehouse."

"Any other occasions?" He's looking me intently.

I'm silent for a moment, juggling possibilities. I can't see any harm in answering truthfully. Who knows? Maybe he can even help me.

"I…I don't know. Maybe." I look up from the cards. "It was almost like the same feeling had been lying in wait. Ready to jump out at me again. It was like…the warehouse was a *reminder* not to feel. But I can't remember when the first reminder was."

Max leans back. "Tell me, Meg. Did you notice any changes after the warehouse incident? Panic attacks? Nightmares?"

"No. Well. Actually yes," I say. "They weren't related to what happened at work. Just old nightmares I used to have as a kid. They came back for a while."

"This would be the nightmares about a guy with playing cards for eyes?"

"Right." *And the lady in underwear.* "Are you going to show me your cards or what?"

He lays his cards out. "Not bad," I say. "But not good enough." I rake in the winnings.

"What age did you initially stop having these nightmares?" tries Max.

"Thirteen, maybe. I cured them by drinking alcohol and popping pills."

"Wasn't that the same time your sister left home?"

"Yes."

"And you don't remember feeling much since that time?"

"No. I don't have a lot of feelings for most people. I know that makes me a freak or something. But, honestly, my life is better this way."

Max looks sad. "Something traumatic happened in your childhood," he says.

"I don't remember a lot of my childhood," I say. "Can you be traumatized by something you can't remember?"

"Absolutely." Max is nodding fast. "Memory loss is extremely common with trauma." He studies me some more.

"I'm sensing a theme with you, Meg," he says. "Lack of bonding with the group. You mention you broke all contact with your dad."

"He wasn't my dad. My mom screwed him out of years of false alimony. He must hate me."

"You never took the risk of finding out. Have you considered you abandon people before they have the chance to abandon you?"

"Why would I give someone the chance to abandon me?"

"I suppose because sometimes they won't?"

We're interrupted by the beep of his pager. Max looks at it. "Excuse me just a moment. One of the nurses needs a prescription checked urgently." He stands and heads for the door. "I'll be right back."

As he closes the door behind him, my eyes fall on his open notepad, left on his desk.

Is this a test? Is someone watching me? In the corridor I can hear raised voices.

I lean across and pick up the notepad. Max has written about my childhood memories. Scrawled snippets of things I told him.

I flip back, past more writing, then stop. On one page, the notes are punctuated by larger block letters. Capitals rather than flowing script.

WHO WOULD WANT HALEY DEAD? DIAMORPHINE 1 BOX = 22MG
JADE TRANSFERRING CODEPENDENCE TO HALEY?

I stare and stare.

My fried mind can't quite compute this. There's a noise at the door. The handle turning.

I just about manage to throw myself back into the chair as Max returns. My heart beats a slow steady thud.

"Sorry about that." Max is back. I try to look calm.

"OK." I'm only half listening. The fragile pieces of my brain are piecing together what Max's notepad could mean. Max is trying to solve Haley's murder. He suspects Jade.

CHAPTER FIFTY-SIX

CARA

I stare at the internet pages, my mind whirling.

The police were right. Dr. Lutz changed his name. He ran a corrupt rehab. In Florida.

The drug-testing company we use.

Pro Lab Florida.

Is there a connection? A reason Dr. Lutz was reluctant to share the test results with the police. I already searched the company online and found nothing. I try again, and for the second time, the Florida shuffle documentary I was watching earlier pops up. Paused at the point I stopped watching it.

Strange. Is there some mention of Pro Lab Florida in the documentary that I missed?

I click it.

The TV personality stands in the dingy crack house with the police officer. Both grim faced.

"Addicts are tricked into relapsing?" asks the host, adding a degree of shock to her voice. "Why would anyone do that?"

"It's an insurance scam," explains the officer. "Addicts are in the shuffle. Detox in a clinic. Relapse in one of these so-called sober houses. Return to the clinic. And the whole time, their insurer is paying out."

OK.

On my screen, the host steps nearer the camera.

"At the heart of the model"—she holds a plastic testing cassette close to the camera—"is this. A five-dollar urine test. Companies use them to prove to insurers that an addict has relapsed. But they're also quick to cash in on yet another chance for profit."

The camera switches back to the police officer, and the host extends her microphone.

"It's a very lucrative business model," the policeman explains. "You take a thirty-dollar urine test. You charge the insurer $300. Run seven of those per patient per week. It's huge."

"That's fraud, right?" The host nods.

"Actually it isn't," says the officer.

The woman makes a show of looking shocked.

"How can it not be fraud?" she demands.

"We're working to change the law," agrees the policeman. "That money comes from the shared pot. While rehabs are lining their pockets, there's less money for basic operations and lifesaving procedures."

No mention of Pro Lab Florida so far.

I scroll to the comments, as the video rolls.

There are a bunch of remarks. How disgusting the whole process is. People who have personally experienced the Florida shuffle, and relatives of those who died during the process of repeated relapse.

It's all so sad.

My eyes zoom in on one. Here. A mention of Pro Lab Florida. It's from…a mother whose daughter was caught up in the shuffle. It's a long account, and she complains of receiving huge bills for tests. The testing company billing her insurance was Pro Lab Florida.

I put this together. So Pro Lab Florida is a testing company associated with disreputable rehabs.

Another possibility hits me. Bills. Accounts. It occurs to me that I've been looking in the wrong place all along. Maybe I should have checked out how much we were charging patients for Pro Lab Florida tests.

I massage my temples. Open the one folder I never thought to check.

Billing and accounts. Haley Banks.

Right away I see it. The numbers. They *must* be wrong.

I personally order the urine tests from the drug company every month, and the bill comes to a few hundred dollars max. Around two dollars per plastic test cassette and testing solution. But Haley's bill runs to hundreds of thousands of dollars. My eyes scan. Three hundred dollars per pregnancy test. The drug profile tests were billed at *five hundred* dollars each. That's...I make a quick calculation. A 5,000 percent markup.

One day alone, the charges for various tests and treatments came to over $22,000.

Haley's running total ran to over $100,000 and counting. She had another six days left in rehab when she died. Potentially another $20,000 plus of treatment to be charged. Haley Banks was a cash cow.

The documentary is still rolling.

"Some insurers have gotten wise to it now," continues the police officer. "But the companies keep evolving their strategies. STI tests. Pregnancy tests. Specialist new treatments. It's a huge business. Huge."

I swallow hard. This is what we're doing, isn't it? Here in the Clinic. Marking up drug tests and charging insurers.

The video times out, and the enormity of what I've discovered hits me.

CHAPTER FIFTY-SEVEN

MEG

As I leave the therapy room, my mind is fixed on Max's notepad.

Jade transferred her codependence to Haley.

What can it mean? I imagine Jade and Haley breaking into the medication room. Sharing medications. It's easy to picture.

I need my oxycodone. This super-long therapy session meant I'm badly in the red.

Get to the women's dorm, I decide, *pop a few pills, then hunt for Haley's phone.*

But when I arrive at the dorm, I can't quite take in what I'm seeing. For a full few seconds I wonder if I'm actually imagining things. The whole room has been completely trashed. Ransacked.

My eyes drift over the drawers of clothes pulled free. Nightstands overturned. Covers pulled off beds and pillowcases scattered. What the…?

I step into the room, taking in the devastation. There's a certain methodological feel to it. Like someone was looking for something, rather than blind destruction. What would someone have been looking for? Drugs is the most logical reason.

Or Haley's phone?

The oxy urge twangs at me. *Think this through later. First. Medicine.*

I step a little deeper into the room, crunch on glass. Jade's bedside lamp lies in pieces, her oak nightstand upended.

My eyes land on the picture of Jade and her little girl lying in the debris. Smashed glass. I notice something else too. A foil package of prescription pills hidden behind the picture.

I pick them up. And my reaction spins again. I was expecting a familiar drug. Something sold on the street. What I'm not prepared for is to see the word *Rohypnol* running in diagonal lines across the back of the pack.

A few things come together in my mind.

Jade keeps date-rape drugs on her nightstand.

Jade has transferred her codependence to Haley.

I stand, my legs shaking. OK. Enough detective work. I need the oxy.

Just in that moment, Jade steps out of the shower. She sees me. Sees the room, and then yanks out a set of earbuds that I didn't realize she had in.

"Meg," she says. "You skipped group. We were all waiting…" Her eyes take in the room. "What the fuck?"

"Who are you?" I demand. "Tell me the truth, Jade. We've met before, haven't we? As kids."

She holds up her hands, placating. "Meg, I don't know what you're talking about."

In reply, I hold up the pack of pills. "Rohypnol, Jade?" I demand.

Jade's lips move slightly as if she's trying to make sense of what I'm saying.

"Did you trash the room?" she asks finally.

"You're codependent," I continue wildly. "You latched onto Haley. Gave her drugs when she was trying to quit, then killed her."

I turn to see Dex enter the room.

"What's up?" he says uneasily, looking between me and Jade. "I heard shouting."

"Meg trashed the room," says Jade. "Then accused me of killing Haley Banks."

Dex is shaking his head. "Meg. Are you serious?"

I feel like there is white noise crashing around me.

"She's codependent," I point a finger at Jade. "Jade gets off on getting other people high. Max's notes say she transferred it to Haley. Now Haley's dead and Jade has fucking date-rape drugs in her nightstand."

"That's not what 'codependent' means." Madeline has walked in now, with Sierra. "You should try getting some education before you accuse people," she says. "Codependency is when you take on other people's dramas as a way of avoiding your own feelings. It's got nothing to do with feeding them drugs."

"Max is helping me not to take on everyone's grief about Haley," explains Jade. "I do that. When someone dies."

My mouth opens and shuts. I really, *really* wish they would all vanish so I can take my oxy.

"What about Rohypnol?" I demand. "I know everyone *loves* Jade and all. But can *anyone* think of a reason to keep roofies on your nightstand?"

The pain in my shoulder has spread like an ache to my whole body.

"Are you talking about my sleeping pills?" Jade says finally. "They're in my cupboard. I don't take them all the time 'cause they're strong."

"Rohypnol is used for bad sleep issues," confirms Dex. "I took it for the first three nights here."

"Why hide them?"

"I didn't." Jade looks genuinely confused. She looks so certain

I'm doubting myself. Maybe the packet was lying under the frame. Maybe it isn't a hiding place.

My eyes meet Jade's. She looks confused, hurt, even a little afraid of me. I take in her posture, the slight curl of her hands, the way the shoulders are held.

No tells. No subterfuge. No secrecy. She's an open book.

"But…I know you," I say helplessly. "We met before. I'm sure of it."

Jade's brown eyes soften.

"I think…that's a rehab thing, chick," she says kindly. "Transference. Emotions get mixed up. Other patients become like your family. Maybe…it's the first time you felt that?"

The shock of that hits me like a physical thing. Because she's right. I never had a family whom I felt close to. The shame of it knocks me sideways.

"Jade wasn't even *here* when Haley died," says Madeline. "She checked in Thursday. Day after Haley left in a body bag."

Oh. Fuck.

"What the fuck is with you, Meg?" demands Madeline. "You haven't been straight with us since you got here. You don't engage in group. Art class is like some joke to you. Go home if you don't want to get better."

Everyone is looking at me with various expressions of anger and disappointment.

"I need to get out of here," I mutter, striding out. My shoulder hurts. I'm shivering. Nothing is making any sense.

Did I really get it so wrong?

First thing I do when I'm out of sight is call Harry, my hands shaking.

"I'm fucking it up" is the first thing I say.

I hear him take a breath. "Hello to you too," he says. "OK. What did you do?"

"Accused Jade. Everyone hates me."

"Not great," acknowledges Harry. There's a long pause.

"What?" I demand. "Tell me."

"We got the fingerprints back," he admits.

My heart pumps faster. "You did? And? Jeez, Harry. Don't keep me in suspense. Whose were they?"

There's a pause.

"The fingerprints were Haley's."

CHAPTER FIFTY-EIGHT

MEG

I'm clutching the phone in my hand, hardly able to believe what Harry is telling me.

The fingerprints were Haley's.

What does that mean?

"You are absolutely sure?" I ask Harry. "Haley's fingerprints?"

"Yeah. Her prints were on file for a DUI." He pauses. "Guess she must have handled that paper before she died."

"So that means…" I try to catch my thoughts, but I can't.

"The person who gave you that note was organized enough to wear gloves," says Harry. "And they were close enough to Haley to get to things she touched before she died."

"That doesn't make sense," I point out. "Whoever left me that note couldn't have known I'd be able to fingerprint it."

"You're dealing with someone very methodical," says Harry. "A planner. Kind of person who leaves nothing to chance."

There are too many thoughts in my head. *Sierra said she and Haley were friends. But…Dex. He had a key to Haley's room, didn't he?*

"I can't get my head straight," I tell him. "There are all these people. They're messing with my thinking. I can't deal with it."

"OK, OK." I can picture Harry frowning. "Just...take a moment, OK?"

"I don't *have* a moment, Harry!" My voice is rising. "I'm living with four people who all have a reason to kill my sister. It's like a really, really bad game of Who's Who?"

"OK, Meg. Work with me. Like you said before, it's a poker game, right? You wouldn't walk into a poker game and expect all the answers right away."

"You're gathering data," I agree.

"Right. And how do you get intel?"

"You give out intel," I say begrudgingly, realizing what this means. "Share dark secrets and people feel inclined to tell you theirs."

"But have you told anyone a single true thing about yourself, Meg? You know, in the spirit of making some real friends."

"I've been keeping a low profile," I admit.

I hear Harry blow out. "If you want people to talk to you, you are going to *actually* have to be vulnerable. For real."

I sigh. "That's what my therapist keeps saying. Bond with the group. He wants me to read out this big honesty statement saying all the messed-up stuff I've done."

"So do it."

"I don't know if I can. If I do the honesty statement, the next step is digging up childhood trauma. I'm not ready for that, Harry."

"Haley was remembering childhood stuff in rehab, right?"

"Right."

"So maybe you and Haley's past with this guy is the key to what the fuck is going on."

"What are you talking about, Harry?"

"You're not going to like this, Meg. But to solve your sister's murder, you might need to solve yourself."

There's a pause. I sniff. Rub my face.

"Meg," says Harry gently. "You've been there almost a week now, and it doesn't seem like you're getting better. Are you still taking those pills?"

I pause for too long. Harry is about the only person I don't lie to.

"Thought so." The disappointment in his voice is too much.

"I'm going to stop," I tell him. "I quit the booze and…"

"Meg," he says, anger spiking his voice. "Don't kid a kidder. OK. I'm coming to get you."

"No! Please, Harry. I'm getting closer to finding out what happened to Haley."

"You're getting closer to making yourself crazy is what you're getting."

"Just. A few more days," I plead. "They put me in for treatment. I remembered stuff and…"

"Bullshit, Meg."

"Two more days."

There's a pause. "Two days," he says finally. "Then I come get you. Check you into someplace that will actually help you quit."

I let out a rush of air. "OK. Deal." I take a breath. "I gotta go. Harry…"

"Yeah?"

"I… Never mind."

He must understand what I'm trying to say, because he replies like I said it.

"You're welcome, kid."

CHAPTER FIFTY-NINE

MEG

When I hang up, it feels like my whole body is attacking me.

A wave of pain hits me as I walk to the bathroom. Either I didn't take enough oxy or I'm needing more. Fuck. It hurts. What hurts worse is I think Harry might be right.

Feelings. The ones I don't feel. The ones the oxycodone keeps locked up tight. Underneath the opioid buffer is something sharp and icky. Something I don't want to confront.

I have an awful intuition it could be related to why Haley died.

I need another treatment.

But I need my oxycodone.

Locking the door of a stall, I slip my pack of pills from its hiding place. Twenty left. Just about enough to last. Maybe. I take a long, deep breath.

I think about what Max said. How drugs numb your feelings. I think about when I first started using. After Haley left home. The things I don't remember. Or don't want to remember.

The pack of oxy is reassuring in my hand. Promising to turn it all off. But there's something unfamiliar in my body. Something so deep I can only brush it with my fingertips. A drowsy truth that has rolled over in its sleep.

To solve your sister's murder, you need to solve yourself.

Slowly, I pop every last pill out of the pack. They lie in my hand. I flip my palm and drop every last one into the toilet. My hand is shaking so much I can barely push the handle.

"I'm going to find the answers." I tell the oxy. "You can't hide them from me anymore."

For a pure five seconds, I feel nothing but victorious relief. No more sneaking around. No more fucking myself up. I'm going to go back to those memories wherever they take me and face up to it all.

I watch the pills spiral out of sight. Then the momentousness of what I've done hits me.

Fuck. I plunge my hand into the toilet. It's too late though. They're gone. Different emotions are buffering me from all angles like a five-strike punch in a knockout combo. If I could, I'd get in head first and swim down the cistern.

It's only a second later that a wave of pain hits my shoulder so hard I'm breathless with it.

Too late. The pills are gone.

I'm not ready. I'm not ready at all. I stand up, a sick feeling of dread rippling through me.

To solve your sister's murder, you need to solve yourself.

There's no going back now. Only I don't think I'll like what I'm going to find.

CHAPTER SIXTY

CARA

I'm packing my suitcase when there's a knock at the door. I open it to see Dr. Lutz.

"Miss Morse," he says. "One of the nurses told me you were leaving. I didn't believe it, of course. You of all people would give a professional amount of notice, should you require urgent leave. Are you unwell?"

"You lied to me," I tell him. The reaction is not at all what I wanted. I expected him to flinch, to deny it. Instead he simply looks at me.

"The Florida shuffle," I say. "You ran a rehabilitation center in Florida that was closed down for patient brokering and drug kickbacks."

"Yes." He tilts his head very slightly. "It was a very disagreeable business. Sadly, my good intentions were subverted by several unscrupulous individuals. Fortunately, they are now in jail. But I was forced to make the very sad decision to close the rehab, though we were helping a great many people."

"You're telling me...you weren't complicit?" I don't know how to process this information.

He frowns now. "Of course not. Since the age of twenty-two, my sole passion has been rehabilitating addicts."

I take in what he's saying. It's true. It doesn't fit that someone with his past would keep patients addicted for profit. Dr. Lutz's expression is of such genuine disgust that I find myself believing him.

"How could you have no idea people were being brokered to your facility?" The anger has gone from my voice. "Then pressured to relapse?"

"I'm sad to say my commitment made me an easy target. It was only after I began noticing the same people returning again and again that I had the slightest idea. I assumed that everyone was like me. Committed to fighting addiction."

He smiles sadly. Opens his hands. "The court case is a matter of public record," he says. "The judge ruled very definitely on my side. He even expressed regret that given our excellent success rate, the facility's reputation was sullied to the point that I elected to close."

I hesitate. It's true he wasn't convicted. He would have been sent to jail.

"What about the drug test cassettes," I say. "I've seen the accounts. We make a 5000 percent markup."

"There's nothing illegal in that," says Dr. Lutz with a faint smile. "The markup represents the cost of our medical staff, our time, and the high-quality facility in which the test is administered."

"But it's...completely immoral!" I say. "You're taking money from healthcare providers."

Dr. Lutz considers this, hands folded in prayer.

"You're correct of course," he says. "The insurers think what we're doing is terrible. I happen to have a very low opinion of what they are doing too." He pauses for effects. "The budgets they afford for rehabilitation are an insult. A legacy of an archaic system that regards addicts as self-indulgent." He pauses, animated. "We take what is needed, Cara," he says. "To do the good that needs to be done for these traumatized people. If insurers need to adjust their finances, so be it."

"You're asking me to choose between what's right and what's necessary," I say quietly. "I don't know if I can."

"If you don't like impossible choices, don't work in medicine," says Dr. Lutz.

I clear my throat. "What about our staff?" I say. "Six staff members, all with criminal records?"

Dr. Lutz's expression lowers by degrees. "It is not illegal for a nurse to have a criminal record," he says, shaking his head. "Naturally, I have rehabilitated former addicts and placed them on staff. To me, their past is behind them. You see how police operate, Cara?" he says. "To take a noble act of trust and give it a nefarious edge."

"Hanson suggested they had links with organized crime," I say.

"Drug addicts often have those associations. The circles they move in to acquire their substances are almost universally populated by organized criminals."

That makes total sense. So why do I get such a shady feeling about several of his male nurses?

"Why didn't you tell me?" I ask finally, realizing this at least can't be answered reasonably. He strokes at his bushy beard.

"I am an overly logical man," he says finally. "My personality does not easily entertain the inefficiency of catering to people's egos and emotions. I leave that to Max."

"If we're to work together," I say. "You'd need to keep me informed."

He hesitates. "Employee relations isn't my strength," he says. "We all have different roles to play. Mine is practical and financial.

Imagine a surgeon who vividly imagined how the wound felt. A war president who empathized with the men he must conscript."

"There'd be a lot fewer wars." It pops out of my mouth.

Dr. Lutz gives a shrug of disdain. "You only need watch televised singing contests to know the common empathetic person cannot be trusted with leadership. Portray a participant who has survived cancer, and a whole nation is baying for the blood of their rival. We couldn't have a world run by people who show barely more intelligence than a flock of chickens pecking at one another. Positions of authority are held by people like me. Who separate our emotions from key decisions. That is why Max and I work so well together." He hesitates. "You are aware of my failings now and must decide if you can work around them. I will say, you are doing exceptionally well in your administrative role. You are the perfect manager."

It's hard not to feel good about the praise.

It's a relief, I tell myself. I got it all wrong. Nothing terrible or illegal taking place.

Just completely unethical. Or is it?

"Does Max know?" I ask. "About the insurance markups?"

"Of course," says Dr. Lutz. "Max has worked in rehab for almost a decade. How about you talk to Max and consider giving us one more week? If you are unhappy with our model after that, then by all means leave. We will honor your bonus as if you'd worked out the year."

Maybe I've overreacted. I can't very well leave them without a manager with no notice.

"I'll work the week," I say. "And if I still decide to leave?"

Dr. Lutz opens his eyes wide. "Then, of course, you are free to go."

CHAPTER SIXTY-ONE

MEG

The next day I wake up feeling like I have the worse flu of my life. My head aches, I can't breathe through my nose, every muscle hurts.

Oxy. I need the oxycodone.

I'm hit with sheer blank panic as I remember how I flushed it. What the hell was I thinking? I manage to sit up in bed, but it's like each individual muscle holds a bruise.

Goose bumps randomly appear in patches on my skin as I shakily pull on my clothes.

No one is talking to me at breakfast. It's the least of my worries.

Get through the day, I tell myself, as I try to get a mouthful of dry toast past my shaking lips without heaving. *That's all you have to do.*

First I have a session with Max. He's reading the assessment we did yesterday as I walk in.

"Are you OK, Meg?" is the first thing he says. "You look terrible."

"I'm fine." I notice I'm scratching at my arms and stop. "Just a little fallout with Jade."

His mouth compresses. "I heard."

I maneuver myself to a chair and sit, wincing. My scalp prickles with cold electricity.

"I'm ready," I announce. "I'm going to read my honesty statement to the group."

Max's eyebrows rise. "That's...good," he decides.

"After that it's another treatment with Dr. Lutz, right?" My hand has started scratching again, and I clasp my palms together to stop.

"Right," says Max. "If you feel you're ready."

"I get memories back, right?" I lean forward to take a tissue for my nose, which has started running, the movement sending a fresh sluice of acid through my tender muscles.

Max hesitates. "Commonly, yes. Fugu treatment is very successful at unearthing traumatic memories that have been suppressed."

"Fugu?"

"It's the drug you were given in treatment. To relax the body," he explains.

Something leaps into my brain. A disjointed image from the past. *Haley. Mr. Priest is holding her by the hand. He's leading her into a bedroom.*

My hands start shaking. I try to focus on what Max is saying.

"Unprocessed memories mean the brain goes into a constant state of hypervigilance. Irrational anger. Sleep disturbances. The kind of mental torture that pushes people to addictive substances."

"So you're saying...it's not my fault? That I'm an addict?"

"Fault and accountability are different things. But what happened to you as a child? No, that wasn't your fault."

Not my fault. It's somehow obvious and not obvious at the same time.

Max talks on. "When you're drinking and using drugs, your brain is foggy. You can't get to any normal emotions. But you're also saving yourself pain. Addiction is actually a very intelligent solution in many ways. People only tend to come to us when the cost of numbing those feelings become too high."

I think about this.

"You need to be prepared," continues Max. "Treatment is extremely tough. Extremely emotional. We help patients process trauma in a way that's manageable. But it's still trauma. Memories can surface that will change everything you thought you knew."

Something Haley used to tell me as a kid drifts back.

I pay for all of us, Meg. In more ways than one.

I look at Max. He's studying me intently.

I nod, thinking. "Group therapy is right after this, right? I mean. I could do my reading right away?"

"If you felt ready." Max considers my face. He looks directly at me. "If you're ready to feel some of your painful feelings."

Everything hurts. My shoulder is a nauseating ache. I think of Haley.

I need answers.

"I'm ready."

CHAPTER SIXTY-TWO

MEG

As I walk into group therapy five pairs of unfriendly eyes swivel in my direction.

My body can't be relied upon to relay messages to my limbs, and I'm moving like a puppet. I have the strangest sense that my head is about to wobble off my shoulders and smash like a melon on the floor.

"Meg," says Max. "You're sure you want to do this now? You're shaking."

I ignore him. "OK, listen up." I address the room. "First, I didn't trash the dormitory."

"No one cares about the dormitory," says Madeline. "We care about you accusing Jade of drugging Haley."

I take in the cold stares.

OK. They still hate me. Bad start.

"I owe you all an apology," I say. There's a pause. "I haven't been engaging in group."

"There's an understatement," mutters Madeline darkly. The unrelenting pain in my body pushes me on.

"It's not 'cause I think I'm above you or anything," I add. "It's… This is really hard. I never tell anyone my feelings." I sigh, look around for my chair, and sit.

My face is sweating. I wipe it distractedly.

"Honestly, I don't really *have* feelings much. I got really, really good at pushing them down." I risk a glance around. Expressions are sympathetic. "Now they're coming back." I take a deep breath. "And to be honest, it's fucking terrifying. I mean, it's the scariest thing I've ever had to deal with."

Jade's head is tilted in sympathy, her lips pursed, eyes glittering. The heavy bruising on her face is fading now, giving her a green-yellow visor effect around her brown eyes.

"And I'm…embarrassed…I guess. I don't know. Anyway. Whatever." I sway on my chair slightly and use a hand to right myself.

"Meg," says Jade gently. "You look bad, chick. Like you're going to pass out."

"I'm OK." I pull a dog-eared piece of paper from my pocket. "Here it is. My big confession. Sorry it's late."

I look down at the page and start reading the words in a fast staccato. I'm half expecting Max to stop me but he doesn't.

"When I worked at the casino, I had a great system. Stealing drugs from the amnesty box. We have a place at the door where people can drop any illegal drugs," I add. "No reprisals. Smart, huh?"

I glance up. The expressions aren't what I was expecting. No one hates me yet. I read on.

"I used to tell myself because I only took pills from the box, I wasn't a junkie," I tell them. "But I know different now. We're all trying to block out feelings. Doesn't matter if we use heroin, prescription pills, food, work, whatever," I add.

Jade and Tom have been nodding sympathetically throughout, but I notice Madeline's eyes widen at this. She nods too. Sierra is leaning back in her chair, like she's deep in thought.

The room shudders, with a strange vibrating sound effect. No one else heard it, I realize. It's in my head.

I look down at my paper. "This time around, these pills in the box were stronger than I thought." I look up, playing the comic timing. There are nods. Smiles.

"Because I was high, I didn't realize a loan shark had pegged me as undercover," I continue. "I thought the sting was going well, and I accepted an invitation to take a ride with them to another gambling joint."

I glance up. No one is smiling now. Jade's face is stricken, her chest visibly rising and falling.

I plunge on.

"They took me to an old warehouse, poured gasoline on me..."

Jade gasps, her hands covering the lower half of her face. Everyone else is looking horrified too.

I read faster. "I was so wasted, half of me didn't even care. Dislocated my shoulder getting my arm free. Didn't even feel it."

I lose my place on the page, find it again. "If my backup from the casino hadn't followed my tracer, I would have been killed. It was a very dangerous situation that I would never have gotten into if not for the drugs," I conclude woodenly.

There is a long silence when I finish.

"That's freakin' *dark*, dude," says Dex, messing with a ripped strand of his T-shirt.

"Thank you for sharing that with the group," Max says formally.

Jade's jaw opens and shuts like she's chewing gum. "Meg," she says. "What the actual *fuck*?"

"I know. I'm a jerk," I say.

"I don't think you're a jerk," says Madeline. "For the record, we've all done dangerous stuff. Stupid stuff. I slept with a guy, 'cause I knew he had drugs in his apartment."

We hold eye contact for a second, then Madeline looks away.

Jade tilts her head. "What happened in the warehouse after you got loose?"

I frown. "I beat the crap out of the guy with the gasoline can. The other guys liked the show so much they backed off long enough for my buddies from the casino to arrive."

Max breathes out. "It sounds like an extremely"—he chooses his words—"fucked-up world you work in."

I'm only half listening. My sweat glands are doing something weird. Like someone is poking sharp itchy needles in everywhere that sweat comes out. I can't stop myself from scratching under my armpit, even when I notice Tom's eyes glued firmly to the gesture.

"You're kind of making a joke of it," says Jade softly. "I do that too. Sort of underplay it."

I hesitate. "Yeah. Well…" I manage to stop scratching.

Might as well go for total honesty.

"The truth is I nearly killed that guy. I *would have* killed that guy if the team hadn't arrived. That's…a weird thing to know about yourself."

A shock wave passes around the room. It all happens so fast I only get a few faces. Sierra looks thoughtful. Like she's reassessing me. Dex, Jade, and Madeline. They all look…troubled? Guilty? It's too close to call, and there's too much information to get a strong match. My eyes switch to Tom and stay there. For a second I could swear he looked excited.

Something is dripping onto my lap. It takes me a moment to realize my forehead is pouring with sweat.

"I think you should take a break, Meg." It's Max. "You're very pale."

"I'm good." I try wiping my face with my arm and yawn without meaning to. Why are they all looking at me like that? Then the weirdest thing happens. One moment everyone is the right way up. Then they're on their sides.

I can feel hard floor on my cheek and under my palm, and I'm wondering what this means when a world of pain hits every part of my body. The whole world is shaking. Things come in snatches.

"She's having a seizure." That's Max. "Everyone keep calm. It looks worse than it is. I'm calling for help."

"Meg? Meg, it's OK." Jade is by my side. "They're getting help."

And that's when I see her. The lady. Standing in the doorway.

She wears the same horrible smile I remember from my childhood. Lipstick stretched across her perfect face. Vintage-style underwear. Suspenders. A pointy-cupped brassiere in snowy white.

The queen of hearts.

I've let her in. Without oxy, she can come back.

"Get her out of here," I stammer, trying to point. "She can't be here."

Jade turns. "There's no one there," she whispers, looking pained.

"You're not real," I hiss at the lady. "I made you up." But the lady smiles and smiles.

CHAPTER SIXTY-THREE

MEG

When I wake up, it's night. I'm shaking, sweating. I need to throw up, but every part of me hurts.

The lady is leaning in the doorway, like she's always been there. Details come into focus one by one. Deep-red lips. Large blue eyes, with long dark lashes and a fifties flick of black liner.

I haven't seen her since I was thirteen.

"Go away," I croak. "I don't believe in you."

"I'm sad to hear that." The face transforms. Max. Looking deeply concerned.

I try to sit up and groan in pain.

"Easy there," says Max. Sweat bubbles up on my forehead.

"Where am I?" I demand.

"You're back in the dorm," he says soothingly. "The nurses put you in your bed."

"She's here," I tell Max urgently. "She's in here. Only she's in *here*, you know?" I tap my head.

"You're going to have to explain what you're talking about."

I put my head in my hands. Rub my face. When I take away my hands, the lady has gone.

It's Max. You're talking to Max.

"OK. I'm seeing someone who isn't real. A lady. I remember her. She stands in doorways. Blocking exits. And you know how you said I don't feel things? Well, I'm fucking terrified of her."

"I need you to take a few deep breaths. You've had a fairly epic seizure. That's not very common for opioid withdrawal, but it's not unknown. When it does happen, it's usually recurring, so we're medicating you with anti-seizure drugs. It's key to avoid stressful situations," he adds. "They could bring on another seizure."

I take this in. "I've been taking drugs this whole time," I admit. "Oxycodone. I flushed the last of them down the toilet."

Max's expression clouds.

"I know I've broken my contract. I know you're supposed to kick me out. But. I think I can change."

Max nods slowly. "Thank you for your honesty," he says. "This seems like a very big step for you."

I wrap my hands around myself and shake, shivering. "Help me. Please. I'm dying."

Max frowns. "You're not dying," he says. "But you are going to feel that way."

"Can you put me back in a coma? *Please?*"

He shakes his head. "I'm sorry. No. You're going to have to tough this one out. The other patients will take care of you. They've all been through detox at some point. I can give you some medication to help you sleep…"

"Anything." I'm nodding.

"And something to help with the psychotic episodes you seem to be experiencing."

"Thank you." I'm pathetically grateful. I grit my teeth as I'm hit by another explosion of cramps.

He catches the expression. "The main thing to realize is this will come in waves," he says. "You'll feel like you're going to die. But it will pass. Then you'll feel OK. But that will pass too."

"Great." I'm shivering uncontrollably.

"This would have been a lot easier if you had not brought oxycodone into treatment," he points out.

"Are you going to make me leave?"

There's a long pause. "Not yet," he says finally. "What I will say is you're here by the skin of your teeth. If it was up to me you'd probably be packing your bags."

"Dr. Lutz?" I guess. "You think he'll let me stay?"

"In your case, I think...yes." Max looks very unhappy about this.

At some point Max must have left, because the room slides in and out and he's gone. I try to close my eyes. But the moment I do, I'm seized by nausea.

I make it to the bathroom, limping across the floor, a prickling stab accompanying every muscle movement. I gag repeatedly, stumbling toward the toilet.

As I hang over the bowl, all my skin, from my legs to right up my back and across my shoulder blades, writhes like insects. Somewhere between here and the bathroom I've been flayed alive and covered in a wriggling swarm of wasps. I dig in my nails to scratch and it drives the swarm into deeper itchier places under my arms. I want to tear off my own body.

I convulse as my body dry heaves over the toilet, sending a fresh wave of stabbing pains through my legs and a repulsive new undercurrent down my swarming skin. I shudder, heave. The room swims.

When I open my eyes again, Jade is leaning over me.

"Hey," she says. "I think you passed out. Can you stand?"

I paddle my legs and they skid on the tile floor. "Maybe not."

There's someone else there now. Madeline, hauling me up.

They half carry me back to the bed.

"You finally gave up those pills, huh?" says Madeline.

"Max told you?"

Madeline snorts. "Figured it out long before. Why do you think I was so mad at you all the time?"

"We've all been through it," says Jade. "We're not stupid. The good news is you're doing it now."

"It's like my own body is torturing me."

"You're gonna feel like that for two days at least," says Madeline.

Another spasm of pain hits me, and I curl up in the bed, my body jerking.

"Fuck," I hear Dex's voice. "She's bad." I see him lower himself to my level and take my hands. "Stick with it," he says. "You're a fighter, Meg. This is the worst part."

I feel a cool cloth on my head. It's Sierra. "Keep still," she advises. "It's worse when you move around."

"You don't have to be so nice to me," I manage, my words labored. "I lied to you all."

Dex grins. "You know we're all junkies, right? Lie, cheat, steal to get our fix. You're one of the crew now, Meg. If there's one thing we all understand, it's lying to people."

Jade puts the covers around me. "Here," she says. "Just rest."

"Max says she's booked in for treatment tomorrow," I hear Madeline say. "The rest of us had at least a week of detox first."

"I know," says Sierra, sounding afraid. "Dr. Lutz will make her remember everything that made her an addict. What happens if she's not ready?"

CHAPTER SIXTY-FOUR

CARA

Dr. Lutz has arranged for Max and me to meet in the library. I'm standing, waiting, feeling increasingly nervous.

"Sorry I'm late," says Max out of breath as he jogs in. "I was with Meg."

"How's her withdrawal?"

He looks pained. "She's having hallucinations. Dr. Lutz wants her booked in for treatment."

"You think that's a good idea?"

"She'll be closely monitored."

A half answer, I notice. "In any case," he corrects himself, "it isn't why we're here. Dr. Lutz wanted us to have a talk."

Max clears his throat. "Dr. Lutz says you had some concerns."

I eye the door. "I guess you could put it that way. I had my suitcase packed this afternoon."

Max's eyes widen.

"He didn't tell me *that*."

I fix him with a look. "Did you know about the marked-up tests? Scamming insurers?"

"I suspected," admits Max.

"Then why…?"

"I didn't question it because the fugu is working, Cara." Max looks earnest. "Better than we could ever have hoped. It could save the lives of countless addicts all over the world."

"You're telling me you turned a blind eye because your treatment is working? Tests being marked up by 5,000 times the net cost?"

Max sighs. "Dr. Lutz isn't doing anything illegal. Or anything a hundred other rehabs don't already do. I've worked with addicts long enough to know this is how things have to be done. The companies that play fair with insurers, that don't mark up the tests and push for extra time...their addicts don't stand a chance. It's not cost-effective to run a good rehab on what insurers pay out. And certainly not a luxury one."

I turn this over in my mind.

"Every rehab does this? That's what you're telling me?"

"No." He sighs again. "Just the ones that have any success." He lifts his eyes to mine. "We're doing important work here. Sometimes you have to weigh those things. Do you know what standard medical insurance covers?"

"The better ones cover rehab, right?"

"Three days," says Max. "Just enough time to clear drugs. They treat addiction as purely physical, and it's wildly ineffective." His face darkens. "My time in public hospitals was spent begging insurers to pay for a few more days. I've lost count of the patients who walked out of rehab and died the next day." Max pauses for effect. "But a drug-based treatment like fugu could potentially treat millions of addicts. Not just wealthy ones."

He waits for this to sink in.

"You think fugu can replace months of expensive therapy?" I ask.

"We're proving it." He nods firmly. "Using fugu, brain waves drop into delta on the very first session."

I close my eyes, trying to figure a path through all this information.

"I don't know if I can ignore the poor ethics of overcharging insurers," I say.

"If it makes you uncomfortable, I wouldn't want you to." His face is serious. "Dr. Lutz knows I want you to stay, Cara. He expects me to try to persuade you."

"Why would you want me to stay?" The question sounds more loaded than I mean it to be. There's a tense pause, while a reason I had never even considered insinuates itself into the silence.

"Apart from you being about the only normal person here?" He smiles and his eyes have a mischievous quality. I get the impression he's dodging the question. "In any case, Dr. Lutz fully expects me to tell you only what you need to hear to stay. But since I think you should use your own judgment…"

His scheduler beeps. He frowns and checks it distractedly.

"Saved by the bell," he says. "I need to help Dr. Lutz prepare for Meg's treatment." Max swallows. "You deserve a full explanation. I'm fully booked for therapy sessions for the foreseeable. How about dinner?"

"Dinner?" It sounds strangely romantic.

"The formal dining rooms will be available after the patients leave," says Max. "We can talk more then. I'll tell you everything."

CHAPTER SIXTY-FIVE

CARA

The atmosphere between Max and me is strained as we meet for our prearranged dinner. I've spent the day becoming increasingly anxious about what he might tell me. By his expression, he's nervous too.

Max moves to the dining table to pull my chair out, then hesitates as if suddenly realizing we're not on a date.

"Sorry," he mumbles, "English boarding school habit."

"You seem anxious," I say.

"Yes. Dr. Lutz undertook Meg's fugu treatment today and I'm... concerned. Meg has such similar brain scans to Haley Banks."

"How did Meg react to treatment?"

"Her elevated heart rate was a concern. It's the aftereffects I'm afraid of."

"Disassociation and anxiety?" I think of Dex.

"Meg is so unstable, she could even suffer separation of self. Her scan suggests deep trauma."

"You think she could have some kind of psychotic breakdown?"

We're interrupted by a nurse bringing plates of food. We both thank her, neither of us commenting on the strangeness of being brought preordered meals that neither of us requested.

"It's carrot and ginger venison today," I tell him, since I help the chef design the menu. "Something to do with balancing winter energies."

Max gives me a lopsided smile as the nurse retreats. "I should remember to eat here more often," he says, eyeing the beautifully laid-out plate. The frown reappears. "I wanted to tell you about Dr. Lutz. His…past."

I'm holding my knife and fork perfectly poised, waiting.

He takes a breath. "Dr. Lutz qualified as a surgeon as a younger man in Switzerland."

I nod. I know this.

"He didn't leave to study drug rehabilitation in India," says Max. "He left because his clinic was investigated for criminal connections."

"*Criminal?*"

"They were accused of supplying black market surgical procedures. Bullet removal. Trauma surgery. Cosmetic alterations. Nothing was ever proved. But the reputation stuck. 'The mobsters' surgeon.'"

My own unfortunate social media associations come to mind. Gold digger. Man-eater. Some horrible photos of me without makeup flash before my eyes.

Max's eyes slide to mine. "That's why Dr. Lutz left for India."

"Do you think the clinic was guilty?"

"Probably," says Max. "But I also think Dr. Lutz had an epiphany in India. He really does believe in drug rehabilitation."

"What about Florida?" I ask. "Dr. Lutz was implicated in a Florida shuffle scandal. Patient brokering. There was even a suggestion of sex trafficking female patients."

"He was cleared," says Max. "I had a private detective look into

Florida before I agreed to work with Dr. Lutz. His conclusion was the judge got it right. He investigated very thoroughly." Max nods. "With Dr. Lutz, it's not illegal. But it's probably immoral. You have to ask yourself how comfortable you are with that." He looks at me a fraction too long.

"What about Haley Banks?" I ask finally. "Do you think Dr. Lutz had anything do with her death?"

There's a loaded pause.

"No," says Max. "Only a patient could have gotten to Haley that night. Fugu is an extremely effective muscle paralyzer. It's not a magical brainwasher. And even Dr. Lutz can't talk someone into murder." He sighs. "I think you have the wrong impression of Dr. Lutz," he adds.

I consider this. "What about the insurance markups?" I say. "Surely you're not happy that the Clinic is doing that?"

"I've been in rehab long enough to change my opinion on what ethics means where addiction is concerned." Max manages a half smile. "I'm a lost cause. I've seen too much misery. For me, it's the greater good. It's not the same for someone like you."

"Someone like me?"

I give him a look and he laughs. "Only...you seem to be an upstanding citizen. Someone who doesn't cut corners. It's often the case in addictive families where one child has to be the perfect one," adds Max. "Atone for the sins of the addict. Prove to the world that it's not the parents' fault. Be perfect."

"This is far from perfect," I sigh.

Max nods. "Welcome to the world of addiction treatment. It's extremely hard, and I still never get over it when my patients relapse."

I cut a piece of meat and spear it on my fork.

"Were you always like this?" I ask. "So keen to make everyone better?"

He nods immediately. "Even as a little kid. Not easy when the boys in your dorm bully the younger kids as a bonding exercise." He takes a breath. "But it's all worthwhile when I see them walk out sober. And even better if they stay that way." He gives me a little lopsided grin. "That even happens sometimes, you know?"

I can't help but smile back.

"Dr. Lutz was right about one thing," says Max. "We need you, Cara. This clinic can't run without you. I can't imagine anyone else giving even half the dedication."

I sigh. "I'll stay for a week. See how we go from there. On one condition."

"Which is?"

"You let me read Haley's file. All of it."

Max hesitates.

"Haley died after fugu treatment," I point out. "If you want me to stay working here, I need to know everything."

"I'd have to ask Dr. Lutz. But…I can't see him denying you that."

I nod, feeling reassured. Part of me had been expecting a problem. I smile at him. "I'm the only normal one here, huh?"

"Can you think of anyone else?"

"Might as well make our own normal bubble."

"I'll take that as a compliment." We chink glasses.

I don't mention I'm also planning to look more deeply into Dr. Lutz's affairs myself. Because surely Max can't be naive enough to think two serious criminal scandals would attach themselves to Dr. Lutz by sheer coincidence?

I look into Max's blue eyes. Something about how he's looking at me…

Why do I feel like I've stepped onto quicksand?

"Dr. Lutz wants me to schedule another treatment for Meg," I say, looking back down at my food. If my plan was to break the moment between us, it worked perfectly. Max's face falls.

"Yes," he says. "Meg will have another treatment tomorrow."

CHAPTER SIXTY-SIX

MEG

I lie awake, unable to sleep, listening to the ocean crashing outside my room. Finally I doze off. But what seems like only minutes later, I wake to the sound of footsteps near my bed.

Something's wrong. I can feel it. Opening my eyes to slits, I make out the shape of a person at the foot of my bed.

I'm wide awake now, lying completely still under the covers. I've made out a vital detail that sends ice shivering through my limbs. Whoever it is wears a fedora hat. Just like the man in my nightmares.

You're dreaming, I tell myself.

But I'm not. I can hear the other women sleeping in the room. Gentle breathing.

The figure at the end of the bed moves toward me.

I want to get up, to move. My limbs are paralyzed. It's overwhelming, all consuming. My breath is fixed in my chest, coming in shallow scoops. *It's a dream. Just a bad dream.*

He's standing over me, face shadowed in the dark. Then his hands reach out and around my throat.

It isn't a dream.

Pain explodes in my larynx, behind my ears where his strong

fingers are squeezing. The air constricts. I flail, panicking, unable to catch a breath. My hands grip his forearms, but he's strong, and when I try to cry out, no sound comes.

My thoughts drag themselves to my immediate surroundings. My nightstand has a lamp and a water glass. Grab the water glass, I decide. Swing it.

My limbs feel like soup but somehow my arm obeys. My finger touches smooth glass but only topples it, sloshing water and smashing. A fizzing sound comes from the floor, like electricity. Then an alarm sounds, high and loud.

The pressure on my throat vanishes. The man drops to the floor and out of sight. For a moment, all I can see is black dots. When the room finally comes into focus, I see emergency lights go on. Dim green glows by the door.

Madeline sits up in bed, an eye mask pushed up askew, forcing her dark hair into a mound at the front. "What the fuck is going on?" she demands.

The man has vanished. *Did I dream him?*

"There was a man," I say, uncertain now. "In a fedora hat. He tried to kill me." My hand is on my throat.

Jade slides her legs out of bed and crosses over to me. "There's no one here, Meg. Just us." She puts a hand on my knee over the covers. "I think you were having a bad dream," she says.

Sierra is stirring now. Madeline is by the main light switch, flicking it on and off. Her eyes zero in on the smashed glass by my bed. "Did you spill some water on the plug socket? Looks like you tripped a circuit."

"No one can get in here," says Sierra, with a nervy expression like she might be afraid of me. "Security is double tight. You had a bad dream, spilled your water, and woke us all up."

"It wasn't a dream!"

"Meg says she saw something." Surprisingly, it's Madeline who believes me. "Shouldn't we at least check the room?" She pads about, checking inside the bathroom.

"What about the drapes?" I suggest. I don't want to admit it, but drapes were my main fear as a kid.

Madeline heads for the drapes as if this is a completely sensible suggestion and pulls one back. "Nothing," she says. Then on the way back to her bed, she stoops and picks something up.

Madeline holds it out. A fedora hat. It's small. Women's style, in checked red and white.

She looks at me. "This what you saw?"

"That's mine," says Jade, staring.

"How did that hat get on the floor?"

"No idea." Jade is looking at me, like maybe she believes me now. "It was in my dresser," she says.

Thoughts are turning. *Did someone in this room put that hat on to freak me out?*

"What's happening?" A very sleepy-looking Dex is standing in the doorway.

"Meg had a bad dream," says Jade, looking at me. "Right, chick?"

"Is Tom in bed?" I ask, realizing how possible it would have been for anyone from the male dorm to flit in and out fast.

"Yeah. He's passed out. Didn't want to wake him." Dex looks at me. "Sorry you had a bad dream." He rubs his face. "Night."

Sierra lies back down in her bed. "Good night," she announces pointedly.

Everyone lies back down in bed, but Madeline stays near me and leans in close so no one can hear her.

"Want me to check under your bed before I turn out the main light?" she whispers.

I nod, wondering where this sudden concern comes from.

She glances under, then pops up. "Nothing," she says, meeting my eyes. "All safe."

"Thanks." There's a silence. "Do you believe me?" I ask.

Another silence follows.

"Someone used to come into my room at night when I was a little kid," Madeline says finally. "I have dreams about it sometimes. Wish I had someone to check under my bed. Just to let me know I'm safe."

I absorb this. Suddenly I feel differently about Madeline.

"I'll check for you," I tell her. "Anytime you want someone to look under your bed, just ask."

There's a pause. "It's weird how you dreamed about a hat," she says. "Haley. That was what she started saying. Stuff about a man in a fedora. Right before she died."

CHAPTER SIXTY-SEVEN

CARA

When the alarm sounded, I more or less fell out of bed and started pulling on clothes. A nurse radioed, telling me it was a false alarm, Meg had a bad dream, as I reached the patients' quarters.

It was on the way back to my room that I saw it. A door that should have been closed.

Leading to the medication room.

I put out a confused hand. Closed it. Headed back to my room, trying to disprove what I know this means.

Is a patient getting in and out of the medication room?

There's only one route in. The door was closed when I went to bed. It would have been impossible for a patient to come this way without being seen.

Unless there's another route in the patients' wing.

I'm turning this over, halfway back to bed when I hear a knock. Given the weird hour of night, I try not to feel spooked, crossing my semidarkened apartment.

"Cara?" It's Max's voice. I pull open the door.

"Is everything OK?" I must look and sound as flustered as I feel.

"Oh, yes. Everything is fine. I wanted to check you're OK."

"*Me?*"

"The last time the alarm went off, someone was dead," he says bluntly. "I thought I was going to have an actual heart attack when I heard it. Assumed you might have similar feelings."

"Oh." I relax a little in the doorway. "Yes," I admit.

We're silent for a moment. I'm suddenly wide awake.

"In any case," Max's eyebrows rise expressively. He holds up a bottle. "I was going to have a nightcap and thought you could use one too."

"Sure." I eye the label. "Single malt whisky? Isn't that contraband?"

"A gray area," says Max. "It's an affectation of us English nobility." He smiles disarmingly.

"I'll get some glasses." I stand aside to let him in. The weird thing about Max being in my apartment in the middle of the night is it's not weird at all. It's nice, actually.

"Are you really English nobility?" I'm getting better at telling if Max is joking, but this one has skipped me by.

"More or less. My brother inherits."

I take two glasses from the kitchenette and put them on the coffee table of my hotel-like living area. Sofa for one and an extra chesterfield-style chair that I sit on as Max pours.

"Does that bother you?" I ask. "Not inheriting?"

He shakes his head fiercely. "God no. He has my deepest sympathy. Nowadays inheriting an English pile is a life sentence in roof repair and smiling nicely at tourists. Cheers." He holds up his glass.

"What are we drinking to?"

He looks thoughtful. "To rehabilitation," he says, holding his glass high. "New beginnings."

"To new beginnings." I sip. "Gah!" The whiskey burns my throat. "This is strong."

He sips. "I know. Alcohol is highly toxic." He grins.

"You make it sound so classy."

"Can't help it. It's the accent." He turns the glass around in his hands. "You know. For a moment there, I really thought... I was fully expecting another fatality. That's the way with trauma, isn't it? Tends to leave an imprint."

"Stress hormones supercharge your memory, right?" I'm quoting his research. "Trying to protect you from making the same mistake twice."

"It's one of nature's cruelest tricks," agrees Max. "No wonder people with terrible childhoods seek to ease their turmoil with drugs. And how sad that these people who most deserve our sympathy are treated with the most disdain."

My mind floats back to the mysterious open door.

"Max," I say. "Do you think one of the patients could still be using?"

"Why do you ask?" He looks concerned.

"I think someone is still accessing the medication room. The door was open when I went to check just now."

His eyes widen. "That isn't possible," he says.

"That's what I thought," I agree. "The only way a patient could have gotten to it unseen is if there's some other route to the medication room that I don't know about."

"Dr. Lutz designed the building," says Max. "There's no way he would have designed a medication room with such an obvious breech."

"You trust Dr. Lutz?" I say. "Implicitly?"

"Of course I do. I wouldn't be working here if I didn't."

Max stands abruptly, glass in hand, and begins pacing my tiny living area.

He looks at me. Angry. Something else. "If you don't trust Dr. Lutz, then leave."

"You want me to leave?"

"I want…" he hesitates. "From the start I wasn't sure someone with your personality is suited to this Clinic."

Things are sliding into place. His coolness toward me. He didn't want us to have a working relationship because he thought I couldn't do the job.

"What do you mean by that?" The insult shows in my voice.

"Nothing. We're both tired. Best get some sleep." Max walks past me toward the door. He reaches for the handle and hesitates, looking down at me.

"It's only because I care about you, Cara," he says quietly.

"If you care about me *so* much…"

Suddenly Max is kissing me.

Oh my God.

My hands wind around the back of his neck. I know I should stop. I know I should break away. I can't. It's Max who pulls back first.

"I'm sorry," he says sounding confused. "I–I apologize."

"Rehab romance syndrome," I say quickly. "Small number of people crammed in together. No one else to talk to. Let's forget it ever happened."

We look at each other for a long moment.

"Right," says Max finally. "Right. Rehab romance syndrome." He stares at my face a little longer as if hoping I'll say something else, and when I don't, he shakes his head like he's actively trying to dislodge something.

"I'll keep out of your way," he says, nodding firmly as though to convince himself. "Good night, Cara."

As soon as the door closes, I lean against it, my eyes shut tight.

It's all so confusing. I don't know what to feel. The only thing I'm sure about is he's right. We need to keep away from each other from now on.

My body is telling me something different. I think about what Max said about trauma. The basic part of your brain not understanding that events aren't still happening.

Not just trauma that gets stuck in that part of the subconscious, I decide. *Max. What have you done to me?*

CHAPTER SIXTY-EIGHT

MEG

The morning I'm due for a second treatment, I've mainly been getting over the worst physical cramps, vomiting, and headaches of my life. And I'm still nowhere near normal.

I'm struggling to put clothes on. My fingers won't work zippers.

"You got the detox fingers, chick?" Jade comes over to help me.

"Yep," I tell her. "Fuck," I add. "How long until the tremors stop?"

"Couple of days. Maybe three. You scared?" asks Jade. "About treatment?"

I consider this. "I don't get scared so much. Not since I was a kid. Now it's more like biofeedback. My body gets agitated but I kind of separate it."

"That's all about to change," says Madeline, padding toward us with a yawn, her dark hair messy. "You're about to get those feelings back."

Jade smiles at me. "How is your biofeedback?"

I meet her eyes. "I think it's scared."

Jade appears to make a decision. "Come with me," she says. "Salt cave."

I shake my head, holding up my wrist. "I have free time."

"Nope," Jade loops her arm through mine. "You're coming to join us."

"Who's us?"

"Everyone."

"Why?"

"You'll find out."

The salt cave is like an igloo made of salt block. Craggy walls are lit from behind, giving the whole place an eerie orange glow. Slabs of rosy salt bricks form pillars leading to a beehive-shaped roof, and the ground beneath my bare feet crunches with a deep layer of crushed salt. It tingles on my lips.

Blocks are arranged in a circle for us to lie on. I stretch out on the nearest. Which is about as weird as it sounds. The air is salty, with the scent of unfamiliar herbs.

Jade is next to me in a surf-brand pink bikini, and her tanned stomach protrudes a little over the bottoms.

"You gonna tell me what this is about?" I ask.

"Not until the others arrive." She sits up slightly. "Right on time."

Tom enters wearing only a towel, stooping to get through the igloo-style entrance.

He takes the slab next to mine. He stoops and pours himself a large measure of mint tea from a flask and chugs.

It's hard not to want to shift away from his muscular, hairy body. After seeing him knock Jade around, I can't stand Tom.

He's followed by Madeline and Sierra. In a black string bikini, Madeline could easily pass for ten years younger, though her breast implants have pulled stretch marks into her cleavage. Sierra looks like a lithe little athlete. Hardly an ounce of fat on her tiny body and wearing the kind of sensible extra coverage bikini that girls wear when they're trying to pretend they don't care about being sexy.

"So, we ready?" Sierra asks, snatching a glance at me.

"Dex isn't here yet," Madeline points out.

On cue, Dex streaks through the entrance in black cargo pants.

"Fuck! Fuck! Fuck!" he yelps, half skipping across the warm floor. "*Fuck!*"

Jade sits up, eyes wide. "What happened to *you*?" she says, staring. "Dex. There's steam coming off you, mate."

"Cryotherapy." He grins. "I'm obsessed. It's a fucking rush."

"So what's the deal?" I ask warily as Dex sits. Jade wipes sweat from her forehead. "Could someone please tell me what the fuck this is about?"

"We're staging an intervention, chick," says Jade.

"None of us think you're ready for another treatment," Madeline adds, her gravelly voice echoing around the cave. "With the nightmares and…"

"And thinking people are trying to kill you," chimes in Jade with characteristic bluntness.

"You seem…kind of on the edge," supplies Sierra.

"And by that, she means crazy," says Dex. "Tom saw you talking to yourself after treatment yesterday."

"I wasn't talking to myself…" I stop. I'm not about to tell them I was talking to a nightmare lady from my past who dresses in underwear and has begun slinking into the corner of my vision.

"Treatment is tough," says Tom, concern on his aging, even features. "No shame in taking it slow."

"We think you should wait a few days," concludes Dex.

But I don't have a few days. Harry is going to turn me in unless I have answers.

"Why are you doing this?" I demand, exasperated and confused.

There's a pause. "Maybe we actually care about you, Meg," whispers Jade.

Something in me bubbles up. Like. Is this actually real? People caring about their fellow addicts? My casino buddies are more about ripping into each other. We're close. But it's kind of a collusion in *not* talking about how we feel.

Then I remember. Someone here doesn't want me finding answers.

I look at them all one at a time, trying to spot any tells.

Dex looks nervous. Jade…concerned. Madeline is twirling her hair in that way that means she has a bad hand. Which I guess she does, since there's no way I'm delaying treatment.

I look up at the sweltering brick ceiling. Sweat prickles my eyelids.

"I appreciate your all thinking of me," I say slowly. "But…"

"But you're doing treatment anyway," says Jade. "That's what Dex thought you'd say."

"I said that too," says Madeline, lying back on her slab so her hair tumbles over the edge in a dark wave. "Meg is the most bullheaded person I ever met." She shoots me a little smile. "Worth a shot."

Sierra is looking at me with concern. "Do you have any friends or family you can talk to?" she suggests. "Before you go in?"

"You mean someone who'll talk me out of it?"

She smiles. "Maybe."

I close my eyes.

Harry.

"There was someone before the warehouse stuff," I say quietly. "A guy at work. I thought we'd move in together. Get a dog. Dumb, huh?"

"I thought that about my third wife," says Tom. "We both came from abusive homes. Thought we could fix each other, you know?" His eyes light on mine.

"Did you divorce that junky gold digger yet?" asks Madeline.

Tom flinches, then recovers himself. "My finances are in bad shape," he says, hardening his features. "My manager won't even put me forward for auditions if I'm married to a junkie. So yeah. I serve her papers today." He looks miserable.

I sneak a glance at Jade. Her face is giving nothing away. Maybe she and Tom really were acting a scene.

"What's everyone doing next?" I ask, trying to move the conversation away from me.

"Tom's going to join me in the cryotherapy room," says Dex.

Tom laughs, shaking his head. "Once was enough for me. I think I got icicles on my ear hair."

"We all have free time," explains Sierra. "Spa. Gym. Anger rooms. We'll be thinking of you, Meg."

Everyone files out. I hang back in the salt cave. The heat and dark feel good. A momentary relief from thinking about what's to come.

The door bangs. Tom pops his head back in.

"Meg. You coming out?"

"I… Yeah sure."

He leans on the doorway, looking at me carefully. "Someone was listening in," he says, "when Jade and I were having a private conversation. I heard their scheduler go off."

He looks at me meaningfully.

"I thought private conversations weren't allowed." My heart has a low, steady beat, I notice. If this was a poker game, he'd be calling my bluff right now.

Tom looks at me for a long moment.

"You should be more careful," he says finally. "Hanging out alone in confined spaces isn't smart. Especially if you think someone is trying to kill you."

His handsome face moves strangely. Is he joking? I can't tell.

CHAPTER SIXTY-NINE

CARA

It hasn't been easy to keep out of Max's way. But I've mostly managed it. He seems happy to avoid me too. Which shouldn't bother me. But it does.

Dr. Lutz is about to begin a second treatment with Meg. Which gives me a half hour to search for another entrance to the medication room. The more I look at plans, the more I'm sure there could be a way through the anger rooms.

I walk quickly to that part of the Clinic. My feet stop outside the familiar sign, warning to wear goggles and safety equipment.

I've never actually been inside. Always too professional, too in control to even consider it.

Ear defenders and plastic goggles are hung outside. I ignore them, pushing open the padded door. There's a tinny smell to the interior. The walls and floor are concrete. I survey the tables of breakable items.

Old computers. Printers. TVs. Glass bottles.

In the corner is a bin filled with weapons. Baseball bats and crowbars. I take a good look around. But there's nothing.

I hunt around for another twenty minutes, looking in every

corner, under tables, up at the ceiling. No secret doors. Nothing strange about the construction.

Eventually, I accept I got it wrong. If there is another entrance to the medication room, it isn't here.

I pick up a bat. Whirl it in my hand for a moment. I don't know what possesses me exactly. But I bring the bat down on a computer.

The casing shatters and thick glass fragments spin free. It's… kind of therapeutic.

I bring the bat down again. This time the computer smashes clean inward, revealing shining innards. A flash of adrenaline flares in the pit of my stomach. Now that I'm halfway to destroying it, I'm gripped with a desire to finish the job. I swing the bat again and again in a frenzy.

From nowhere, a sob emerges. As I pound the bat repeatedly, fracturing plastic and glass, I'm crying. My face is all screwed up but I don't care. Suddenly I'm crying for my brother. For myself. My childhood. Jerks who take their wedding rings off at work.

I pause, bat in hand, not sure what to make of what I'm feeling, when the lights go out.

What the?

The door opens and shuts, and a figure slides inside.

"Hello?" I call into the dark.

I'm answered by creeping footsteps. I hear a bat being slid out of the container.

"Who's there?" I demand. The whole atmosphere of the room has shifted. Like I've suddenly gone from the aggressor to the target.

In answer, I hear silence, then something smashes.

"Fucking *bitch*!" I think the voice is female. But it's so distorted with fury I can't place it. In the dark, the words buzz with malice. Sweat breaks out on my palms.

"Hey! Who's there?" I shout. I'm holding the bat defensively against my body, backing toward a wall I can't see. Something smashes right by my leg, and a chip of plastic flies up and cuts my cheek. It burns.

"Why can't you leave me alone?" comes the voice again. My heart is thumping. I'm scared now. I start moving around the edge of the wall, trying to feel my way to the door.

Something smashes by my ear, and I throw up my hands, letting out a whimper of terror.

"Please," I whisper. "Stop."

What did you expect, Cara? says a strangely familiar voice in my head. *This is what you get for being angry.*

"I never wanted to kill you, Haley." More smashing sounds. An invisible weapon destroys something near my feet, and pain sears into my ankle.

I inch along the wall in the dark. *Keep quiet*, I decide. *Try to get out.*

My fingertips locate a straight groove. To my massive relief, I think I can feel out the sides of the door.

"How could you *leave me*?" Smashing sounds echo through the room. "I never would have hurt you."

The voice clicks into place.

I know who it is now.

My fingers fan desperately. The door handle. I have never been more relieved to grip a door handle. I push it down, and light floods the room.

CHAPTER SEVENTY

MEG

This time around, I arrive at the treatment room to see Max is there.

"Did things just get serious?" I joke.

"Nothing to be afraid of," says Dr. Lutz, catching my wary expression. "You had some physical reactions to treatment last time. We want to be sure you're safe."

I lie down slowly on the bed. Max doesn't look at me as he fixes the straps. Dr. Lutz positions the needle.

"You'll feel a pinprick, as before," he explains. "It should all happen much faster this time. Your body will remember."

As the needle withdraws, I can already feel the fugu working. Blocking out muscles. I try to wiggle my fingers and find I can't.

"Can you say your name?" asks Dr. Lutz.

"Meg," I say, the word coming soft.

"Good. Excellent." I hear a beeping sound. "Last time we spoke, you were telling me about a lady in a doorway. Shall we start there?"

I want to swallow, but those muscles aren't engaging right.

"You were frightened of this lady," he prompts.

He's right. I am so frightened of this lady I can barely get my words out. She's seared on my mind in her baby-pink negligee with shapely legs peeking from underneath.

As that thought solidifies, reality and dream seem to merge.

"She's there," I whisper. My voice comes out strained. Like a little kid voice. "In the doorway."

I hear voices from outside my dream. A nurse.

"There's a lot of activity showing on the EEG," she says.

"This isn't regular," I hear Max say. "She should have no anxiety at all in this state."

"I want to go home," I say. "Please let me go home."

I want Haley.

Dr. Lutz's face is over mine again. "Why won't this lady let you leave?"

"She doesn't want me to see what my sister does with the playing-card man." I try to take a breath, but it gets stuck and shakes.

"He's taking her into a bathroom. My sister can't stop crying."

The memory levers off a lump of emotions from some hidden old place, and it spins dangerously in my chest, a soft sphere with sharp edges.

"Heart rate is rising," says the nurse. "Blood pressure is up."

"I think we should stop," says Max.

You'll never know what I protected you from, Meggy.

She wasn't all bad, my older sister. When I was a little kid, she would look out for me. Before I started getting a mind of my own. Images roll through my mind. Haley standing up for me at school. Sneaking me sips of liquor from Mom's cabinet. Showing me how to hide pot from teachers. Haley pushing me under the bed as Mom screamed at her, blows raining down.

"What's in that bathroom, Meg?" asks Dr. Lutz.

"Something *terrible.*" My voice sounds babyish. I see myself walking toward the bathroom, opening the door.

Haley is on the floor in her nightdress, hunched over the bathtub. She turns when she hears me come in.

Don't look, Meggy.

Mr. Priest is closing the door, shutting me out. He throws a pack of cards up into the air.

They rain down, and suddenly, the lady is everywhere. She leans suggestively against the wall, a redhead in a black negligee and matching suspenders. Lounges on the couch in a graduation gown, brunette hair, stocking legs kicked up coquettishly.

In the doorway, she's blond again. White baby-doll pajamas. Another version sits legs stretched wide on the round rug. Platinum ponytail. Cowboy boots and pigtails.

They're all my characters, I realize fuzzily. The roles I play at the casino. Different outfits and attitudes. Angry Little Rich Girl, Hustler Francine, Pro Patty with the coke problem. Small Town Susie. Underneath them all is the lady.

The queen of hearts.

She steps forward. Red bra. Suspenders.

"You lose, Meg," she says. "Queen of hearts. You lose."

Haley steps in front. She's holding out a gift-wrapped box. "Happy birthday, Meggy."

"Bring her around." It's Max's voice. "Do it now."

This time, when Dr. Lutz clicks his fingers, I spring back into the room.

"How are you doing, Meg?" asks Max. He can't hide the concern from his voice.

"I…I'm fine," I manage. Everything hurts. But something important has turned into place. Gifts from Haley. *Birthdays.*

Haley's password, from when we were kids. I think I just remembered it.

And if I know her password, I might be able to track her phone.

CHAPTER SEVENTY-ONE

CARA

The anger room has a particular smell to it. Something about the smashed computer components, mixed with my own fear and confusion. It twists into something else as the face in front of me slides into focus.

"Sierra?" I'm staring at her furious expression, baseball bat raised.

"Cara?" The famous face collapses in shock and surprise.

It's then I realize she's wearing ear defenders. Sierra takes them off, looking horrified. She lowers the bat, little mouth turned down, thick eyebrows scrunched.

"Oh my gosh. Are you OK?" She is the picture of concern. The complete opposite of the woman confessing murder ten seconds ago.

"I… Yes. A little shaken up," I admit. "What was all that about?" My eyes are on the lowered bat.

"Well. Um. So I suffer from obsessive thoughts." She adjusts the bottom of her skirt. "And Max encouraged me to get in here and sort of…treat them like a bully in my head, you know? Beat them up a little."

Sierra swings the bat idly at her side. "I have intrusive thoughts about people I get close to. Ideas that I might…harm them. You know?"

I hesitate, turning this through. Sierra's strange confession.

I never wanted to kill you, Haley.

"You…thought you would harm Haley?" I say.

I probably shouldn't be asking that, I realize. But I also want the answer.

Fear flashes across Sierra's face. I feel bad for asking.

"Sometimes." She takes a slow breath. "Sometimes I think I could hurt a lot of people. Max is helping me realize. They're just thoughts, you know. Just thoughts. Doesn't mean I have to act on them. I got closer to Haley than anyone else here," she adds. "My thoughts get worse when that happens. I worry about…germs… mainly. Infecting people. I know that sounds dumb."

"It sounds…exhausting," I say with feeling. "I'm sorry to have intruded on you." I don't know what to say.

"Well, I'm a little embarrassed," Sierra admits, picking at the edge of the bat. "You don't expect anyone to be listening in." She shuffles her feet, childlike. "The vacant sign was up."

The vacant sign. Missed that one.

"Sorry if I scared you," she adds. "I'm not myself today. I had a call with my bandmates. They're not sure they want me back. Think I'm scary." She says this last part in an acted comedy voice without meeting my eye.

"I'm so sorry." Sierra isn't the kind of person who naturally shares her setbacks.

She manages a small smile. "Thanks. Were you using the room?"

My first impulse, shamefully, is to lie. Tell her I was in here checking things, tidying up.

"I thought I'd try out, being angry," I admit. "See how it fits."

"You don't seem like an angry person."

"I think I keep it hidden," I say. "I didn't grow up in the kind of home where it was safe to be angry."

"Me neither." She nods. "You were angry in my neighborhood, you got beat."

This isn't what I meant, but I've typed up Sierra's notes and can't help but picture her as a little girl, scared of gang violence. Anxiety turned up to the max.

There's a pause. "I was angry with Haley," she says. "For dying. I don't know. Haley was so difficult. That last day. I thought we were friends." Sierra's dark eyes lift to mine, brimming with tears. "I even kept it secret, that Haley was screwing Tom. Then…Haley *knew* I liked Dex. And she goes and does…you know, that last group session."

I don't know, because I don't have Max's notes for that. But I nod like I do.

It sounds like Haley was sleeping with Dex *and* Tom. I try to pass through what this could mean. If either found out about the other.

Sierra sighs. "Maybe there was a sweet little girl under there. I don't know. She was really messed up."

CHAPTER SEVENTY-TWO

MEG

I leave treatment with Dr. Lutz shaking with excitement. Haley's phone. If I have the password, there's a chance I can find it.

I mentally map the Clinic. What did Sierra say? The rest of the group had free time. Where are people unlikely to be?

The hypoxic chamber, I decide. Otherwise known as the deserted gym.

Behind the glass walls is a bunch of purple-lit exercise equipment that no one seems inclined to try out. Low oxygen levels and exercise doesn't appeal to everyone. Go figure.

I head inside the glass-walled room. There's a low hissing sound as a machine pumps in a steady stream of air. I vaguely remember this being explained to me by Jade. Lessened oxygen means more effective workouts.

The lighting is strange inside. A low neon that I guess has something to do with the air emissions. The thin air catches me right away. I steady my breathing.

Sleek, modern fitness equipment is dotted about the room, shining and futuristic looking. I take a seat on a weight machine.

Opening the cloud app on my phone, I hastily enter the email my sister always used. Titanium_cowgirl@haleybanks.com.

The password screen pops up. Taunting. Tantalizing.

Could this actually work?

Haley's password used to be my birthday.

My fingers shake as I put in the digits. I am totally unprepared for the wall of emotions that slams my chest.

Haley always did remember the date too. After she had gotten famous, she'd take me on big days out. Toward the end, she had her PA send lavish gifts. But she always remembered. Always.

Easier to think Haley was all bad. Black and white. Now I'm seeing the gray, and it's horrible. Confusing.

Nothing is happening on the screen. My heart sinks.

Haley must have stopped using my birthday as her password. Most painful is knowing I've been deleted from her life. Her sleazy boyfriend-manager, Frank, would have most likely taken over access to all her accounts.

The screen flashes as I lower it, defeated. It's then I realize I'm not looking at the log-in screen anymore. It's a map.

Oh my God. The password worked. It fucking worked.

And right there, an image of a phone and a button, offering to "find your phone."

I can't believe it. I'm one click away from finding Haley's cell. I take a breath, press the button.

A circle turns, and then the screen is zooming in, hurtling through seas and continents. An overlapping chaos of streets and buildings. Then the roads and landmarks vanish and there's nothing but forest and ocean. An outsized hexagonal shape.

The Clinic.

Haley's phone is here. The circle turns, drilling down, zooming in.

Not in the bedrooms. Not in the lunch hall. Not in the therapy rooms.

I stand up, and the weight machine I was sat on clangs in protest.

The phone symbol gets larger, circles. Stops. A squarish shape. Large, with other square rooms attached at the edges. I mentally follow the corridors to this part of the building.

The spa. I knew it. Haley's phone is in the spa. But...wait. It's *moving.*

Someone in the Clinic has Haley's phone. Right now.

I'm on my feet, ready to move, when I'm hit by a wave of dizziness. I stagger, putting a hand out to the wall. It shifts and waves.

On the screen, there's a time delay. The location jumps.

The phone is much nearer to me now. Just along the hall.

I'm momentarily distracted by a strange hissing sound filling the room. Steamy air is pumping from ducts above my head.

Something weird is happening to my breathing. Like I can't get enough air.

What did Max say? You'll feel like you want to die. Then you won't. It comes in waves.

This will pass. I tell myself. But it doesn't. Now I'm starting to panic.

I gasp, trying for deep breaths. No air is getting to my lungs. I'm wheezing now. Did something go wrong with the air in the room?

The hypoxic chamber. It works to lower oxygen. Did someone alter the settings?

I take two steps toward the door and fall to my knees. Walking is impossible. I need air. My head feels like it's swelling up to burst, and my eyes are straining against my skull. I crawl, each inch feeling like a mile. I've covered about two feet of the twenty-foot distance when even raising my head is too much effort. I shuffle my body, inching over the padded floor, face lolling downward as I pant for oxygen.

Summoning all my strength, I risk a glance up. The door is out of focus. Too far away. But the transparent wall… Something about the way the air is flowing has condensed in a mist on the outside of the glass.

There are…letters…writing.

Meggy.

I try for the rest of the words.

No more treatment, Meggy.

I feel something hard and cool against my face. The floor. My eyes droop. There's nothing left in me to get to the door. I manage one last scant lungful of air before everything fades to black.

CHAPTER SEVENTY-THREE

CARA

I head away from the anger rooms, wondering if I've got it all wrong. Perhaps there is no secret route to the medication room.

My radio is reverberating, and I pick up distractedly.

It's Dr. Lutz. "Cara, the delivery truck is delayed," he says. "We've got freezing fog rolling in, and they won't risk the woods."

I hesitate, mentally logging our supplies.

"There's plenty in store," I tell him. "We can wait for next week's delivery."

"That's why I hire you," he says, sounding pleased.

I arrive back at my desk and double-check the weather distractedly. Nothing serious. Just your regular Northwest mist with a side order of cloudy gloom for the next day or so.

No big deal but I should check in with the chef. Something else occurs to me. Matthew Priest. He was scheduled to come by and pick up Haley's belongings. I should let him know the weather is too bad.

I'm about to do that when I see a file lying on the desk.

Haley Banks. Clinical Notes.

Max kept his word then. The file is here. Ready for me to read. I open it to see that attached to the top are a sheaf of roughly ripped pages in handwriting.

The missing journal pages.

I'd forgotten they were put in Haley's file. I lift the sheaf and flick right to the part that was obscured in the picture sent me by housekeeping.

I can see both intertwined hearts up close now. The names underneath are clear.

Tom and Dex. A little heart drawn around each. Then thickly slashed through in angry pen.

I read underneath.

Group session I looked Tom right in the eye and told people some of the most shocking things I had done with Dex.

About thirty seconds after therapy ended, me and Tom hooked up. I can't help myself sometimes. I try to be boring. Then I get bored.

That was what Sierra said, wasn't it? Something about Haley making some ugly admission in therapy. My mind drifts back to Sierra. I can't quite think about her the same way since encountering her in the anger room. I'm actually a little afraid of her.

I leaf through Haley's thick file, the pages and pages of clinical notes and observations. Toward the back is official data. Prescriptions. Insurance details.

Frustrated, I drum my fingers. What about… I check through the admissions documents. Insurers don't cover the full cost of the Clinic, so supplements are due.

Now I see something strange.

Haley's account. Paid in full. But where the supplement should be, is nothing. A zero.

I scan back to see if there is some mistake, but there isn't.

Haley was never charged the supplement.

I stare at that for a long while. That means…

Haley was $20,000 short of the treatment cost when she died. But that doesn't make sense. Haley was a multimillionaire. Wasn't she? World famous with platinum-selling records.

My mind floats across possibilities. Could Haley have been in financial trouble? Extorting money for her treatment? Blackmailing?

What am I missing?

Insurance payouts. Haley Banks.

The Florida courts found Dr. Lutz innocent of patient brokering. And there is no evidence he had connections with clinics who engaged in human trafficking.

So why do I feel like these things are linked?

Haley Banks's murder. Patient brokering. Insurance fraud.

The silence that follows is broken by an ominous buzzing sound from my desk phone. I look down to see an incoming call light I've never seen flashing before.

Dr. Lutz's treatment rooms. I pick it up, checking my scheduler distractedly, wondering if I've messed up. No one is due in that room now.

I hold the receiver to my ear.

At first all I hear is heavy breathing.

"C-Cara?" It's Tom. But he sounds dreadful.

"Tom? Why are you in the treatment room?" I demand.

"Haley Banks," he says. "I know...who killed Haley Banks." He starts laughing. It's an eerie sound.

"Tom. Are you high?"

"I know who killed her, Cara." He's still laughing, but now it's jerky. Like maybe he's crying too.

"Who?"

The line goes dead.

CHAPTER SEVENTY-FOUR

MEG

I open my eyes to find myself on the floor of the hypoxic chamber. The air is…normal. I can breathe again. I sit up, gratefully pulling in lungfuls of oxygen.

Two yoga-socked feet arrive in my eyeline.

"Meg?" It's Sierra, dressed in sleek-fitting yoga wear, brown hair smoothed back in a bouncy little ponytail. She bends down and I can smell her perfume. "Can you stand?"

Weirdly, I can. Now that I can get breath in my body, I feel completely fine.

"Detox attack?" asks Sierra, pulling me to my feet with a concerned expression.

I shake my head. "I don't think so." My hand moves to my throat. "Something happened to the room. I couldn't breathe."

Sierra glances back at the door, her famous eyebrows jerking upward. "Did you change the settings before you came in?" she asks. "There was a red light flashing outside, and some oxygen sensor thing going crazy."

I shake my head. "Did you shut it off?"

"No. I think some emergency override kicked in. You're not supposed to alter the settings," she adds. "It's dangerous."

"I didn't alter the settings!"

"OK. If you say so." But her expression suggests she doesn't believe me.

"There was a message..." I begin. But no more words come. I wheeze. The writing on the wall has blurred to almost nothing, I notice. The steam must have started to clear when Sierra opened the door.

"Can you see any writing on the glass?" I ask, pointing. The letters have all but vanished now. Only the barest shapes of them left.

Sierra twists her head. "Um. I think that's how the steam runs down." She has that expression people have been using with me a lot recently. Like they think I'm crazy but they're scared to rile me up.

"There was a message," I tell her. "Telling me not to do treatment."

I watch her for tells. But she's so damn neurotic, it's impossible. Every part of her body is a permanent jangle of twitching nerves.

Sierra looks concerned. "Just...rest up a moment," she suggests. "I'll get a nurse. Treatment can be pretty rough for a few hours afterward."

"No nurse. I'm fine," I lie quickly. "Just give me a second." I lean against the nearest wall and close my eyes. "Why are you here, anyway? I thought you were on the other side of the building."

If Sierra feels this as an accusation, her face doesn't show it.

"Got some bad news," she admits miserably. "Did the anger rooms, then came in here to work off some emotions." She takes a long breath. "The band are not sure they want me back, even if I get clean." Sierra stares straight ahead like she's trying not to cry.

"Fuck 'em," I say. "Go solo. You're the best singer by miles."

She stares at me.

"What? It's true. You carry those sugar pop bitches."

To my surprise, she laughs. "You've gotten a lot nicer since you were first admitted."

"Yeah. I'm sorry if I wasn't friendly."

She rubs the bridge of her nose. "It's OK," she says. "I know I'm a little high strung. Probably why...you know...I go crazy." She mimes swigging from a bottle. "Self-medicating."

"Maybe you should be yourself."

"Easy for *you* to say, white girl." From nowhere, she beams a big smile, like sun coming out from clouds. It makes her face look completely different.

I get to my feet, feeling surprisingly normal. I'm wondering how to get out and search for Haley's phone without seeming obvious. Then I realize that Sierra might know something about who altered the settings. It could even have been her.

I pick up some boxing wraps and start winding them around my fingers.

"No way." Sierra grins. "You box?"

"I used to," I say, aiming a few jabs at the bag. "My trainer kind of kicked me out after I showed up high one too many times."

"You look pro," she says, wincing. "Can you show me some moves?"

I deliver two more upper cuts. "Sure."

I show her how to put on the wraps, winding the long webbing strips around her wrists and knuckles.

"Where's everyone else right now?" I ask casually, as Sierra aims a weedy little punch at the bag.

"I think...Madeline went to the spa."

The spa. Where Haley's phone is.

"Jade and Dex were daring each other to do the sauna and

cryotherapy room. Tom… Something was wrong with him. He went off alone."

The air seems thinner. Hard to take in who was where.

Who doesn't want me finding out more about Mr. Priest and Haley?

I adjust Sierra's shoulders. "Follow through with your body," I tell her.

Sierra makes a few more girlish jabs, then hangs back. There's a silence. Machinery whirs.

"Meg," says Sierra. "I've been meaning to ask you something."

"OK."

"Remember when we first met? I thought I'd seen you before?"

For a moment it's hard to catch my breath. "I don't think so."

She doesn't take her eyes off me. "After my last treatment, I had the strangest flashback I met you at a party once. With Haley."

She was so wasted at that party. There's no way she can be sure it was me.

"Treatment puts all kinds of weird stuff in your brain, right?" I deliver it perfectly. Casual indifference. Slight questioning inflection. Almost immediately I wonder if I should come clean. For the first time I'm imagining how everyone will react if they find out I'm not who I say I am.

Sierra turns back to the bag.

"I guess so," she says. "But I didn't think you could remember things that hadn't happened."

This time, when she hits the bag, she does it with a force that come from nowhere. A jab cross that wouldn't look out of place in a boxing gym.

CHAPTER SEVENTY-FIVE

CARA

I'm running to Dr. Lutz's treatment room, paging Max and every staff member as I go. Having written up Tom's sessions, I'm not keen to put myself alone with him in a room. Particularly not when he seems to be losing his mind. It's the first time I'm mildly grateful for the previous criminal convictions of Dr. Lutz's nursing staff.

What did Tom say?

I know who killed Haley Banks.

Was Tom…confessing? Did he find something out? Or was he losing it?

As I near the treatment room, the radio at my hip blares. Max's voice.

"Cara? Can you hear me." I lift it to my mouth, slowing to a walk. "Can you meet me in the treatment room?" I ask. "Tom's in there. He called reception, and he sounded maybe high or something."

"He's relapsed?"

"I don't know. He said he knew who killed Haley Banks."

There's a pause. "Don't go in there alone," says Max. "I'll be right there. Did you call any nurses?"

"Everyone I could page."

"OK. Good. Don't try to take on Tom alone, OK? He has a history of violence with women."

"I'm not stupid, Max. Why do you think I paged you?" I'm outside the treatment room now, slowing to a halt. The door is wide open, offering a full view of the many security screens and the stretcher bed where patents are sedated with fugu. Even from this far down the hall, I can see there's no one inside. An unhooked telephone receiver lolls on a metal table, blaring fretfully.

I watch the room, lifting the radio. "Max? Are you still there?"

"I'm about a half minute away." I can hear the wheeze in Max's voice. The lung condition. He must be sprinting.

"I don't think Tom's here," I say.

"You're sure?"

I angle my head. "Yes."

Another pause. "OK," says Max. "The only way back from the treatment rooms is toward the gym and my office. I can go check."

"Max?"

"Yes?"

"Be careful."

There's a pause. "You too."

It's the first time either of us have properly acknowledged that someone dangerous is inside the Clinic. I wonder if Max knew it all along.

I move into the empty treatment rooms, where the flat whine of an unhooked telephone resounds. Set it back on its wall cradle. Make to leave.

It's a weird room. Dr. Lutz's many security cam screens all facing inward like so many sets of giant eyes. I suppress a shudder.

There's a large walk-in medical fridge at the back of the room, and the door is open.

Strange.

Instinctively, I move to close it. And it's only when I actually put my hand on the cool metal that it occurs to me that Tom could be lurking inside.

He isn't. Of course he isn't. Nothing inside but shelves of medical packages.

I let out the breath I didn't know I was holding and shut the door, managing a tight little laugh at my own anxiety.

"Stupid, Cara," I whisper to myself. "Tom's not lurking in a fridge, ready to pounce."

Even so, I'm glad to leave the room.

It's only on the way out that I notice something else strange. A drawer in a medical cabinet has been pulled all the way open. And inside…I lean forward to confirm what I'm seeing. It's a collection of surgical tools.

But we don't perform surgery here.

The tools look dated. Medical antiques, even. There are calipers and knives arranged on a velvet panel. Beside them is an array of… I actually jerk in alarm.

Eyes. Human eyes.

Twelve single eyes glare accusingly up at me.

I step back, breathing out, hand on my heart. "Jesus. What the…?" I peer back. Are they real?

Porcelain, I realize. The eyes are set into a neat matrix by order of color. From fairest blue to darkest brown. Disturbingly, each eye is set within a clay eyelid, each slightly different, as though handcrafted, making them appear horribly real. One blue iris is pointed down, exposing white along the top, as though gazing at some unseen horror below. A brown eye stares directly out as if in unspeakable terror.

I try to understand what I'm seeing.

Is this...a hobby of some kind? Dr. Lutz's background is in surgery, I recall. Maybe he collects old tools of the trade. But why keep them here? In his treatment rooms?

"Cara?" It's Max. "I came from the medication room. It looks like diamorphine is missing."

"Heroin?"

Oh no.

"Was it Tom?" I ask.

"Couldn't say for sure," says Max. "The cameras show him headed to my office."

"Did Tom even use heroin?" I'm struggling to remember.

"Tom used more or less everything by the time his third marriage rolled around," says Max. "He and his second wife were into injecting speedballs together."

"You think Tom's planning to get high in your office?"

"Or he already relapsed," says Max. "Maybe we're not too late. I'm going now. I've called the nurses."

I glance at my scheduler. "They're five minutes away. I can be there in one."

"I think you should go back to the lobby." I can hear the wheeze in his lungs.

"Absolutely not," I tell him, remembering Tom's crazed tone. "If there's a chance we can stop Tom from relapsing, every minute counts, and you need all the help you can get."

CHAPTER SEVENTY-SIX

MEG

As soon as I can get away, I leave Sierra and walk in the direction of the spa. Trying to ignore the muscle cramps and light-headedness that start up the moment I do.

Stepping into the steamy cedar-clad changing room of the spa feels like I'm entering another world. Leaving the stark lines of the clinic far behind. My mind is still half in the last treatment session, and I'm jumpy. Expecting to see figures from my childhood waiting in doorways. The oxy withdrawal has taken on a kind of surrealism. My body feels attached to my mind by the barest thread right now. Anything more detailed than walking to the spa is completely insurmountable.

Once I'm completely sure there's no one else here, I take out my phone and see several missed calls from Harry. There's a soft feeling in my chest. I hit Redial. No answer. He must be at work. I fire off a quick text, noticing the letters warp and enlarge as I press them.

Hunting for Haley's phone. Think someone tried to kill me in the gym.

I look back at the message. Something not quite right about how it reads, but I don't have time to overthink it. Someone could come into the spa and stop me searching.

I hit Send, then enter Haley's password combination into the cloud tracker.

This time the locator is immediate.

I take a quick breath, hardly able to believe it. The phone is here in the spa.

Within thirty feet of where I'm standing. My initial surge of victory is buffered by the limitations of the tracker. It can't give me a more accurate location than the entire spa area. Which is vast.

The tracker app has an option to play a sound on a lost phone. I press the button. There's the briefest of pauses. Then a steady eerie beep sounds from somewhere deep in the spa.

Yes! Her phone is here. I'm going to find it!

I wait for a moment, listening.

Faint but unmistakable.

Beep, beep, beep.

Pushing my phone under a towel, I wade, fully clothed into the echoey water-filled first chamber, following the sound. The long, dark walls close around me, tuning everything out.

Beep, beep, beep.

It's here. It's in here.

It echoes confusingly through the interlined tunnels. The warm water is lapping at my hips.

Beep, beep beep.

Wading further, I turn the first corner toward the middle cave. The scent cave. A chain curtain divides it from the wider black-walled entrance, and the chains drape over my shoulders as I push through, like ceremonial jewelry.

Beep, beep beep.

Inside it's just me. I breathe out. It's louder in here. Even with the whirring of the fan, wafting essential oils from a central aromatizer.

There's an underwater bench, tiled in gray slate. Above, the tiles continue up the wall. The beeping of the phone is coming from here. My eyes zero in. The outline of one slate tile, is glowing. As though a light is flashing behind it.

Haley's phone! I splash toward the rectangular light. As my hand touches the edge of the tile, triumph flashes through me. I was right. I pull the tile free. This part is hollow behind. Someone has dug out the grout and carefully removed a tile. The backer board behind is thin concrete with a ragged hole. A perfect hiding place.

I feel down, searching for a shape.

Aha. When my fingers hit the edge of duct tape I know for sure. I peel away where it's stuck down, hardly daring to believe it. A plastic bag comes free. I'm terrified I'm going to drop it, but I manage to sit, hands clear of the water. It's the kind of bag you wrap food in. Thin. Semiopaque.

Inside is a cell phone.

For a long moment, I hold the phone in my hand. The first thing I think, stupidly, is I don't recognize it. But of course I wouldn't. I hadn't seen Haley in two years. The edges show a rose-gold phone. Shiny new but with ugly scratches on the casing. I turn it on.

The same thought is looping around my mind. *Haley's hiding place. Haley's phone.*

The phone flashes up a screen.

Haley's screen saver. A desert island, with *Dream Big!* in looping text. No pass code. It opens right up.

The very first thing I see is a note screen with a six-digit number on it. And "door code." Guess this was the number Haley used to break into the medication room.

I pause, my finger held out, wondering where to start. Texts, I decide.

A row of messages opens up. I open one from her boyfriend Frank. Hundreds of them, asking where she is, who's she's with. They stop when she gets into rehab. Guess she never told him she was taking her phone.

I scroll down. Another message thread from a different name. My eyes fix on it, shocked.

Madeline.

CHAPTER SEVENTY-SEVEN

CARA

I'm in the treatment room, about to leave for Max's office, when something catches my attention. A movement on one of the security screens. It's Max. But he isn't heading for his office like he told me. He's stopped. Talking animatedly to someone, his expression furious.

I hesitate, staring at the camera. I've never seen Max look angry before. The person he's speaking with steps into view. It's Dr. Lutz.

Wasn't Max racing toward his office to stop Tom from relapsing? What is so important that he's stopped to talk with Dr. Lutz?

It goes against every professional instinct to be watching this. But somehow, I can't help myself draw nearer the cameras. I notice a volume switch below the screen and turn it.

I'm rewarded with a burst of earsplitting static. I wince, pulling back. As I do, I hear Dr. Lutz's voice.

"You think…find out…what you did, Max?"

More words come.

"Telling…my nurse…less fugu…Meg."

I try to work this through. Did Max secretly give Meg less fugu than Dr. Lutz asked for?

Another voice sounds. Distorted. I'm getting every other word. Slowly, I turn the dial down, smoothing out the volume.

"Psychologically dangerous," says Max. "Hallucinations. Paranoia. She… Mental collapse."

The sounds. I curse under my breath, twisting at the volume. For a time there's nothing at all. Then suddenly Max's voice. Very clear. And angry.

"That is a monstrous suggestion. You know full well we are very close to achieving clinical results for fugu."

"Cannot risk Hanson…" begins Dr. Lutz. There's another blare of static. "I cannot have important decisions made by softheaded sentimentalists who let their personal feelings cloud their logic. I told you," continues Dr. Lutz. "If you didn't get the results, I would find another use for fugu. Your time has run out."

Dr. Lutz walks away, and Max turns, heading now toward his office.

Swallowing, I leave the room, going in the same direction as Max, wondering what I heard.

Dr. Lutz will find another use for fugu? What?

I'm wondering what this could mean, when I literally collide with Max.

"Cara!" Max has a strained look on his even features. "Sorry, I was talking with Dr. Lutz. It held me up a few minutes. Let's hope we're not too late."

I hesitate. Not sure whether to admit what I heard.

"Important conversation?" I suggest.

"Nothing you need to worry about," says Max. "Let's concentrate on finding Tom."

I nod in agreement, thinking over what this could mean. Max starts toward his office, and I jog to keep pace.

"How did Tom sound?" asks Max. "When he called you?"

"He sounded crazy," I say. "But...do you think he knows something about Haley's death?" We're at the office corridor now. Max's door is at the end.

"Tom filed divorce papers today," says Max. "I was expecting it to have an impact on him. I figure he isn't in his right mind but... Maybe he knows something."

"Tom and Haley..." he begins. "Never mind."

We're outside the office. Max turns the round handle, and the door creaks ominously as he pushes it open.

"Stay behind me," he says. "If Tom is high, you can expect some fairly unreasonable behavior."

I follow Max inside. From behind, I see his shoulders tense. The office comes slowly into view, Max's old-fashioned wooden desk, with locked filing cabinets at the back. The leather chair where patients sit.

"Tom's not here," I say.

But Max is shaking his head. It's only when I move to where he's standing that I see it.

Tom is lying on the floor under the desk. His head is tilted too far back, and his legs are splayed unnaturally. Tom's lips are blue and his cheeks hang slack.

I recoil instinctively.

"Tom!" Max runs to him, but we both know it's too late. I walk slowly behind as Max fruitlessly checks Tom's pulse.

"Max. Stop."

Max is performing CPR, checking the airways, applying pressure to Tom's chest. My throat constricts.

"Stop," I tell him. "Max. Stop. He's dead."

CHAPTER SEVENTY-EIGHT

MEG

The warm waters of the spa feel distant. Like they're happening to someone else.

Madeline was texting Haley? I can't get my head around it. I press to open the message.

Haley, delete your messages from me. M.

Okaaaaay.

So Madeline was texting Haley. And didn't want anyone to know.

Question is, did Haley delete the messages? Knowing Haley, she didn't, and that thought makes me smile.

Scrolling up, I read the earlier messages.

They seem…transactional. Madeline is sending flight details. Meetup addresses. Panning right to the top, I check the dates. The very first text from Madeline was sent two months before Haley even checked into rehab.

This is my number. Good party last night. I talked to the guy I told you about. He wants to meet you. Madeline.

My mind is in overdrive trying to figure out what all this could mean.

Which man?

Then, from behind me, I feel two powerful hands grip my shoulders.

Everything is happening at once, and I can't get a fix on any of it. Before I know what's happening, I'm pushed hard under the water. My legs pitch straight up, and my hands flail wildly.

Haley's phone cracks screen first against the tiled seat, then spins from my grip. The world turns to water, and all the air leaves my lungs.

I punch out, trying to reach backward at my unseen attacker, and slam into hard wall. The grip on my shoulders is relentless, horribly strong. I try to twist, but I'm pinned.

A whole world is flashing past me. Haley. The man with the playing-card eyes. Then suddenly, the pressure is released. The dark shape behind me vanishes. My face breaks the surface and there's air. For several seconds I can't see anything but black spots. The room comes back into view, into a completely different orientation than what I was expecting. I'm stretched sideways, and what I thought was the dark ceiling is a wall, dappled in beads of water.

Then someone is pulling me out, laying me on the half-submerged bench. The light touch of the small hands is so different from the iron fingers that held me under that it does something physiological to me. Like, my whole body reacts.

Haley?

My vision rights itself. Not Haley. A face tight with alarm. Dark-brown eyes so close I can see the ring around the iris.

"Meg? Meg? Talk to me." It's Jade's warm voice.

I cough. And then cough some more, hunched over, my whole body convulsing. Jade waits, patting me uncertainly on the back.

"Meg. What happened?"

I shake my head. "I don't know. Someone grabbed me from behind. Pushed me under." I cough some more.

Jade watches me like she's weighing this. "Are you sure?" she says finally.

The annoyance is back. "Yes, I'm fucking sure. Jeez."

"It's just… You got out of treatment with Dr. Lutz, right?" Jade's round eyes are wide with concern. "You couldn't have maybe… imagined it?" she says cautiously, tucking her honey-brown hair behind her ears.

"I didn't imagine it. You saw them, right? Someone must have come out of the spa."

She shakes her head. "I heard a lot of splashing as I came in, so I called out. When I came through into the cave, it was just you here. You were kicking your legs, and you had this weird look on your face. Like you were possessed or something."

My mind tracks the labyrinthine tunnels of the spa.

"Probably they heard you come in and left before you got here," I decide, mentally mapping the way out. It would just about be possible, I guess. Unlikely. But possible.

"Meg. You have to stop, OK? Stop accusing people. It's bad for the group dynamics."

Her eyes are locked on something behind me, and I turn to see Haley's phone submerged beneath the water. The obliterated glass shows black water bubbles.

Fuck.

"Is that yours?" asks Jade.

I take a breath, deciding how much of the truth to tell her.

"I think it belonged to Haley Banks," I say finally. "I found it here. Maybe why someone pushed me under."

Jade's small fingers reach beneath the water and pluck up the phone.

She looks at it for slightly too long. Like it reminds her of something. Then shakes her head as if dispelling demons.

"No use to anyone now," she says finally, taking in the water-logged screen. "It really isn't yours?"

"I know I haven't always been honest with people here," I say. "But it isn't my phone. And I really am sorry, Jade," I tell her. "For accusing you of all that stuff. I fucked up. I got paranoid. I like you, OK?" It's very hard to get the word out.

"It's OK." She smiles, looking me right in the eye. "And I believe you about the phone," she says.

I try to thread back what I've discovered. Madeline lured Haley in. She could have slipped me the note. But it wouldn't explain the text I got from Haley's phone.

I catch a flash of something in the doorway. A familiar person.

The lady has started popping up everywhere, in various fifties lingerie. I stare at her, and she flickers in and out, then vanishes.

No time to think about why she's showing up everywhere now. I need to find Madeline.

CHAPTER SEVENTY-NINE

CARA

Tom's lifeless body seems to take up the entire room.

"What happened to him?" I ask, taking in the blue lips.

"I don't know," says Max. His eyes fall to where Tom's sleeve is rolled up and a spot of blood is beaded on his inner arm. "Looks like he was injected with an opioid. Prone position. Blue lips. It fits. The body forgets to breathe."

"Heroin?" I suggest.

"Heroin was missing from the store. Tom had a lot of demons"—Max shakes his head, breathing hard, looking devastated—"but I don't think... I don't think he would have done this."

"If something was injected, I don't see the needle here," I say.

We look at each other.

Max leans on the chair for support, and I hear the wheeze in his lungs.

"Are you OK?" I move to his side.

He looks dreadful. Max waves a dismissive hand.

"I'm...fine," he manages. "Just my lungs sometimes...react to... stress."

I help him to a chair and he sits, putting his head in his hands. Max takes measured breaths.

"Do you think someone did this to Tom?" I can't bring myself to say "murdered."

Max is thinking. "I guess...if Tom could have arranged to meet with someone else here. He struggled with impulse control."

"Who could he have met with?" I ask.

Max's face clouds. "They're all on free time. Anyone could have gotten in here. I *need* to know what is going on," he says, teeth gritted. "If a patient is capable of this, I should know. I'm a *therapist*." Max sits with his head in his hands. "What does it all *mean*, Cara?"

My eyes settle on the body.

"First thing. We need to alert the police," I tell Max, moving to pick up the phone on his desk.

Max nods blankly, unable to take his eyes from Tom's dead face.

His gaze swings to me as if noticing for the first time what I'm about to do.

"Cara, wait," he says. "Before you call the police. You need to hear what I have to say."

CHAPTER EIGHTY

MEG

I find Madeline in the giant futuristic library, a stack of books at her elbow. Glossy curved white shelves are arranged in concentric circles widening outward. She sits in the open-air center smoking a cigarette, slightly reclined on a white seat.

I have too many questions to formulate a clear plan right now.

She doesn't see the book until it hits her square in the jaw. The cigarette goes flying.

"Hey!" Her hand flies to her face and she pops up, confused, angry.

"You fucking lying piece of shit," I growl at her. The second book bounces off her raised hands as she tries to deflect it.

"You're working with Dr. Lutz, aren't you!" I demand.

"What?"

I move in close and grab her by her T-shirt, pinning her to the wall and bringing my face in close. "I know you brought Haley Banks here. And you're going to tell me exactly what is going on. Did you kill Haley?"

Several things flit through her eyes. To my surprise, she doesn't look especially afraid. Just weary.

I slam her against the wall. "Tell me."

"OK. OK." She pulls at my hands. "Cut it out. I've been wanting to tell everyone anyway."

"Tell everyone what?" My hands are still gripping her shirt.

Madeline sighs. "I have a kind of a...deal going. With the owner, Dr. Lutz."

"A deal?" I loosen my grip.

She nods. "Patient brokering."

"What the hell are you talking about?" I've let her go completely now and she takes a step back, smoothing her shirt.

"It's like where you hang out at a particular club and keep an eye on anyone who looks like they might be in need of rehab."

I'm putting this all together. "You get a cut of profits from people signing up to rehab?"

She chews her lips. "Kind of. And I get a cut from people who relapse. So...I kind of have people in mind when I'm in. Then I'll hook up with them once they get out and see if I can get them to party. Get them checked back into rehab."

"You convince people to relapse? That's..." I turn through the words, thinking of my own journey here. "That's fucking disgusting."

Her brow descends in one frozen piece downward, giving her a furious expression.

"I know," she says. "Hate me all you want. I'm a dirty addict. But don't forget, no one ever gave *me* anything, Princess Meg. No one ever fed me or put me in clean clothes. I had to do all that on my own. Anyway." Madeline runs a hand through her long dark hair. "As it *happens*, I was already out. Didn't like what they were asking me to do."

"So why did you go after Haley?"

Madeline's face does a strange thing. Like a wobble.

"Haley was a special case."

CHAPTER EIGHTY-ONE

CARA

In Max's office, I pause with the phone in my hand.

"You need to hear this before you speak to the police," Max is saying. "It's over. If you call the police, it's all over, Cara."

I hesitate, hand on the receiver.

"They'll destroy our stocks of fugu," adds Max. "Everything we've been working toward. All our results. We were so close to a marketable formula. Our potential to help addicts. It will all be gone."

My mouth moves of its own accord for a moment.

"Why would the police do that?" I ask, frowning. "It doesn't make any sense."

Max takes a long breath in, then lets it out slowly.

"Blowfish is a controlled and highly poisonous substance," says Max, not meeting my eyes. "It's illegal to own in this country."

I feel my mouth drop. "*What?*"

"Dr. Lutz," admits Max. "I needed someone with…connections. To source fugu. He wanted a therapist for his clinic. At the time it seemed symbiotic."

The phone is gripped tight in my hand. I can't believe what I'm hearing.

"Dr. Lutz is sourcing you blowfish venom illegally," I clarify. "As in…smuggling?"

"I knew fugu could change lives," Max says. "But I needed huge quantities for the research. Getting that approved by the authorities would take years. People are dying of addictions *now*."

"Tom is dead," I say. "You know I have to call the police, Max?"

"I'm not trying to stop you." Max holds his hands up. "But you had nothing to do with this, Cara. If the police start asking questions, you have to deny you know anything about fugu."

"I can't lie to the police," I say.

"Please, Cara," Max's face shows utter devastation. "They could find you complicit. My dream of saving addicts is over. I couldn't live with myself if you were brought down with this too. Importing blowfish carries up to a ten-year prison sentence," adds Max.

I hesitate. "Will you and Dr. Lutz go to prison?"

"There's no way Dr. Lutz would risk prison. He has…a contingency plan."

"Which is what?"

"The cryotherapy chamber. He'll destroy all the stocks of fugu. Extreme cold. Any evidence will be obliterated. Along with my research."

I run over what all this means.

"You told me we weren't doing anything against the law at the Clinic. You *lied* to me."

"I'm sorry," he says. "I thought I could control Dr. Lutz. I got in too deep. Almost as soon as we began working together I regretted it. I was arrogant, Cara. Assumed my understanding of Dr. Lutz's psychology protected me. I thought a Clinic of celebrities would be enough to sate his needs for power and recognition. But when he saw the power of fugu…" Max's voice trails off.

"Dr. Lutz has consignments of fugu that he can simply reroute. If he isn't using it to treat trauma, he doesn't need me or my research. He already knows the dosages."

Things are occurring to me. Dr. Lutz's involvement in the Florida shuffle. Accusations of human trafficking. His criminal past in Switzerland.

"Then he'll sell fugu to the highest bidder," says Max.

"As in…a drug company?" But I already know the answer.

"He has criminal connections who would buy it."

"What for? What for, Max?"

He swallows. "You can probably imagine the uses fugu could have in human trafficking."

Horrifically, I can. "A drug that totally immobilizes people, while keeping them alive," I say blankly. "Max. How could you? You sold your soul to the devil."

There's so much going on in my mind that it's hard to pick a single thought. But somehow I manage it.

"I'm calling Hanson."

CHAPTER EIGHTY-TWO

MEG

Madeline sits down and retrieves a pack of cigarettes from her jeans pockets and offers it to me. I shake my head.

"You've been earning kickbacks from rehab clinics?" I ask her. "For signing up wealthy patients."

"Been doing it for years," admits Madeline. "Modeling work doesn't exactly fly in for women in their fifties." She gives me a look to suggest this is an understatement. Madeline inserts a cigarette into her padded lips and lights it, inhaling deeply. "I needed to fund my own party, right? But I was done. Believe what you want, but I had a crisis of conscience," She waves the cigarette around. "Ready to sort my own shit out. Told them I was out. Problem was, I'm a fucking addict." She snorts in disgust at herself.

"No money for rehab or health insurance." She blows out smoke. "Then I got a call. This guy wants to meet you. Old Swiss guy." Her eyes travel up to assure herself I know who she means. "He'd heard I went to these certain clubs, and he wanted Haley Banks in his rehab." Madeline sucks more on her cigarette thoughtfully. "Deal was, if I could get Haley, it was a fat paycheck and they'd throw in my rehab too."

"You knew Haley before rehab?"

"Sure. Everyone who partied knew Haley."

Only you didn't, I think. Not really.

I put a hand to my forehead.

"Haley wanted to be a different person," says Madeline. "It was really sad. Of all the people I ever enlisted, she most wanted to do it. Succeed. You know? She kept saying she wanted to transform. She was sick of being typecast as this dumb singer."

"She wasn't dumb." I remember that so strongly. How silly it seemed at first when people treated Haley like a dizzy blond. Then it seemed to stick. Almost like she morphed into it.

"She was unhappy with her life," says Madeline. "No one would sign up a country singer with a reputation for partying to a serious project. And she was good. She really was. I honestly thought maybe Dr. Lutz could help her kick the drugs and become an actress."

I study her body language, trying to decide if she's telling the truth. Looks like she is.

"But why," I ask, "did he want Haley?"

Madeline shrugs. "Are you kidding? What rehab wouldn't? But…once Haley was in, she became like a special project. Dr. Lutz was obsessed with her brain or something." Madeline smiles. "Everyone was a little obsessed with Haley, right?"

"Guess so."

Madeline's bloated mouth twitches. Obviously Haley liked the attention. "But…she always seemed sad when she came back from treatment," continues Madeline, nose wrinkling. "No. That's not right. Not sad. Guilty."

"You're saying you had nothing to do with why she died?" I demand.

Madeline sighs. "Look, I don't know what happened to Haley,

OK? She was complicated. But I didn't kill her." Madeline's eyes cloud. "We all saw her body. It was horrible."

"You don't think there was anything suspicious about her death?" I press, desperately trying to cling to an avenue of inquiry I feel sliding shut.

Madeline shakes her head slowly. "Haley started going to pieces right after the time the old guy came for the family visit."

"The old guy?" Electricity sparks along my spine.

Madeline's eyes settle on my face, confused by my interest. She blows smoke.

"I actually only saw him from a distance. But he dressed like vintage-style. One of those old suits and a hat you know?" She hesitates. "Are you OK?"

The thoughts all coming at once knock the air out of me.

Matthew Priest was here. He was a visitor.

The idea that he can get inside this building gives me a sensation I can't explain. Like my body is trying to tell me something I don't understand.

Madeline shrugs. "Honestly, I don't care. I just want to get out of here."

"Why don't you leave her alone, Meg?" demands a deep voice. "Stop *fucking* it up for us." I turn to see Sierra has walked into the library. She points an accusing finger.

Hearing Sierra swear is so strange that I actually find myself tensing up.

"I know who you are, Meg," she says.

CHAPTER EIGHTY-THREE

CARA

Max watches mutely as I call Meyers's direct number. Hanson picks up. I press to put him on speaker.

After Max and I explain the situation, there's a long silence.

"Bad news is you got seven miles of freezing fog just rolled in," he says finally, clearing his throat with a low rumble. "That swamp road is barely a road, and in the dark we risk sinking. Nearest chopper is out near Portland, and they can't fly in fog either. I'll do everything I can. Maybe we can get to you sooner than daybreak. Worst-case scenario, first slice of dawn, we'll get on the road. Can you take any precautions? In the meanwhile?"

"Precautions?"

"I mean," says Hanson in a slow deliberate tone, "if one of your patients is killing people, you need to keep everyone safe until we arrive. Who do you have in there?"

No sense in keeping them anonymous any longer, I decide.

"We have Madeline Murphy," I say. "She was a supermodel a few decades back."

"I know who Madeline Murphy is," says Hanson. "Just 'bout every boy in my high school had her picture on their bedroom wall." He considers. "She's tall," he decides. "Possible physical threat." I don't like how his mind is working. "How about Sierra Johnson?" He adds. "You finally going to admit she's in there?"

"She's in here," I say. My mind floats to Sierra in the anger rooms. "Sierra has a...crazy side," I admit.

"Who else?"

"Dex Adamos."

"The rock guy? OK. Physically you are going to be in trouble if he loses it. Final two?"

"Two more girls," I say. "Jade. An English actress."

"Tall, short?"

"Medium. And Meg. But both of those girls checked in after Haley died."

I don't like how this conversation is forcing me to focus my mind.

Sierra. Dex. Madeline. One of those people killed Haley.

"OK," says Hanson. "And you got at least six nursing staff there, right?"

"Right." I feel better already.

"I suggest you get everyone together in the same dormitory for tonight," says Hanson. "Make up some reason. Water leak. What have you. Set up a night shift to watch them. We'll be there soon as we can."

"OK. Yes. That's a good plan. I have administrator access," I say, thinking aloud. "All the doors lock remotely. I can seal this wing."

"We can't imprison patients in this Clinic without their consent or knowledge," says Max. "It's completely unethical."

There's a pause. "Well, sir," says Hanson finally. "Seems to me that ethics are the luxury of folk with options. And right now, those folks don't include you."

CHAPTER EIGHTY-FOUR

MEG

As Sierra walks into the library, I try not to react.

I know who you are, Meg.

Keep cool, I decide. Deny everything.

Sierra moves to stand beside Madeline and fixes me with a hard look.

"Meg, we all gave you the benefit of the doubt," says Sierra. "You betrayed us."

I shouldn't feel it. I *hate* that I feel it. But I'm devastated. Sierra hates me now.

"Hey, what's all the shouting?" Jade appears in the doorway. She takes in Sierra's expression.

"What's going on, chick?" Her expression is wary.

"What's up?" We all swing to the doorway. It's Dex.

Oh great. An audience.

Sierra points at me accusingly. "Why don't you tell the truth, Meg?"

"What truth?" I demand. Sierra's hair is wet, I notice.

There's a leaden feeling in the pit of my stomach. Everyone is looking at me.

"I found an old party picture," she says quietly. "We met before rehab. You're Haley Banks's sister."

There's a moment like someone has paused a movie. Where time stands still. No one reacts. It's like the news is so big they've all been frozen in the moment, unable to accept it.

Then the reel skips and reality bumps back, along with four faces in various states of shock and outrage.

"She's *who*?" asks Madeline, sounding confused.

"Tell them, Meg," says Sierra.

I swallow. "I can explain..."

"Is it true?" demands Madeline.

"Yes," I say. "But you have to listen to me..."

"You said you were going to be honest with us," says Jade. "Then you kept on lying. The whole time."

Madeline steps forward. "You're Haley's sister?" She looks sad for me.

"She is," says Dex. "She even kisses the same."

"You kissed Dex?" Sierra's voice is loud with shock. I can tell from Madeline's face that I've lost any sympathy she might have had for me.

OK. *Sierra likes Dex.* I hadn't picked that up until now.

There's too much data coming at once, and I can't keep it together.

"You think one of us killed Haley, right?" says Madeline quietly. "That's why you're here?"

I feel a crashing sense of failure, looking at Madeline's disappointed expression.

I'm not used to what's happening. Everyone is angry with me. Usually I wouldn't care. But now...I kind of...do.

"Someone attacked me in the spa!" I hear the uncontrolled accusation in my voice. "Sierra, how come your hair is wet?"

Sierra looks terrified. "I–I took a shower." Her hand rises to her hair.

It's the wrong thing to say. All of them are shaking their heads disgustedly.

I'm desperately trying to think how to defend myself when an alarm sounds throughout the building. High and piercing.

"What's with the alarm?" asks Jade, looking at the frightened faces of the other patients and putting her hands over her ears.

Sierra jabs a finger at me. "It must have been Meg."

What? I point a finger at my chest. "Me? What are you talking about?"

"You were messing with the controls in the hypoxic gym earlier," says Sierra, turning to include everyone else in her theory. "Meg's on some crazy detective mission, isn't she? I bet she broke some door control or…tried to break into the medication room or something."

"You can't go tampering with things in here," says Jade gently.

"I didn't!"

The alarm stops. In the sudden silence, all of our wrist schedulers beep at once.

Reflexively, I look at mine. It shows the plan of the Clinic with several rooms grayed out.

"Looks like…the lobby and treatment rooms have been locked," says Jade, glancing up at me.

There's a pause while we all absorb this.

"Why would they lock the lobby and treatment rooms?" asks Dex, confused.

Because those parts are where the exits are.

Madeline shrugs. "That's where the drugs are, right?" She cuts a suspicious glance toward me. "Maybe someone has been stealing drugs."

"No," I say. "They're locking us in. Something has happened. Don't you see? We're trapped in here."

With Matthew Priest, says a voice in my brain, *and the lady.*

"Where's Tom?" I ask.

"Stop, Meg," says Dex. "Treatment is making you crazy, OK? Just…go to the spa to something."

They're all walking away from me, in pairs. Jade and Dex. Sierra and Madeline.

"Are you going to tell Max and Cara?" I ask miserably.

"Is that honestly all you can think about?" demands Jade. "You betrayed us, Meg."

Sierra lingers for a moment.

"You shouldn't have done that, Meg," she says in a serious voice. "People are here to get better. I'm sorry your sister is dead. But you should…grieve your loss. Not spread it around." She turns and leaves before I can reply.

CHAPTER EIGHTY-FIVE

MEG

As I watch the other patients walk away, my eyes fill with tears. I can't remember the last time that happened.

Outside the library window, evening is setting in, and the weather with it. Cloying fog has rolled in, cutting out the ocean view with the setting sun. A freezing darkness that exactly reflects my inner world.

When I need it most, my armor is gone. Thick-skinned Meg has been replaced by this raw, vulnerable person who I hate.

I wipe my cheeks. Take a breath.

Fuck this. All of it. I need oxy.

One of Max's stupid exercises rises to mind. Distraction. Count your fingers.

The urge dies back slightly, but doesn't go away. Harry, I decide. I need Harry.

I locate my phone, strapped to my inner arm. When I turn it on, I see fifteen missed calls from Harry. He picks up first ring.

"Meg. What the fuck? I was booking a flight to Nowheresville Northwest. You texted that someone tried to kill you?"

I'd forgotten that.

"I'm done," I tell him. "I'm getting out of here."

There's a pause. "OK," he says uncertainly. "Good. That's… smart." Something in his voice puts me on edge.

An idea floats into my head. A nasty little thought that won't go away.

Harry is very sure he wants me to quit. He has my phone number. Access to police technology. Could he have been sending the messages from Haley?

I push the thought away. I can trust Harry. Can't I? Suddenly I'm not so sure. Can I believe anything he says?

"What is it?" I ask.

"Nothing," says Harry. "Come home."

OK. Now I *know* something is wrong.

"What are you not telling me, Harry?"

I hear the breath exit his body in a loud huff. Harry never could lie to me.

"I've been doing some digging," he says. "Occurred to me it isn't just police records people have on file."

"I don't follow."

"Sometimes people commit crimes so crazy they're committed to psych wards. Doesn't necessarily go down on their criminal record."

"Someone here was on a psyche ward?"

"Sierra. She was committed about ten years ago. Her own safety. Safety of others."

There's a pause. Ocean waves crash in the distance.

"Come home, Meg," he says. "I think you're in danger."

CHAPTER EIGHTY-SIX

MEG

So Sierra was committed to a psych ward. I turn it over.

"Did you find out why she was committed?"

"Yep. She has obsessive-compulsive disorder, in a bad way. Back in her late teens she was trying to put bleach in the family food."

"Whoa. That's...crazy."

"Crazy and dangerous."

"So it's like a hygiene thing with Sierra?" I fit this with the immaculate clothes. The constant washing and showering.

"Intrusive thoughts. Fear of spreading germs and hurting people in general."

But something else is buzzing at me. Trying for my attention.

The notes. The phone call.

Game playing.

"Harry," I say. "What if someone in here has been playing with me all along?"

"I think that's exactly what they're doing, kid," says Harry. "Question is, who?"

"What if it's Haley?"

There's a long pause.

I keep talking. "Doesn't that make the most logical sense? Harry, that is *just* like Haley. Playing tricks."

"Meg. Slow down. I don't think…"

"And I found Haley's phone. Madeline deliberately brought Haley into treatment. The phone and the fingerprints. It points to Haley not being dead, right?"

"Meg, Haley died." He says it in a soft voice that makes me want to punch him.

"If she's gone, why do I *feel* like she's here?" My voice is cracking and I hate myself for it.

"Because you haven't grieved. But as the drugs wear off, it'll probably happen naturally."

I don't need to grieve my sister. Because she isn't dead.

More facts occur to me.

"They closed off half the building," I tell Harry. "I think… That's a clue. Like, maybe they found out Haley didn't really die. And now they want to keep her trapped."

"Meg, you're scaring me. For real."

"Harry," I say. "You're not listening. They closed the part with the treatment rooms. Madeline told me that Dr. Lutz was obsessed with Haley's brain. That's where they'll be keeping her. Haley won't be able to move. Or get help. Because of the fugu."

Haley never died. She's alive. But I need to save her.

I scratch at my arm. I see it all so clearly now. Everything feels so…right.

Skin is coming off my wrist, I notice vaguely.

"Meg, that's crazy," says Harry.

"Crazy is right. Dr. Lutz and Mr. Priest could be working together to hide Haley. I need to figure out a way in."

"Meg." I can picture Harry, hands tugging his hair in exasperation.

"There could be a killer on the loose. And your plan is to creep around the clinic alone? Like some bad fucking horror movie?"

"You forgot the part where I am physically incapacitated because of severe oxycodone withdrawal."

"That isn't funny, Meg. Promise me you won't do that."

"I actually feel better now." Max's words bubble back up. *Withdrawal comes in waves. You'll feel better for a bit. Then you won't.*

"That's the problem with you, Meg. You're not afraid of anything. And you should be."

He hesitates. "Look, I didn't want to have to do this, but you leave me no choice. If you don't check out right now, I'm turning you in."

"What?" I'm genuinely baffled.

"I'll tell the Clinic manager who you really are."

"You can't do that, Harry. I'm so close to finding Haley."

"You're acting completely psychotic. Haley is *dead*, Meg. She had her reasons for doing what she did. The fact that you don't understand them doesn't make it less real."

"She didn't kill herself." I stop talking, realizing this is getting me nowhere. "OK, you win," I lie. "I'll check out and come home. You're right. I'm on this new mix of medication. It's made me a little crazy."

He breathes out in relief. "Thank. Fuck. I'll book you a flight."

"Thanks."

I hang up the phone, feeling a rush of energy. There's no way I'm getting on a flight. Next thing I'm going to do is find a way into the locked half of the clinic.

As I leave the library, a familiar figure stands in the doorway. I'm getting used to her now.

She wears a short white doctor's coat, unbuttoned to reveal matching-color underwear. Her blond hair is set in a wave beneath a nurse's cap, and she holds an outsized injection needle coquettishly to her mouth.

"Hello, Meg," she says in a movie drawl. "Time for your medicine."

"I don't have time for you," I hiss, pushing past. "I need to find Haley."

"You know you can't trust anyone?" she says, watching me go. "Not even Harry. It's just you and me now, Meg. Just you and me."

CHAPTER EIGHTY-SEVEN

MEG

Night is falling as I head to the open-air quadrant at the heart of the Clinic. Boxing webbing is wound around my palms.

I've got a plan of sorts, but it isn't a great one. If I'm right about the layout, I can scale this wall and get into the other half of the Clinic over the roof. I'm going to climb the drainpipe. My boxing wraps are long, strong cross-woven fabric. In theory, perfect to hook around and grip.

The fog makes it hard to see. And now rain is falling. Fat drops that soak me almost immediately the second I get outside. I shiver.

There are thick old iron pipes running right up the quadrant to the top. The old-fashioned kind heavily bolted to the wall. When I try feeding the long boxing wraps around and setting my feet, the pipe takes my weight with a mild squeaking protest.

Muscle spasms shoot through my arms, and I drop, falling to the hard ground.

Fuck. Keep it together, Meg. I eye the metal pipe like a boxing opponent and reset the tension, winding the grips firmly around my palms. Glancing back to the door, I start again. No one has seen me. Yet.

I'm a quarter way up the drainpipe when I stop, muscles shaking again.

Don't fall, I tell myself. Gritting my teeth, I ascend another few feet. I've hit the bracket. Didn't think of that. I have to unwrap and reattach over the top. One-handed. My forearms start shaking.

Wind and salty rain whip across my face as I contemplate the maneuver. Then I hear my name. I look down through the fog to make out the shadowy figure of a nurse, wide-eyed with horror, in the quadrant. She's a long way down.

Turning back to the wall, I untie the wraps, jamming a hand behind the drainpipe so I can reattach them one-handed. I lose my grip at the last moment. I fall several feet, one hand still stuck, the other winging free. My attached wrist wrenches up as it takes my body weight. I twist out, feet kicking wildly, pain pulsing up my arm, then swing back, face-first to the soaking-wet wall.

Somehow, I get the wrap back around the pipe, above the bracket. Dig in with my feet. Ignore the pain in my injured wrist. Above me is a windowsill. *OK. Make it there*, I decide. *Rest my arms.*

I take a breath. Not so far to the top. Better get started before my wrist injury really kicks in. The nurse has vanished. Probably going to sound the alarm.

Come on, Meg. Last chance to find Haley.

I don't know how I make the last part of the climb, but somehow I get up on the roof. Now all I have to do is walk across the slippery pitched tiles. I rebind the wrap on my injured wrist, compressing it. Hard to tell how bad it is with the pain in my body already at such a fever pitch.

Cold fog obscures my view. I take a moment to get my bearings on the giant roof. Main clinic. I think that way. Treatment room wing. Over there. My eyes fall on a skylight. Perfect. I make for it. The glass is both easy and satisfying to put a foot through. Tinkling glass falls an indeterminable distance below, allowing me to push through a hand and twist the lever.

A concrete corridor is below. I drop into it. As I do, a familiar sour smell encloses me.

Fugu. I can smell it. This must be the right way to the treatment room.

She's in there, I tell myself. *Haley must be in there.*

I try not to imagine Harry, shaking his head, telling me she died. *You're wrong, Harry. Haley is alive.*

It all looks very different at night. But I recognize it even so. The treatment room. It's up ahead.

I reach the door, fully expecting it to be locked. When it swings open at my first push of the handle, it takes me by surprise. But not so much as what's inside.

I try to control the sob that rises up.

The treatment room is empty. Nothing but Dr. Lutz's security screens, showing empty corridors.

The realization brings with it a terrible certainty.

Haley isn't here.

There's a shadowy shape in the corner, and I realize it's the lady again, perched provocatively on the hospital bed in a silk teddy, bare feet dangling, painting her fingernails scarlet.

"Haley's dead," she says, blowing on her hand. "Queen of hearts. You lose, Meg."

As if in answer, a loud clunk echoes across the hard surfaced floors and walls. Then everything is bathed in blinding white light.

Dr. Lutz is standing in the doorway, flanked by two thickset men dressed in white scrubs. They have the all-too-familiar stance of henchmen. Scenes from the warehouse flood back. Shame. Powerlessness.

"Well, well," says Dr. Lutz. "It seems you are not who you said you are, Meg."

CHAPTER EIGHTY-EIGHT

MEG

Dr. Lutz walks toward me, and the henchmen-like nurses stay shoulder to shoulder.

"You have been lying to us." The way he says it sounds a lot like the way the men in the warehouse spoke, right before they doused me in gasoline.

"You are sister to Haley Banks. I assume you came here to try and discover what happened to her?"

"You're a real genius."

He blinks slowly. "I am very interested in you, Meg. The way your brain operates is quite unique. I should very much like to study you."

"You can't keep me here," I tell him.

"You'll find we can." His lips turn up slightly. He's enjoying this, I realize. I feel my fists ball.

"You entered the clinic with a paranoid delusion your sister was the victim of some...nefarious situation," he says. "While here, you attacked a patient. You hallucinated an attack on your life in our spa. Then you broke into a clinical facility, putting yourself at great physical risk by scaling a sheer wall." He smiles. "Meg. Does this seem like the behavior of a sane person?"

"This insane person fooled you and all your staff," I say, fixing him with a cold stare. "I've seen more professional security in a two-bit motel gambling pit."

That gets him, I can tell. A little anger flares behind the eyes. I've figured out how to rile him. Next trick is to learn not to use it. I never did get that one down.

Learn to fold, Meg.

"I have encountered a great many patients in the depths of psychosis," he says. "Not a single one ever believed they were imagining things. It must seem very real at the time."

"You're a psychopath," I tell him.

Somehow I'm not surprised when he nods calmly.

"I prefer the term 'antisocial personality disorder.'" Dr. Lutz manages a small smile. "I found out by accident while conducting addiction research in India. Imagine my shock to find my own brain scan correlated with those of criminals and murderers."

He pauses for effect. "Over the years I have come to accept it. I consider myself something of a persecuted minority."

"You're serious?"

"Absolutely. My condition has been unfairly maligned. I am not sadistic or violent by nature. My exceptional traits have enabled me to do a great deal for humanity. And I don't pose a threat to other people unless provoked."

"Did Haley provoke you?"

Dr. Lutz shakes his head in amusement. "Not that she didn't try. Fortunately, I am immune to the charms of people like Haley."

That's what you think, buddy, I find myself thinking. *Haley would have played you somehow.*

"An advantage of psychopathy," continues Dr. Lutz, "is I can't be emotionally manipulated."

"But you can kill people for fun?"

He looks annoyed. "That's a tiresome myth. My kind don't kill any more commonly than empathetic people. And if we do, it's not personal. It's far easier to manipulate empathetic people to do cruel and unpleasant things than a person like me. Lynchings and honor killings are not carried out by psychopaths."

"You just take care of all the serial murders," I say.

To my surprise, Dr. Lutz starts laughing.

"What's so funny?" I demand.

"Oh, Meg. Didn't you put the pieces together yet? Your work with Max. Your brain scans. I thought you were intelligent."

"Put what pieces together?"

"You didn't suspect there was a reason Max had such difficulty assessing and medicating you? Did he mention that your brain scans don't resemble the other patients?"

I don't reply.

"Meg." He blinks slowly. "You are just like me."

CHAPTER EIGHTY-NINE

CARA

Max and I have managed to section off the Clinic from the lobby computer.

Patients in one half. Medics in the other. Now we need to figure out a plan to supervise everyone.

"If we keep the sessions the same as usual, there's a good chance no one will even know," I say to Max, reassuring myself more than anything.

"What about the electric fence?" says Max. "Shouldn't we power it down? If there's a fire or…"

He doesn't finish the sentence, but I catch his meaning. If something goes badly wrong, we could all be trapped inside the grounds.

"I'll turn it off," I say. "Patients will be in this half. Medics in the other. But there's an escape route. If we need it."

"But only for medical staff," Max points out. "Patients won't be able to get out onto the grounds."

"I think that's probably a good thing," I say.

"I don't think we should be doing this, Cara," says Max. "Whoever killed Tom, they're on the edge. If we put everyone together in a dormitory, they could completely lose it."

"What other option do we have?" I point out sensibly.

"If we can identify the killer, we can isolate them," says Max. "We have traumatized patients here, Cara. The damage we could do by trapping them together with a killer…"

"Let's concentrate on keeping everyone safe," I say. "We have six nurses. That's plenty. We can all take turns staying awake."

"Tom went to my office," says Max. "Alone. Someone must have lured him there. Most likely female, don't you think?"

"I…"

"Tom struggled with impulse control," continues Max. "He was having an affair with Haley before she died. If you can call it an affair," he adds, forehead wrinkling. "It didn't sound to me like either of them were having much fun."

"Haley wanted Tom to divorce his wife," I say, drawn in despite myself. "Power play."

"So…maybe there's something else we're not seeing. If Tom was also in a relationship with Sierra or Madeline, there could have been jealousy. Enough to kill in unnatural confines like rehab."

"Tom also owed money," I point out. "If he was blackmailing someone, they could have been male or female."

We're both silent, overwhelmed by possibilities.

"Do we know where Dr. Lutz is?" I ask.

"I don't think we should tell him about Tom," says Max. "I'm not sure how he would react."

A cold bolt of fear shoots through me.

"You're suggesting he could harm a patient?"

"Dr. Lutz cares about power and money," continues Max. "In many ways he is psychologically very simple. So long as he has those things, he is predictable. But if he feels threatened, I am not sure what he could be capable of."

As he finishes speaking, my computer screen flashes.

System override.

"I never saw that screen before," I say, momentarily confused. The schedule flashes, then blanks out completely. Every session has been reset.

"Max." I swallow, looking to the corner of his office where the security camera is pointed. "I think there is a good chance Dr. Lutz already knows."

CHAPTER NINETY

MEG

In the treatment room, I stare back at Dr. Lutz.

"I am *nothing* like you," I tell him.

Infuriatingly, he only nods calmly. "Not *exactly* like me," he quantifies. "I am a psychopath. You're a sociopath, Meg."

"Bullshit." I hate that I blurt it out.

"I had the same reaction at first myself, after diagnosis." He smiles smugly. I wanted to punch him right in the face, but that would prove what he's trying to make me believe.

"We had an expert panel diagnose you," he says. "You have twenty of the twenty-three traits of sociopathy. Half of the psychopathy traits. Myself, I have almost the full complement of the latter."

"You're lying," I tell him.

He inclines his head. "I am, of course, a good liar. But only when it serves me, and it doesn't serve me to do so now. Your brain scans show reduced activity in the areas that deal with empathy and processing emotions. Your sister, Haley, had similar configurations. These traits often run in families, although every case is unique."

A slight smile plays on his lips. He's enjoying toying with me.

"Tell me, do you consciously mirror people? Copy their gestures, their body language?"

"I… It's for my job," I retort angrily, mad that I'm even being drawn into the discussion.

"Of course." He nods curtly. "Your job is in many ways law enforcement, correct?"

"Yes." I nod firmly. "I catch bad guys."

As if he needed any more proof I'm not a female Ted Bundy.

"Do you know how many police officers are sociopathic? Neurotypicals mostly can't handle making logical decisions to punish or, seeing the worst of society, being lied to. They fall apart, get divorced, have breakdowns. The same is true of lawyers, surgeons, journalists. Most American presidents score highly on the psychopathy scale. High-adrenaline jobs that require a high level of emotional detachment." He strokes at his bushy beard. "I think you are intelligent enough to notice that you don't yawn when other people yawn, or wince when someone stubs their toe."

I don't answer.

"You are quite special, Meg. Extremely high functioning. You have found the perfect way to train yourself without attracting undue attention. I assume since discovering the power of mirroring body language, you deploy it in all social settings?"

"That's me and every other poker player," I counter.

"Tell me, Meg, do you engage in power play with authority figures? I imagine Cara would have bothered you immensely. Is it impossible for you to back down, even for your own good?"

I don't reply, but Sol's voice is in my head. *When have you ever folded a hand, Meg?*

"Do you, perhaps, have a phenomenally high pain threshold?

Go into rages when you feel someone has crossed you? Rages that go beyond the behavior of the average person?"

I picture the guy in the warehouse. The way I took him out, even with a dislocated shoulder. My response to Madeline's book throwing. The many, many expulsions from school after episodes of violent delinquency.

"I care about people," I tell him, thinking about Harry. Maybe even my fellow patients.

"Ah, the sociopathic inner circle," says Dr. Lutz. "You do know you don't see them as separate from yourself? Don't be ashamed, Meg. There is nothing inherently wrong with sociopathy. As a person with psychopathic traits, I admire your kind greatly. I was born this way. You were forged. Most people are broken by intolerable trauma. You chose to win. Repurposed yourself not to feel stress. Cauterized the emotions that were causing you problems. What a gift, to surgically alter the entire function of one's brain."

I shake my head. "You're trying to trick me, and it won't work."

He sighs. "What a pity. I had hoped for an intelligent conversation with you. Certainly Haley was more able to engage with her dark side, before her unfortunate demise."

He's waiting for a reply from me, and when I don't give it, his face is an unreadable mask.

"I'm afraid the conditions of your staying here are quite clear," he tries. "You signed a form giving us permission to treat you however we saw fit. Max thinks another fugu treatment would be ill-advised in your case, but I am willing to risk it."

Everything about him suggests strength. His stance. The words he chooses. Only a complete idiot would try to call his bluff. So why can't I help myself?

"So do it," I tell him, looking steadily back.

There's the slightest pause when I think maybe my gamble paid off. He doesn't have the nerve to follow through with his threats. But deep down, I know that's not the case.

"Very well," he says. "I'll ready the treatment."

CHAPTER NINETY-ONE

MEG

It took both of Dr. Lutz's heavyset nurses to manhandle me onto the bed, but they managed it eventually.

As they strap me down for treatment, Dr. Lutz eyes the security screens, taps a few buttons thoughtfully. Behind me, the nurse is already injecting fugu.

When the effects kick in, I see but can't feel electrodes being stuck under my collarbones.

My body is completely immobile. The strange sensation of complete detachment spreads through my mind. I could tell anyone anything. It doesn't matter.

Dr. Lutz is leaning over me.

"One final treatment," he says. "I should love to keep you for longer. But unfortunately, you are evidence, Meg. And I can't leave evidence lying around."

He glances across at the security cameras, assuring himself of something. Then returns his attention to me.

The edges of the room are wavering. I can't keep hold of any sensation in my body. And the familiar feeling descends. I don't care about anything much. Why not tell this strange man what comes into my mind?

"We had interesting results when we discussed a house with purple drapes," decides Dr. Lutz. "Let's go back there."

The world drops away a little, and I hear the old ceiling fan again.

Whump, whump whump.

"Tell me more about this house," says Dr. Lutz. "Perhaps it was your family house growing up?"

"No." I'm remembering easily now. "It was the house next door."

"What happened in that house?"

"Haley took us there." I try to blink but I can't. My mouth is having difficulty too. Funny how this image doesn't bother me at all, but I know in some distant logical way, deep in my soul, I'm terrified. "She tried to put me to sleep in one of the bedrooms. But I woke up."

Memories and images are overlapping. There is something in my body now. Like a storm cloud that needs to get out.

"I went out on the landing. He was taking Haley into a bedroom. She was crying."

"Who was taking her?"

"Matthew. The man with playing-card eyes."

"What happened to you, Meg," he asks, "in this house?"

"They shut the door." Some part of my body is sobbing. "They shut me out. He got her. I could hear…at the door. Haley crying. Then *she* came."

"Who is she?"

"The queen of hearts. She wouldn't let me leave."

"What happened to you next?"

"My sister. I couldn't get to her. The lady wouldn't let me."

"What, Meg, what happened to Haley?"

All around me, I can hear medical equipment beeping wildly.

"No," I hear Dr. Lutz say to an unseen nurse. "The larger dose. Give her the larger dose."

This time I feel the needle. A cold flow of paralyzing liquid snaking down my spine.

"What happened to your sister, Meg?" repeats Dr. Lutz.

I try to swallow but my throat won't move.

Your sister needs a little rest. She's not feeling so good right now.

"When she came out of the bedroom," I say. "Haley was gone. She wasn't there anymore."

"She went somewhere else?"

I try to shake my head but it won't move. "Her body was there," I say. "But Haley wasn't in it."

I can picture Haley's violet eyes so clearly. Dead and blank.

So many ideas jostle in my head for space, trying to elbow their way into full feelings. A desperate need to see Haley. Realization I will never, ever see her again.

"He got her," I whisper. "He got my sister."

This time there's no oxy. There's no alcohol either. Nothing to stop the prickle-edged storm of memories from exploding. And then, real sickening pain. Vicious little pockets of despair, growing, insinuating, unfurling like poison vines. They prod into my body stabbing, burning.

"Make it stop," I whisper. "Make it *stop*."

"Where was your mother?"

"Gone."

"You didn't know where she was?"

"I think…maybe the man… Maybe he'd gotten her too."

A picture unfolds in my head. Mr. Priest hitching his trousers, seating himself by a low coffee table. Producing a pack of cards.

He deals, face down. I see myself taking a card.

The queen of hearts.

There's an image on it. The lady. In her white nurse's outfit. She blows me a kiss and winks.

None of it makes sense. Just a series of confusing pictures. But at the heart of it all, a feeling. A feeling I don't want back.

"Her heart rate is elevating." It's a nurse. She sounds frightened. "She's going into shock."

CHAPTER NINETY-TWO

CARA

Max is tapping keys on my computer now, looking at the screen.

It's still flashing override. Refusing to let either of us log on.

"Try the phone," I say. But we both know. Even before Max lifts it.

"Dead," he says.

I snap on my radio. No frequency there either.

There's movement on my computer screen.

"The sessions are rebooking themselves," I say, looking. "They've all changed to…"

"Cryotherapy," says Max. "All the patients are booked for a cryotherapy session. In the cold chamber."

"That's…irregular," I say.

Max is shaking his head. "How could I have been so stupid," he mutters. "Of course Dr. Lutz would destroy all the evidence."

"Max," I say. "If you're still talking about your drug stocks…"

"Fugu," interrupts Max. "It has a half-life of two months in the human body. But it's broken down faster by extremes of temperature."

I'm trying to figure out where he's going with this.

"Cara," Max says quietly. "I think Dr. Lutz is making plans to destroy the evidence."

"I already told you, Max," I say. "I don't care about fugu."

"You don't understand. The evidence that Dr. Lutz means to destroy"—Max swallows—"it's the patients."

CHAPTER NINETY-THREE

MEG

I'm in a blue sky, floating past fluffy clouds.

Playing cards bob in the air. I reach out and take one. The queen of hearts. There's a picture of the lady on it, in a graduation gown. She leans slightly over, a finger pressed against her lips, and smiles at me. Her hair is styled slightly longer this time, brunette, falling free from the square mortarboard on her head.

"The work you have to do is right here," she tells me, her tiny finger wagging. "You're grieving your sister. You need to sit with that grief. Stop running."

"Quit telling me to feel my feelings," I tell her. "I'm like you. There's nothing good back there, OK? It's…an endless well of shame and more shame. It's fucking exhausting."

I let the card go and she floats away. I take another card. Ace of clubs. She's there again in a different outfit.

I pluck cards from the air. Fan them in my hand. The lady is tiny. Just a picture on a card. She wriggles in her two-dimensional prison. Frowns. Pouts.

"Too bad," I tell her. "It's time you went back where you belong."

In reply she freezes into a still drawing.

I stare at the image. *She isn't real.*

The lady is an illustration on a pack of pinup playing cards.

I've come back to earth without noticing, and now I'm sitting at an old-fashioned school desk. Cards are scattered everywhere. Max stands by a blackboard.

"What are you doing here?" I ask him, looking around. We're in my old school, I realize. The last one I attended before I was kicked out for good.

"I suppose I must be a figment of your imagination," says Max. He holds up a fistful of playing cards. The lady is illustrated on each one, in various seductive stances.

"Who was she?" asks Max.

"I think the lady was a drawing. On a playing card," I tell him. "Or…a set of cards. She was a set of cards."

Max spreads them out. Cute pinup girls and playing card suits. It's the kind of deck I would imagine Mr. Priest owning. Vintage.

"I learned to play poker with this particular set of cards," I tell him. "Mr. Priest taught me. The man with the playing-card eyes."

"Likely you played a game of poker in particularly stressful circumstances," agrees Max. "Somehow, this set of cards got printed on your memory. You remember the lady as a person who hurt you. But I think she also became part of you. Perhaps even the part of you that can shut away your feelings."

"I lost." The words come out. "I lost that game."

"Can you tell me anything more about it?"

I shake my head slowly, feeling my fists ball. "I *lost*," I tell Max.

"Yes." He nods. "But *what* did you lose?"

"*Everything.*" I stand and cards go flying in all directions. They're everywhere. In the air, on the floor. "*I lost everything.*"

CHAPTER NINETY-FOUR

MEG

When I come around, for a second I think it was all a dream.

Then I realize where I am. The treatment room. Strapped to the bed.

The fugu has worn off. I try to sit up and realize I can't.

What the fuck happened?

I remember…playing cards. Memories. A poker game.

Things crystallize. The lady was a playing card. From a game I played with Mr. Priest. But…*why* did I make her into such a frightening figure?

Whatever happened between me, Haley, and Mr. Priest is still locked away tight in my head. Refusing to make sense.

Even so, I feel different. Where I had a black void, there is now something.

Sadness, I realize. *I feel sadness.*

Turning my head on the bed, I take in the multiple camera screens that line the inside of the treatment room. No one is on any of the screens.

Then I see movement. One of the cameras is focused on the lobby.

And walking right into reception is…

I blink. Blink again.

It's a man wearing a fedora hat.

My mind buzzes, like a static display, and then it explodes the vision into pieces. The fractured image regroups. Bits have changed. He's walking to the vacant reception desk now. I can see his face.

There are no playing cards for eyes, but I recognize him in the deepest, most frightening part of my being.

It's Matthew Priest. Here. In the Clinic.

"OK, Meg," I tell myself. "You're going insane. No big deal. It was always going to happen."

I look back at the security camera. Can't get rid of the idea that Mr. Priest knows I'm trapped in here and is coming to get me.

As I'm thinking this, he exits the lobby. Entering the main part of the Clinic. Another camera picks him up. The corridor toward the treatment rooms.

OK. Time to leave.

Does he know I'm here? I have a bad feeling Matthew Priest is not coming to send me home with a "thirty days clean" sticker.

The thought pushes me to action. I need to get off this bed. Simple. Just the small reality of being restrained by medical apparatus designed to immobilize crazy people.

Take a breath, Meg. Think calmly.

Much as I hate to admit it, Max's techniques for keeping my head do kind of work. I count slowly down, trying to think properly. Exploring the nature of my restraints.

They secure my wrists. But…my shoulders can move slightly off the bed.

My shoulder. It's how I escaped the warehouse.

"Lucky my shoulder still pops out," I say aloud, trying to

psyche myself up. "No one ever thinks of that when they design restraints."

I tense my arms, stretching out my left. The one with the shoulder injury.

Gritting my teeth, I take a breath, grip the fabric of the restraint, then twist away.

"Fuck!" The pain is indescribable. Oxycodone withdrawal teamed with live nerve damage. It's a white-hot sensation that rolls through my entire body like a heartbeat.

Come on, Meg. Do it already.

I rotate my body in a sharp movement and feel my shoulder slip loose. I'm rewarded with another bout of pain so excruciating, my head swims, and I begin losing my grip on reality.

Focus, Meg. You can't pass out now.

My dislocated shoulder has given me a few inches of slack. Just enough to slide my arm out of the restraint strap, inch by agonizing inch. I breathe through my mouth.

Don't pass out. Don't pass out.

One arm is free. Fuck, that hurt.

On the screen, Matthew Priest has turned a corner toward the spa. He tries a door handle. Finds it locked. Switches direction.

No time for a break, Meg. As fast as my dislocated arm can manage, I unbuckle the straps. It takes every cell in my body, threading small movement, one by one, through the outstretched arm.

The buckle opens. I've done it.

With effort, I stand. My legs buckle and I lean on the bed, breathing hard. *Stop*, I tell my body sternly. *I need you.*

I manage to stand. Lean against the wall. I reach up with my dislocated shoulder arm, like I remember the medics doing the first time around, and push it back into its socket.

I must have passed out for a few seconds, because suddenly I'm on the floor and the side of my face hurts. The left side of my body feels like it belongs to somebody else. Somebody made of red-hot metal.

Stand up, Meg. Time to get out of here.

There are two directions I can take out of the treatment room. One is toward the dormitories and Matthew Priest. The other is to the lobby and freedom.

I just need to pick the right direction.

I get to standing with my good hand and eye the open door. One foot in front of the other. Harder than it sounds.

I make it out, hobbling along the corridor, holding my shoulder. Make a few sharp turns. Picture myself back at work, JD in hand, pack of oxy in my pocket. Time to get back to normal, I decide. Feelings weren't for me.

Ultimately I'm just like Haley. The Banks sisters weren't built to last.

I reach the door that leads to the exit and push down on the handle.

It's locked.

I'm trying not to panic at that when I hear footsteps in the corridor behind me.

Leather-soled shoes. A swish of linen trousers.

It can't be, it can't be, it can't be.

I refuse to turn around, pulling at the handle, a whimper of fear escaping.

"Meg?"

I turn. A man is at the far end of the corridor. He wears a fedora hat.

Kaleidoscope memories play through my mind. His face is hidden, but his familiar suited body is clear.

"Meg Banks?" *That voice.* I feel my skin break out in goose bumps. My shoulder isn't working. My brain won't fit together thoughts. My body is only half-recovered from being paralyzed.

One thing is for certain. Matthew Priest is definitely real.

And I'm trapped here with him. Shut out of the exit. Completely helpless, like when I was a kid.

He takes off his hat, rolling it down his arm in a gesture that fires up a ripple of memories.

"Look at you," he says, "all grown up."

CHAPTER NINETY-FIVE

MEG

Mr. Priest looks older. His hair is grayer. Skin slacker. But his smile is exactly the same. Kind. Caring.

"You don't remember me," he decides, moving closer. I don't correct him. "I'm Matthew Priest. After your mom got sick," he says, "I took care of you and your sister for a couple of days. Haley brought you over to my house because you couldn't be at home. Remember that?" He moves closer.

"I...remember," I say hesitantly.

"You do?" He beams, taking a step forward.

"Why are you here?" I manage.

"I drove here to pick up a few of Haley's effects yesterday," he says. "When I got here, the gate was shut, no one answering the intercom. A fog rolled in and I didn't want to risk the swamp road. Sat in my car for an hour, trying to call reception. Wasn't too warm, I can tell you." He smiles. "When I tried the gate again, it was open, but... I couldn't see anyone on the reception desk." Matthew shrugs. A what-you-gonna-do gesture. "Looks like you beat me to it. That's why you're here, right? To pick up Haley's things?"

I don't correct him. "You visited her?" I say.

He nods sadly. "When I found out Haley was in rehab, I drove out here," he says. "I've got a cabin not so far from Portland. I visited her a few times. When she died, I…" He stops suddenly, face crumpling, tears springing to his eyes. "You know it was only a week ago when I saw her," he says. "How are you?" he adds. "Haley mentioned you and she were having some issues."

There's a paternal concern to his face that completely overlays the nightmare man of my dreams.

"I'm grieving," I say, trying the words out for size.

He smiles, wiping tears. "Do you remember we played cards? I taught you poker."

I manage a half nod. "You won," I manage. "Queen of hearts."

"Straight flush." He nods. "Luckiest draw I ever remember getting."

"Do you still carry the cards?"

"My lucky pack?" He takes out a pack of cards. "Take them everywhere I go."

"Can I?" I take the pack and leaf through. It's the strangest feeling, seeing the lady in her various outfits. I turn cards until I reach the queen of hearts.

Matthew clears his throat uncomfortably.

"Feel a little bad about the imagery there," he says. "Not so appropriate for an eight-year-old. Ashamed to say it didn't cross my mind at the time. You were so determined," he adds with a half smile. "I never saw a kid care so much about winning. You wanted to play again and again, and I had to tell you 'no' in the end. Felt bad about that." He shakes his head. "We didn't know at that point if your mom was going to make it. Trying to keep you busy, you know. Haley very much wanted to spare you the details."

"What details?" There's a lump in my throat.

"Uh. Well. I don't know how much you were told back then. You probably remember how Haley brought you over to my house to keep you safe from all the drama. After she found your mom in the bathtub." His eyes lift to mine, hoping I already know.

When I don't answer, Matthew looks uncertain. Like he's not sure he should be talking about it. "No one ever told you?" He says finally. "Your mom… Well, she tried to end it all. Haley was the one who found her."

CHAPTER NINETY-SIX

MEG

Mom tried to end it all. An icy chill settles on me to hear Mr. Priest say it.

I kind of remember…but at the same time I don't. Mom was always threatening to drink a bottle of gin and slit her wrists in the bathtub. I have a recollection of this frightening me. Then it stopped having the power to bother me. Was that before or after she did it?

"The bathroom," I tell Matthew. "Haley took you into the bathroom. Shut me out."

"She didn't want you to be burdened with it, Meg." He hesitates. "But…I think in rehab Haley came around to the idea that that wasn't right. She was done with keeping your mom's secrets. Thought you should know the truth."

Haley's last voicemail to me. *I need to tell you something. About when we were kids.*

"I thought… I don't know." I frown, remembering the night. The bathroom. "Haley looked so upset. She was never upset. I thought you were some strange guy doing something bad to my sister." I put more things together. "Haley never told me," I say finally. "Not even on the day she died." I feel a lurch of confusion.

"Protecting you, I think." He looks uncertain. "I don't think it was the first time your mom attempted suicide. But…I think maybe for Haley… She was done."

Maybe he's picturing Haley from that night. How her face changed to something blank and cold. Like part of her died.

"Maybe." Knowing Haley, it was more complicated than that.

"Haley and I kept in touch for a while," he says. "Then you had to move again. Next thing I know, Haley's in rehab." He sighs. "I know things weren't great with you two. For Haley, leaving the family home so young was about self-preservation. Her or your mom."

Rationally I know this. But it doesn't stop it hurting, how Haley left me.

I look at Matthew. "Did Haley…did she talk about me when you visited her?"

It's like a toothache I can't help but prod. And I'm sure I know the answer right up until Matthew smiles sadly.

"Sure she did," he says. "From what Haley told me, she cared about you a lot. It's… Your sister had a lot of her own things going on growing up. The legal emancipation thing. Haley's child-acting money went to your mom for quite a while. Your sister had to fight to make sure you were still provided for when she left."

"Haley paid my fees direct to the school," I say. "I thought she was trying to buy me with some grandiose gesture."

He rolls his hat on his arm absentmindedly and lowers his head. "I wanted to help. With your mom, Meg. People told me not to get involved."

"Did Haley seem sad?" I ask. "When you last spoke to her?"

He shakes his head slowly. "You know, I have gone through that in my mind for the longest time," he says. "Whether I triggered something. Mostly we talked about the industry, you know? I'm an agent and she was interested in acting. Seemed to think the moment she left rehab, the world would open up to her."

I nod. Of course I know. That is 100 percent Haley. She kept in touch with Matthew to further her career. And now he's here to pick up her belongings. Even in death Haley manages to get people running around after her.

I manage a smile. "I'm sorry you had a wasted trip."

"Not wasted," he says. "I got to see you." He replaces his hat. "Don't be a stranger, OK? You need anything, you holler."

I realize I've got some of the answers Harry wanted me to find. I know what happened to Haley and me when we were younger. How I conflated memories of Haley's devastation, Mom's hospitalization, Matthew's sudden appearance and made sense of them the best I could.

Mr. Priest never hurt Haley. Mom hurt Haley. And me. Again and again and again.

Suicide attempts. The mood swings, the fluctuating evaluation of Haley's beauty and talent. The way Mom tried to drive a wedge between us.

But now that I know the truth, something else is very apparent.

To solve your sister's murder, you need to solve yourself.

I know now. I know what happened to Haley.

"You can get into the lobby by a different route," says Matthew. "Back that way. I can give you a ride to the airport if you need one."

"No thanks," I say slowly. "There's one last thing I need to do for Haley."

Unmask her killer.

CHAPTER NINETY-SEVEN

CARA

I'm trying to compute what Max is telling me. Because surely he can't seriously mean that Dr. Lutz plans to murder the patients.

"Why would he go to the trouble of putting them in a cryotherapy chamber?" I ask, still clinging to the possibility that it is simply an eccentric treatment choice. "If he wanted to kill them, why not choose another means?"

"I think Dr. Lutz planned this as a possibility from when he first bought the cryotherapy chamber," says Max. "It's clean. Efficient. Done right, you could convincingly argue the deaths were a tragic accident. Most importantly, any fugu in the patient's bodies will be destroyed by the cold. Fugu would still show up in a toxicology report if someone died another way."

"But that's *crazy*," I say. "Dr. Lutz would be putting himself in far more danger by murdering a group of innocent people. He risks life imprisonment."

"Only if he's caught and convicted," says Max. "You're attaching emotion to it. Think about it like a game of chess. Dr. Lutz is risking a worse outcome by killing patients, but his odds of getting away with it are substantially higher. He doesn't see people in the same way you do, Cara. They have no more worth to Dr. Lutz than a set of garden chairs. But any trace of fugu is a smoking gun."

We look at each other. "We need to get the patients out of the Clinic," I tell Max.

Right on cue, a warning sounds from the grounds outside.

"The electric fence," I say. "Someone's fired it back up."

"We're trapped inside the grounds," says Max. "But if we could override the system somehow, we could reschedule everyone to meet in the atrium. Hide them somehow. Until the police arrive."

I think for a moment. "A power cut," I say. "If we could shut off the power, it reboots the system. I'd have maybe a minute or so to log on to the schedule. It might give us enough time."

"The substation is in the medication room," he says. "All the power routes through that room. We can cut a cable."

"Smart thinking."

"Four years at Cambridge. I think it would short out the electric fence too. But let's make sure all the patients are safe first," he adds. "Tackle the gate next."

But as he's speaking, a map of the Clinic flashes onto the screen. A red line races across the system, showing an automatic lockdown of several doors. My eyes fall on our location.

"Go now," I tell Max. "You can make it. I'll stay here in your office. The moment the power comes back on, I can get the system rebooted."

"Cara..."

"Just go."

Max hesitates a moment longer before setting off at a run for the medication room. I watch him go, hoping the corridor will be open long enough.

Where is Dr. Lutz? It occurs to me I should try to find out.

Distract him from finding where Max is going. I tap a few keys on my computer.

The schedule is still locked. But I can log on to the security system. A few basic screens pop up.

"Cara?" I nearly jump out of my skin. It's Dr. Lutz.

His eyes land on Tom's body, lying behind Max's desk.

"What has been happening here?" he asks, in a tone that suggests a glass of milk has been spilled. "Someone has left rather a mess."

I swallow hard. "It looks as though Tom overdosed," I say, improvising.

"Where is Max?"

My eyes track to the computer screen. I can see Max, headed along a corridor. Dr. Lutz doesn't know I can see this, I realize.

"I think he mentioned he was headed to the kitchen," I say, picking the furthest away spot.

Something is turning in my mind. A plan. Of sorts.

I need to keep Dr. Lutz talking.

"Dr. Lutz," I say, "I've got a proposition for you."

CHAPTER NINETY-EIGHT

MEG

Every person in the Clinic has a reason they can't leave rehab. Maybe even something they would kill for. Dex will go to prison. Tom will be cut off by his agent. Sierra will be axed from her girl band. Jade could risk losing custody of her daughter. Madeline can't afford another shot at rehab.

One of those people is the killer.

But I think the reason runs deeper. Haley's death was caused by something in our past. Something that pushed a person in this clinic to do the unthinkable.

My phone. I feel for it, strapped to my inner arm. Calmer than I should be, I call Harry.

"Hey," I say.

"Hey yourself, Meg. What's going on?"

"I figured some things out about myself, Harry. Just like you wanted me to. And guess what?"

"What?"

"You were right. I think solving myself helped me work out what happened to Haley."

"You're way ahead of me, Meg."

"That nightmare I told you about? The playing-card guy? I

think something very scary happened to me and Haley as kids. I think she tried to protect me from it. But…she was only a kid herself, and she couldn't hide everything. The parts I wound up seeing and understanding kind of traumatized me. And her."

"What was the scary event?"

I hesitate, threads of memories coming back. "That's not important. The important thing is I think I know who killed Haley. And I can get them to reveal themselves by going to the medication room."

"You're planning on putting yourself alone in a locked room with a killer."

"If I'm right about who it is and why they did it, I won't be in any danger."

"And if you're wrong?"

"I'll be in quite a bit of danger," I concede.

"You have a backup plan, Meg? For if you're wrong?"

"My backup plan, is 'don't be wrong.'"

"Jesus Christ." He pauses. "Don't do it."

I hesitate. "I think I love you, Harry. Sorry I never said it before."

I hang up.

According to the schedule, all patients are due in group cryotherapy session.

I head toward the room with the chamber and find everyone else already undressing.

I don't know the point when I realized I loved these people. I can't put a finger on it.

"Hey." I hold up a hand. "Where's Tom?"

"Meg?" Jade stands, mouth open. "Tom hasn't shown up yet," she says. "Are you OK? They told us you'd had a bad reaction to treatment."

"Guess I'm tougher than I look. So here it is." I take a deep breath. "I'm messed up."

"You got that right," says Madeline.

I meet her eye. "I know. I...I'm also scared. Absolutely terrified. It's not so easy for me to understand how people are feeling. I have to work hard at it, and I don't always get it right."

I think some more.

"It's like I'm a house. And the other houses have electricity. But I don't," I quantify. "When bad things happen, other people get upset. For me, there's nothing. The lights don't go on."

I'm not sure I can admit that I'm not even sure I want the lights back on. That would kind of make me a monster, wouldn't it?

There's a long silence.

Then Madeline says, "I taught myself to do that too. When the stuff happened to me as a kid. I'd kind of power down. That's how I thought about it."

Power down. That's not exactly how it feels. But...maybe I'm not such a freak after all.

"I can sort of relate," says Sierra quietly. "For the band, I have to be this sweet Latina every girl, watching everything I say in case it comes off too aggressive, or whatever."

I risk another glance up. "The truth is I came here because Haley is my sister. But I am an addict. I did need help. It took this place for me to see it. First step, right?"

I think of Dr. Lutz's accusation that I'm a sociopath and breathe out, reassured.

He's wrong. Sociopaths don't have friends. And I have feelings for these people.

Sierra gives me a small smile. "So, you'll stay?" she asks. "Hasn't been the same without you."

"Nah. My time is up," I tell her with a half grin. "I came to say goodbye. Tell Tom too, OK?"

Jade falls on me, hugging me close.

"Keep in touch, yeah? You're going to do it, Meg. Next time, you'll do it."

"Hope so." I squeeze my eyes tight and realize they've filled with tears. I brush them away, mildly surprised.

"Congratulations for not sleeping with me." Dex shakes my hand earnestly. I laugh.

Sierra steps forward and winds her arms around my neck in a quick little embrace.

"It's been good having you here," she says. "I've learned stuff. See you around, maybe."

Madeline is the last, giving me a heartfelt squeeze and cupping my face in her hands.

"You're OK, Rocky," she says. "Take care of yourself."

"I will. Better care than I've been doing." I raise a hand to all of them.

"See you on the other side."

Now that they're all in front of me, I can't believe I didn't see it before. Someone from my past has been standing in our midst the whole time.

I leave to a chorus of goodbyes. And as I head out the door, I swing toward the medication room.

If I've got this right, I have about five minutes before someone from the group follows after me.

CHAPTER NINETY-NINE

CARA

In Max's office, I'm trying not to let my eyes flick to the computer screen. Max is nearing the medication room now.

I need to keep Dr. Lutz talking.

"I know what you're doing," I tell him. "I want in."

"Oh?" He tilts his head, politely interested.

"You manipulated Max," I say. "You needed him to be your public face. But you always had other plans for fugu."

Dr. Lutz considers this. "I have always found the word 'manipulation' an interesting one," he muses. "If you are driven by strong emotions, can you blame another person for your poor decisions? Max is a free man. I have never coerced him. I took him from a public facility where low funds meant addicts were very poorly treated. Gave him free rein to make people better. It was what he wanted."

"Only your plans were always to sell fugu to your criminal connections for human trafficking. Far easier to transport people when they're not moving, right?"

Dr. Lutz smiles. "I knew you were intelligent, Cara," he says. "But you are not entirely correct. I have rather better ambitions than dirtying my hands in the sordid trafficking business."

His phone rings and he frowns, taking it out to answer it.

"Hello?" He speaks into the receiver. "Yes. Please ready the transport. We will be leaving shortly." There's a pause. "She's here. With me."

CHAPTER ONE HUNDRED

MEG

When I reach the medication room, I am disappointed by how ordinary it looks. Like a regular door to a cleaning closet. I punch in the override code from Haley's phone. Inside, I'm not prepared for my reaction. A sweat breaks out under my arms.

It's like a drug addict's dream. Shelves and shelves of pharmaceutical medications. I'd been so fixated on finding Haley's killer that I never stopped to think I was putting myself in harm's way.

I close my eyes. *Resist it, Meg. You're never going to solve this if you're high.*

My body is shaking, and another thought occurs to me. Maybe I *need* this. Maybe this isn't something I can do while coming off drugs. I've done the alcohol, haven't I? Not had a drink in a week. One thing at a time, given the circumstances. I step toward the drugs, over looping electricity cables.

There's an entire section actually labeled "opioids."

I drift toward it, thinking of Haley, pull some packages free from their shelves and examine them. "Doesn't hurt to look," I mutter. My hands are shaking.

I'm fairly certain whoever killed Haley is about to walk through the door.

One week without drugs. One week and anyone has made a good start.

This might not be the right week, though. If something unexpected happens, maybe I should be prepared. Protected. That thought is occurring to me when the whole room skips a beat.

Weird. I hold my hands up in front of my eyes. The edges of my fingers are blurred, and the palms in hyperfocus.

Oxycodone would make this go away.

Max also told me I would be prone to seizures. But I haven't taken the anti-seizure medication he prescribed since yesterday.

I'm at risk. It's a nice thought. Since I couldn't name the medication I'm supposed to be on, I *need* to take oxycodone. To protect me.

It's while I'm thinking this that I hear a door shut in a corridor not far away.

Someone is coming.

Very slowly, I move back from the opioid shelf and breathe out slowly. The world warps in and out. Ten breaths. If I made the wrong choice, it's too late to regret my decision. Whoever is in the hallway is at the door.

I wait, heart beating steadily. The gentle peeping of a door code and the whir of the entry mechanism.

The handle pushes down and the door opens silently. The bottom rushes out of my reality.

Holy shit. I guessed right. The tells were all there. I knew it right from the start.

As the familiar person enters the medication room, I'm hit with a wave of uncertainly. Am I really in no danger?

I stare at her. She stares at me.

"Jade?" I breathe.

MEG

Jade's rounded face settles in annoyance when she sees me in the medication room.

"What the fuck are *you* doing here?" she says, sounding not like herself at all. Far more confidant. Far more *entitled*.

"I could ask you the same question," I say.

She gives a dramatic sigh. "I'm here for the drugs. Obviously." She's completely absorbed for a moment, scanning the shelves. Then she grabs a box. "Cocaine hydrochloride," she says. "Medical use. Weaker than I'd like, but it works."

"It was you, wasn't it?" I ask. "Trying to warn me off. You wrote the notes?"

"Yup." She opens the bottle, pressing down to release the cap. "If only you'd listened, huh?"

"The spa," I say. "That was you too? Pushing me under the water?"

She considers. "I'd like to say sorry about it. But you have to admit it was kind of funny. Me pretending to be the one who saved you."

Her accent is slipping now. The English giving way to American.

"The trashed room," I say. "Was that you too?"

"Uh. That wasn't personal, Meg. I was…having a moment. Forgot where I put my stash."

"Did you stand by my bed too, in a fedora hat?"

"'Fraid so." She tips the bottle up to her mouth. "Fuck. For weak stuff, this sure tastes bad." She glares at the bottle accusingly. "Just assume everything weird that happened to you in here was probably me."

I rub my forehead. "*Why?*" I demand.

"Duh. I wanted you to stop investigating. Come on, Meg. You used to be so smart." She turns to look at me. Takes in my face. "You know, right?" she says finally. "You worked it out? I killed Haley Banks."

I breathe out, feeling the ground unsteady beneath my feet. Because I do know it. I know that way of making jokes. I've seen it a hundred times.

I should be angry. But I'm sharper now. More in touch with myself.

I take a breath. Then another. There's a feeling building in my chest, and for the first time in a long time I don't push it down. Everything I felt about Jade. It was instinctive. And *right*. Only twisted, in the wrong order.

"How did you know it was me?" says Jade.

"You called me Meggy," I say. "When we first met."

She begins rubbing her powder-laden finger on her gums. "Recognition dawns," she announces.

"I had to work out some of my own stuff before it became obvious," I say. "You look completely different."

"I know, right?"

"You never died," I say. "You never even left. You've been here all along. Haley."

Jade puts the jar down, and for a moment I think she's going to tell me I got it wrong.

Then she reaches up and pops out a contact lens. Beneath is a deep-blue eye. Almost violet.

Piercing. Familiar.

"Hi, Sis," she says with a grin. "You miss me?"

MEG

I'm staring at Jade's single blue iris, watching Haley emerge.

"Dr. Lutz is still working on some adjustments," she says. "Even after a lot of surgery, I'll need another operation for the nose. She touches the slightly upturned nose with the edge of her finger."

"The black eyes, when you were admitted?"

Haley nods. "Not from falling-down drunk," she says. "Bruising from the face surgery. He changed my nose, the shape of my eyes. Injected filler just about everywhere. Most of the work was on my eyebrows. Apparently that's how humans mainly identify one another. Go figure."

She touches around her forehead. "I have these face-lift cog things on threads that lie under the skin," she says, feeling one out. "They adjust the shape of my features. I spent the last month eating enough food to get Jade's fat ass." She grabs her butt disgustedly. "Gross, right? And I shifted my fake tan brand to a different shade, dyed my hair."

"It's…convincing," I admit. Even knowing who she is, it's hard to match. Only the deep-blue eye gives her away. "You sound different too," I tell her. "It's not just the accent."

"Great job on the voice, right?" she agrees. "That was some

keyhole thing they did to my vocal cords with lasers," She touches her throat. "Hurt like hell. I don't sound like me at all. It's like the Little Mermaid. I gave up my voice to win the prince." She affects a dreamy tone. "Only the prince, in this case, is Hollywood."

"Hollywood? What are you talking about?"

"No one warned me," says Haley. "If I became a singer, I wouldn't be taken seriously as an actress. My career was basically over at twenty-seven." There's a mean glitter in her eyes.

It's easy to forget this about Haley, when you haven't seen her for a while. How petulant she is. How she blames everyone else.

"I should win an Oscar, right?" she says. "I even fooled my own family."

"They held a funeral for you," I say, my voice low. "How could you do that?"

"Like you care." Haley gives a little laugh. "Like *Mom* cares. She took everything from me, Meggy. You were too little to remember. My whole childhood was about recreating her career. I don't owe her a goddamn thing."

"What about me?" I ask quietly.

"You don't even like me," she says breezily.

"I did. I do. Sometimes."

"Gee. Thanks, Sis."

I put a hand to my forehead. "Were you ever going to tell me?"

"Sure. I was waiting for my moment. I never expected you to come *here*." She smiles. It's so familiar, that smile. My heart hurts. "I did everything I could to try and scare you away."

"You held me under the water, you fucking *psycho*."

"Takes one to know one. What kind of person doesn't leave a rehab when someone is trying to kill them?"

A wave of dizziness comes over me. I want to sit but instead

I lean against the wall. What's bothering me most about this crystallizes.

"Why would Dr. Lutz agree to change you into someone else? What's the catch?"

She chews a fingernail uneasily and I know. I know she's promised something awful.

"What did you do, Haley?"

Her eyes meet mine, and for a second I can see her consider lying.

"It's me," I remind her.

Haley sighs. "OK. So Dr. Lutz is starting this…business…is all. For people like me who want to change identities."

"People who want to change identities?" A slew of faces run through my mind. At least half the goons I have arrested at the casino would pay huge sums to use this service. Then it slots together.

"Fugu," I say. "He's using the fugu, isn't he? To fake deaths? Is that what you agreed to?"

"I'm, like, the pilot episode." She does a little halfhearted hip shimmy. "He wants me to show how convincing the process is. Then I get to go live my life."

"Except you don't," I tell her. "Haley, did it ever occur to you the kind of people who would want to change identities? You think Dr. Lutz will keep you alive?"

"Of course he'll keep me alive," says Haley. "But I can't say the same for you. Really, Meggy, your only chance is to join us."

CHAPTER ONE HUNDRED THREE

CARA

Dr. Lutz finishes his phone call and gives me a long look.

"Tell me, Cara, do you know how many people need to disappear?"

Is that a threat? I don't answer.

"The process of false identities used to be little more than a wig and a new name, Cara," says Dr. Lutz. "But very exciting developments have been made. Demand for transgender operations have supercharged this process. Facial fillers and threads can alter the set of an entire face. We can adjust the pitch of a person's voice. Change their hairline, body shape."

I blink at him, confused. "This is...your business plan? False identity? But this has nothing to do with fugu."

"It has *everything* to do with fugu," says Dr. Lutz. "With fugu, we can now fulfill the entire process."

It takes me a moment, and then it suddenly all makes sense.

"A fake death," I say. "Fugu induces an extremely convincing deathlike state."

"But not any amount of fugu," says Dr. Lutz. "Thanks to Max's very precise formula, we can assure our clients safety. And trust me, Cara. A legitimate death certificate is worth an unbelievable amount of money."

"To criminals?"

"An unhelpful label." Dr. Lutz waves a hand. "I don't make distinctions. How people earn their living is up to them. Our facility will accept anyone who can pay. Our fee is ten million per customer, and we already have seven eager to utilize the process once they're assured of our results."

"Your results?"

"That is my genius. Haley Banks is our poster girl."

"Haley Banks? But she's dead."

"Is she?" He looks delighted. "Haley has been under your nose the entire time. She walked past you daily, Cara. Yet you never knew her."

My mind is racing.

"Jade," I say. "She checked in for processing right after Haley died."

"I knew you were intelligent. Haley is dead in the eyes of the world. We tour her in front of our buyers, and they will understand the power of what we offer here. A true new life. Enter rehab, and be reborn." His eyes glitter. "People are willing to pay preposterous sums."

"You'd need to supply a dead body," I say, working things through.

He nods happily. "This is the easiest part." He pauses. "Have you any idea how many unidentified drug overdose victims are removed from Seattle every day? More than I would ever have a use for. Empathetic people, for all their talk of family and love, are rather careless with one another. Particularly when drug addiction is concerned. Commonly, they would rather not ever engage with the troublesome addict again."

I think of the morgue pictures Hanson showed me. The suspiciously practiced needle marks on the dead girl's arm.

"The coroner identifies the wrong body," I say, "after you've secured plenty of witnesses to attest that they saw the person they knew dead."

"We can make adjustments," he says. "Tattoos, a few facial alterations, to more closely resemble the deceased. But you'd be surprised how little it takes."

I'm trying to equate this with what I know when Dr. Lutz raises his eyes to mine.

"The strangest thing, Cara. Before you came here, Max was seen by one of my nurses heading toward the area where the power supply is routed. It seems quite a coincidence that you would suddenly become so talkative at the same time."

My eyes flick to the computer screen. Max. A nurse has him at gunpoint.

I feel like the heat has drained out of the room. Dr. Lutz is watching my expression hungrily.

He knew all along. He was toying with me.

Dr. Lutz shakes his head. "Cara, I had you extensively profiled before you started work here. Do you honestly think I believe you would break the law?" He makes a sound that could be a laugh.

Dr. Lutz removes a small pistol from inside his jeans pocket and points it at me.

I stare at the small muzzle. It's such a totally surreal situation that part of me wonders if the weapon is fake.

"If you shoot me, you won't get away with it," I say weakly, realizing I sound like a bad line in a soap opera.

"You'd think so, wouldn't you?" agrees Dr. Lutz. "That is the delightful thing about regular people and their rules. A crime can be blindingly obvious, but careful disposal of evidence means conviction is impossible. It's one of my favorite things about the modern justice system. Once the residues of fugu have been frozen out of our patients, there will be none. Even the local police won't be able to prove anything once the cryotherapy session is over."

The bitterness with which he speaks about the police takes me by surprise. Something hits me that I didn't realize before.

"Hanson won," I say, finally understanding. "He and Meyers saw through you. You needed Haley Banks to be ruled a simple suicide."

An animal flash of rage flares somewhere deep in Dr. Lutz's blue eyes.

"Hanson has not *won*," he hisses. "He will be forced to close the investigation eventually. *I* have won. I will leave with Haley Banks and enough fugu to buy myself a small island."

"But this isn't about money," I say. "It's about power. It always has been. The power of transforming people in your clinic. You lost. And if you fire that gun, you'll be wanted for murder."

Dr. Lutz is shaking his head furiously.

"Your death will be a tragic accident, Cara," he says. "Your body will be found along with Max's."

CARA

Dr. Lutz is walking me at gunpoint along the corridors.

We reach the door of the cryotherapy treatment rooms. He unlocks the door and I see Max already inside, sitting on the bench. Behind him is the giant rocket-ship-like cryotherapy chamber.

"Cara!" He throws his arms around me, then turns to Dr. Lutz. "Put the gun down, Alexander."

"You will both be joining our guests in the chamber." Dr. Lutz sounds bored.

It's then that I notice movement behind the thick safety glass panel on the chamber door.

The patients are already inside.

I hesitate.

"Please be aware," adds Dr. Lutz, "that while I am not a sadistic man, I am afraid several of my staff members are. It makes no difference to me which death you choose, but I should rather think you would prefer the death of minutes rather than hours. I am told death by cold is peaceful."

I look at the cryotherapy chamber. It's taken on an otherworldly quality.

I hesitate for a moment. Max takes my hand. I look into his face, and something about his expression calms me. The lower corner of his eye twitches. He's trying to tell me something, I realize.

Max has some kind of plan.

I run through what I know about the cryotherapy chamber. I have a feeling I know what Max is thinking.

"It's better this way, Cara," Dr. Lutz says. Max opens the door. We both step inside.

The damp smell of cold closes around Max and me.

My eyes fall on Dex, Madeline, Sierra. They're dressed in swimwear, with the regulation padded mittens, socks, and masks to protect their extremities. The nitrogen isn't pumping yet, but it's cold even so. The insulated chamber has retained a chill from previous treatments.

"What the hell are you two doing in here?" demands Madeline. "What's going on?"

"Supervised session," improvises Max. "Cara wanted to join us."

"Fully clothed?" Sierra raises a thick eyebrow.

"Let's get this thing over with," scowls Madeline, wrapping her arms around herself and shivering. "You know I hate this fucking place. We've been waiting in here twenty minutes at least."

There's a heavy clunk of the door seal locking. Right on cue, an ominous hissing sound starts up. Liquid nitrogen fills the air.

MEG

The concrete floor of the medication room doesn't feel as solid as it should. My eyes aren't focusing properly.

Haley shakes herself.

"It is such a relief to be free of fucking sugar-sweet Jade," she says, a hardness settling in her eyes. "She was a piece of *work*, right? So interested in how everyone is feeling. Looking after little baby Meggy. Jade was exhausting."

Something about how she says it doesn't ring true. Like she's trying to kill Jade with pure spite.

"The sketch you drew of the mom puppet master," I say remembering. "That was real, wasn't it? That was our mom. You as a puppet."

Haley nods. "You never saw it," she says. "You were too busy feeling sorry for yourself and resenting me."

"You were Mom's favorite," I admit. "The pretty one, the talented one."

"But Mom didn't *actually* love me more. She used me to live out all her dreams. Max told me that's a thing, by the way, with people like Mom. Playing the kids against each other. One good, one bad."

I think about this. It fits. I remember if Haley and I were getting along, Mom would suddenly blame me for something. Or heap praise on Haley.

"Jokes on her though, right?" Haley grins. "Because the Banks sisters don't love *anyone* now."

"You changed," I say. "Right after Mom tried to kill herself."

"After everything I did for her, she tried to leave me anyway. It taught me never to rely on anyone but myself."

Haley reaches in her pocket and produces a phone. One I haven't seen before.

"Like I said before, the best chance you have of living through this is to join us."

"I catch bad guys, Haley," I tell her steadily. "I don't work with them."

"Dr. Lutz showed me your diagnosis. Agreed by leading experts. Antisocial personality disorder. You can't fight what you are."

Fury boils up inside me, threatening to overspill.

"You're wrong about me," I say.

What frightens me most is how familiar the feeling is. How comfortable. It's all the sensations I feel right before I do something reckless. The last few weeks are flashing before my eyes.

"I don't need the diagnosis, Haley. I fold."

Her face twitches in confusion. "This isn't a game, Meg."

"Everything is a game with you, Haley. You just gotta be smart to figure out the rules, right? You got some good cards," I say. "I don't have good empathy. I can be prone to manipulating people. I do get angry. I'm different. Maybe I am a sociopath."

I can't believe I said that out loud.

She smiles hopefully. "So embrace it, Meggy."

"I said I accepted your diagnosis. That doesn't mean I accept your solution."

"Meg. People with antisocial personality disorder—"

"Are not so hot at empathy. I know."

"It's a lot more than that, Meggy, and you know it. You'll always be a periphery. An outsider. Dr. Lutz can help you too."

"Help me with what? Getting a nose that doesn't suit my face?"

She frowns, then recovers. "Why not? Sisters together again, right?"

"What about the other patients?" I ask.

She wrinkles her new narrow nose. "What about them? We don't need anyone else, right?" She takes my hands. "I never wanted to leave you, Meggy. It was Mom's fault. We had fun, remember?"

It's what I always wanted to hear Haley say. But not like this.

I shake my head slowly. "I don't care about a lot of people," I say. "But I do care about a few. And right now some of those people I care about could be in trouble."

"You should let go of all that stuff. All the rules. Like Dr. Lutz says. It's liberating."

"He's using you, Haley. Like Frank used you. Like *Mom* used you." I watch her face. "You know Dr. Lutz was bragging to me? How your charms had no effect on him? How he couldn't be played?"

Haley's face registers a quick spike of fury.

She always did have to win. Her face sets in petulant frustration.

"When you stop being useful," I tell her, "Dr. Lutz will kill you."

"You can't *know* that."

I shrug. "It's what you would do."

"True," agrees Haley. "Good thing I'm useful."

The whole room is bending. I screw my eyes up tight waiting for it to pass. Instead, a wall of cramps hits my body.

Stressful situation. I'm probably having a seizure, I hear myself thinking, in an abstract way. As though it's happening to someone else.

"Haley," I manage. "There's oxycodone... It will help..."

The next thing I know, I'm flat on the floor, and Haley is standing over me.

Jade would fetch me oxycodone. Help me up, tell me it was all going to be OK. But this isn't Jade. It's Haley.

"I'm sorry, Meg," Haley says. "I won't let anyone stand in the way of my dreams. Not even you."

CHAPTER ONE HUNDRED SIX

MEG

I open my eyes to see bundles of thick black cables creeping up the walls, and out from the floors. They bend in tentacle-like folds into metal housings or bright-colored switches.

I'm still in the medication room. I've been bound with cable ties to the edge of a small generator, with a low metal ledge that makes a rudimentary kind of seat.

Dr. Lutz is looking into my face. Under his arm is a heavy pair of bolt cutters.

Not good. I give a hopeless tug at my bonds. *Cable ties. Smart. No getting out of this with a dislocated shoulder.*

"She's awake," he announces, sounding far too happy about it. I blink to consciousness and see Haley, phone in her hand. I take in the full weight of her betrayal.

"You told Dr. Lutz we were here?" I accuse her.

"I told him *I* was here," says Haley. "It isn't all about you, Meg. Stop taking everything so personally."

"Perhaps this situation is to everyone's advantage," says Dr. Lutz. "I have been looking for someone like you for a long time, Meg. High functioning. Lacking the emotional baggage. Surely you have envied the life of the criminals you pursue."

"Cut me loose and we'll talk." I eye the bolt cutters.

"I would rather not take my chances," says Dr. Lutz. "I am aware of how dangerous you can be, Meg, even if you are not."

I ignore him, turning to Haley. "You can still leave," I tell her. "You don't have to do this."

Haley's eyes flicker. She walks to Dr. Lutz's side. "You wouldn't believe what it takes to get famous, Meg. There are a lot of twisted people in Hollywood. You chose to beat them. I chose to join them. I have done things you couldn't even imagine. Whatever it takes. Like he says, we're outcasts. No one wants people like us." She tries for a smile. "C'mon, Meg. You used to be fun. You want to go back to that crappy casino job? Catching low-rent hustlers and loan sharks? You don't care about catching criminals. You care about winning. So come join the winning team."

"And if I don't?"

Haley's eyes skirt nervously across to Dr. Lutz. I think she knows the answer but still hopes for something different.

"Then I am afraid we'll have to kill you," says Dr. Lutz.

"Haley." I look helplessly at her.

Dr. Lutz shakes his head. "She won't help you," he says. "I think you must know that, Meg. Haley will only benefit you if it helps her. She relies on my protection," says Dr. Lutz. "And Haley knows she can't play her games with me."

Haley returns his smile, but I'm certain I see a glint of icy annoyance in her eyes.

"Particularly," continues Dr. Lutz. "Since Haley is now guilty of murder."

I stare at my sister. She looks unconcerned, but I can tell she's faking to a degree. At least I think so.

"Is it true?" I ask her.

"Tom," she says nonchalantly. "You know how bored I get, Meggy. I wound up reigniting our little affair. But...I changed my whole face, voice, demeanor. Forgot about that tattoo on my hipbone, remember it? The little 'heartbreaker' one. Tom figured out who I was and tried to blackmail me. Luckily he was dumb enough to meet me for one last fling. Heat of the moment, I stuck a needle in his arm. I don't feel bad," she adds. "And I know you wouldn't either, Meg. Tom beat up all of his wives and girlfriends. He would have OD'd sooner or later. I just sped things along." But her face is troubled. Like she can't quite match the reality of that.

"As you see," Dr. Lutz says, smiling like a proud parent. "Haley has accepted her nature. No more following the herd. Being restricted by their nonsensical rules. Regular people will never accept you, once they know your diagnosis. Trust me. I have first-hand experience."

Haley is staring into the middle distance now, with a blank expression I recognize immediately. She looked the exact same way the night my mom went to the hospital. The night she shut me out of the room with Matthew. Tuned out. Somewhere else.

Dr. Lutz slides the bolt cutters from under his arm.

"Haley," I try again.

But my sister isn't there.

CARA

The pain of ice hitting my skin is intense. Every hair stands on end like a stabbing needle.

"Fuck!" Madeline is shouting. "This hurts!"

"Keep calm and breathe," says Max. He turns to me, lowering his voice. "Cara, it's OK. The cryotherapy chamber has an automatic cutoff."

Thank God.

"The secondary cutoff," I agree. "Works even if Dr. Lutz overrides the time. When does it kick in?"

Max hesitates. "Five minutes."

Hope drains away. "*Five minutes?*" With the icy blasts scouring my face, it's hard not to feel absolute despair. We're only a few seconds in, and it feels like I'm dying. "That's easily long enough to kill us," I whisper to Max. "Three minutes is the maximum, and even that can be dangerous."

"We can do this," says Max, but he doesn't sound sure.

"I'm g-going to try the door." I tell him, stuttering with cold now.

I hear his soft tones reassuring everyone, telling them how well they're doing, as I examine every inch of the metal door and mechanism. There's no internal shutoff. Only a countdown clock LED display. An incongruously old-fashioned thing. We're at thirty seconds.

Max continues talking as I scout around the wood-clad interior for anything to help us. But there's nothing. Bolted-down seating.

One minute gone. Four minutes left.

The cold has transformed to something else now. It feels more like burning.

Sierra sits silent, shaking, arms wrapped around her body, head down. Dex jogs on the spot, breath coming out in jagged gasps.

"Cara...take my jacket," says Max. He's struggling for air, removing it.

"No." My face is stricken. "You need it."

Max passes it to me. He grits his teeth and shudders. "You're offending my aristocratic manners."

"That isn't funny." But he's not taking no for an answer, putting the wool blazer around my shoulders. It helps. The freezing blasts are still penetrating right into my bones. But the painful scouring of my skin by the frozen air is buffered.

"H-How long. Have we...d-d-done, man?" Dex shakes out each word through gritted teeth.

"Three minutes," says Max. "Better not focus on the time."

"I can't do this!" Madeline is sobbing, but the tears stick to her face, frozen. "I'm dying. I'm not kidding. I can't breathe."

"Sierra?" I ask. She's gone silent and no one has even noticed her. I slide next to her to see she's curled in a frozen ball, arms wrapped around her legs, barely breathing. Her eyes are wide in pain.

"Try to squint up your eyes," I whisper. "Hurts less that way."

But Sierra is somewhere else. A lost little girl hiding out from gunshots under her kitchen table. I put my arms around her, bringing her under Max's jacket. After a moment, she turns, like she's only just seeing me.

"I need to…see my mom," she whispers. "I promised… I promised her…" Sierra can't finish the sentence. Her blue lips aren't working. I glance up at Max, who is looking at both of us. He doesn't look well, leaning against the wall.

My eyes fix on the clock. Thirty seconds left.

"We can make it," I tell them, though the words won't come out properly through my numb lips. "Almost there."

Twenty-five seconds.

Madeline is breathing little sips of air.

"We need to huddle together," I decide. But it's like no one can hear me. Sierra can't or won't move. Everyone is in their own private hell.

Fifteen seconds.

"Fuck! It's hot!" I turn to see Dex pulling at his protective mitts, trying to take them off. "I'm burning up, man," he says, to no one in particular. "Someone needs to turn the fucking heat off."

"Dex!" I shout. "Stop!" He ignores me.

Ten seconds.

"Nearly there!" I tell everyone. "Hold on."

My eyes are glued to the timer. This is the longest ten seconds of my life. I look back at everyone else. We're going to make it. I think. Max looks…dreadful. He's wheezing. His thin shirt is soaked through from the damp blasts of nitrogen.

"Please, Max," I beg, "take your jacket back."

He shakes his head.

Five seconds.

There's a loud *clunk* and suddenly the lights go out.

"What the fuck?" whispers Madeline.

"Nothing to worry about," mutters Max through gritted teeth. But it is. We both know it is. Someone has cut the power somehow. The override won't work and the door is sealed. We're trapped.

MEG

While I watch, Haley pulls a giant cable untidily free and severs it badly with the bolt cutters. The butchered ends lie prone on the concrete floor, spitting futile sparks. As the power shuts down with a sonic sigh, the large red wall light dies.

Green emergency lighting gives an eerie glow to the snaking cables, like the interior of an organic alien spaceship.

Dr. Lutz checks his watch. "Timed exactly," he says, looking pleased. "Even with our small disruption." He glances in my direction. "Max will be counting on the cryotherapy chamber having an emergency override. How disappointed he will be to discover that a power cut prevents it from working. A technical flaw I was careful to shop for when I selected that particular chamber." He gives a self-satisfied smile.

I'm putting it together. The other patients. Max. It sounds like he's gotten them in the cryotherapy chamber.

"Haley and I shall be flying to India this afternoon," says Dr. Lutz. Haley smiles a stupid villain's girlfriend kind of smile that makes me want to hit her.

"Your acting always was fucking terrible," I tell her.

She frowns. "I don't let negativity bring me down, Meg."

"Life is not perfectly tidy," mutters Dr. Lutz, looking mildly unhappy. It's not clear if he's referring to Haley and me or the ragged ends of the cable. Letting go of perfection seems the kind of thing Max would advise, I think vaguely, wondering if Dr. Lutz has tried therapy himself.

"Haley," says Dr. Lutz. "I am afraid Meg's time with us has come to an end."

He's talking about killing me, I think in an abstract way, *as if he's making plans for a late lunch.*

"My sister won't do it," I tell him. "She won't watch while you kill me."

"Haley has never yet disappointed me," says Dr. Lutz. "And she won't now. You underestimate her. She doesn't let pointless emotions decide her success."

They exchange a meaningful look. I wonder what else he has her complicit in.

"We're a team, like you said," Haley tells him.

I swallow. "You won't let him hurt me, Haley," I say. "You could have told Dr. Lutz I was here right from the start. You didn't. You tried to warn me away."

Haley gives me a cute smile. "You know how much I love games, Sis." She shrugs her little shoulders. "How could I resist?"

She's so believable. But somehow I'm not completely convinced.

Dr. Lutz nods, then turns to me. "It's nothing personal, Meg."

He steps back. The frayed power line lies in two pieces at his feet.

Lifting one piece of cable, he advances toward me.

Warehouses. Gasoline. It's the same thing all over. Only this time, there's no duct tape to wriggle out of.

CHAPTER ONE HUNDRED NINE

CARA

Inside the cryotherapy chamber, the lights go out. All is black, save a small shaft of light from the plate-glass panel on the door.

My nose feels like it's filled with snow. My lips are frozen. Every breath is agonizing.

"It's…a power cut," I say, trying to quell the sudden urge to cry. "The nitrogen is switched off, but so is the door-opening mechanism."

The skin on my legs ripples with stabbing pains.

"What does that mean?" asks Sierra, voice straining against the cold. "We can't get out?"

"The subzero cold air has stopped," I say, choosing my words. "But the insulation of the chamber means it will stay cold for hours."

"What the fuck are you talking about?" demands Madeline.

"It means we're trapped in here," says Sierra. "Dr. Lutz has left us to die. Isn't that right, Cara?"

I couldn't have put it better myself. I don't know how she knows. Lifetime of fearing the worst, I guess.

"He knew," I whisper to Max. "Dr. Lutz must have known about the five-minute override. He cut the power to make sure."

Dex has pulled a glove off and is working at the other with numb fingers.

"Max," I whisper. "Help me."

His blue eyes land on my face. His Adam's apple jerks up and back.

"I needed more time," Max is saying. "More time."

I'm shaking my head, shivering. "Your patients need you," I tell him. "*You*. Not your miracle drug."

Something happens to Max's face. His eyes fall on Dex.

"Dex, stop." His voice is rasping. "It's a condition of hyperthermia to feel hot," he says. "Trust me. It's cold."

Dex looks up. His fingers stop fumbling.

"Put your glove back on," says Max. He turns to Sierra.

"You need to huddle for warmth," he says. "While I try to break the door mechanism."

Amazingly, Sierra manages to stand. She shuffles toward Madeline. Dex is struggling to pick up his glove.

"You know there's no way out," I tell Max. "That door is three inches of metal."

He doesn't answer, only wheezes, looking straight ahead.

"You have a lung condition. At least let me help."

"No...you...won't," he says, each word a pained breath. "H-huddle."

"Your jacket. Take your jacket back." Max only shakes his head. Tears are freezing on my face now, rivulets of ice. The dark chamber blurs as I collide with the shaking cold limbs of the other patients. We're dying. All of us.

CHAPTER ONE HUNDRED TEN

MEG

Dr. Lutz touches the end of the electrical cable to my chest. A white-hot pain radiates across my ribs. As though someone has a hand around my heart and is squeezing. There's a high-pitched noise and it's only when he pulls the cable away that I realize it's me, screaming. My heartbeat is inhumanly fast, then it stops. Just for a moment, and I'm seized with a cramping pain so bad I retch. Something skips, and blood pumps loud in my ears.

"Cardiac arrest," says Dr. Lutz. "Common in drug addicts who go through sudden withdrawal."

I look at Haley who is blank-eyed, distant.

"Haley," I say. "I know you protected me. From what happened to Mom. I know you stopped me from finding her after her suicide attempt."

She turns in my direction, but there's no emotion. "That was when we were kids," she says. "You don't know me now."

"Bullshit," I tell her. "You left me notes. You tried to warn me away. And why call me the night you took the fugu? I think you were having regrets."

"I always did love a little drama, Meg," she says airily. "You know how I am."

Dr. Lutz is speaking. "I think, two more," he says, considering the cable in his hand. "To make it look realistic. I can't risk leaving the cable on long enough to make a burn mark," he explains to Haley.

He steps forward and presses the raw end of the cable to my chest for a second time. Now interlaced with electric pain I feel heat. Burning heat. As though my skin is actually bubbling. The world skips in and out. When he draws the cable back, I collapse forward. I'm wheezing, struggling to catch each breath.

It takes every ounce of energy to lift my head.

"Haley…" But she isn't even looking my way. Dr. Lutz glances back to confirm it.

There's an expression of excitement on his face.

Something crystallizes. Something about these last few weeks. A feeling.

"Jade," I blurt out, gritting my teeth against the pain. "It wasn't a coincidence you chose to act Jade. She was the fairy princess. From when we were kids."

Haley's face flicks up toward me, confused.

"You had a golden wand," I tell her. "You made our family perfect."

There's a spark of something in her eyes.

My body is shaking, and it's hard to get words out.

"She's still part of you, Haley. The part that's my sister. You thought you left Jade behind to escape Mom, but you didn't."

Something happens to Haley's face. An uncertainty. Like her expression switches to a confusion Jade might feel.

Very slowly, she bends and thoughtfully picks up the frayed end of the cable nearest to me.

The vision breaks into a thousand pieces as Dr. Lutz's cable hits my chest for the third time. I buck in my seat, every muscle iron hard, white hot, like a clamp is being tightened on every part of my body.

I'm dying. I can feel it. I'm actually leaving my body. It doesn't feel bad or painful anymore. There's a tunnel of light around my periphery.

For a moment I'm back in the room again, with the agony and the stench of burning flesh. And now Haley is close behind Dr. Lutz. Like time has skipped forward.

Is she trying to touch the end of the live cable to Dr. Lutz?

If she is, it won't work. It's too short and won't reach.

Haley looks again at the gap between her, Dr. Lutz, and the cable and appears to reach a decision.

She stretches out her arm, clasps Dr. Lutz's hand tight. At the contact, Dr. Lutz turns, surprised, free cable end swinging. The torrent of excruciating pain leaves my body.

Haley's expression is calm, knowing, with a hint of excitement.

She looks like when she steps onstage.

"I might not have been the best sister," Haley says, "but I was *your* sister. Remember that, Meggy."

"Haley, let go," hisses Dr. Lutz, the fury of betrayal setting on his face. He tries to pull his hand free from hers.

You can see from the confusion on his face, he has no idea what Haley is doing.

"Don't forget me, Meggy," says Haley.

Oh fuck. She's saying goodbye.

She locks eyes with Dr. Lutz.

"You can't be played, huh?" she asks. "I guess you never played *me*."

Haley slides her grip to the exposed end of her cable. I know what she's doing even if Dr. Lutz doesn't.

Haley is connecting the circuit.

"No!" I watch helplessly as electricity pours from the frayed metal end into her hand and through her body.

There's an ominous hum, then a crackling buzz as the entire substation power passes through her and into Dr. Lutz. A flash of light erupts from his end of the cable as the massive voltage leaps the small gap between his hand and the live end.

Together, their bodies form the connection.

A bolt of bright-blue electricity shoots through Haley and Dr. Lutz as the full current of electricity courses through them, powering up the substation. There's a static noise and the power light glows on.

All across the Clinic echoes the wave of everything electric powering up again. The lights. The computers. The cryotherapy chamber.

Dr. Lutz and Haley stand frozen in time, looking into each other's eyes.

On Dr. Lutz's face is an expression I've never seen before. Eyes wide, jaw set. Maybe this is the first time he ever felt truly afraid.

Haley looks peaceful. Victorious. Like she just played her ace.

You don't play games with Haley, I think, looking at Dr. Lutz's agonized features.

My sister always, always wins.

CHAPTER ONE HUNDRED ELEVEN

CARA

In the dark cryotherapy chamber, there's a loud click, and suddenly the lights are on.

"The power is back!" I say, staggering toward the door.

Thank Christ. It opens, and a rush of warm air hits.

Madeline is out behind me, followed by Dex. We're all still shaking uncontrollably.

Just as suddenly, the power dies again.

"What happened?" asks Sierra. "Why did the power flash on and off?"

"Who cares," says Madeline. "Let's get the fuck out of here."

The tiles of the heated floor beneath our feet have kept their warmth and feel impossibly good. My entire body is racked with muscle-spasming tremors.

"Where's Max?" says Dex.

I don't answer. My body isn't working.

"We need to get him out," he says.

But I don't know if any of us can. My muscles literally will not cooperate. Everywhere is pins-and-needles numb.

Madeline gives an all-body shudder, like she's trying and failing to muster the energy.

Dex staggers forward into the still-freezing chamber. I lunge after him and only succeed in falling painfully to my knees.

He emerges seconds later, dragging Max's body, gasping. This time, Madeline manages to help him. They somehow get Max's unconscious form onto the heated floor. He's barely breathing.

"How the fuck," pants Madeline. "Did you go back in there?"

"Life onstage," says Dex. "Always something left for an encore." Suddenly he starts crying. Big heaving sobs. Dex lies over Max. He looks like a little boy, sobbing his heart out for the father who never cared.

Madeline is first to recover, raiding the cupboard for towels, throwing them to each of us. The heated floor is slowly restoring us.

"Put these on," she instructs. "Keep warm."

I realize I'm still wearing Max's jacket. My hands aren't working, and every single muscle in my body is juddering.

I don't know how many minutes we sit, shaking convulsively beneath our towels.

To my great relief, Max opens his eyes. "Cara?"

"Holy moly," says a familiar voice at the doorway. "What in the world happened to you?"

It's Meg.

"Couldn't leave without my favorite fucked-up crew," she adds. "You too, Cara."

I don't mind her rudeness so much, suddenly.

"Cara, I need to tell you something." Max is coming to his senses. He lets me help him to a sitting position on the warm tiles and glances at Meg, who is examining the cryotherapy door with interest.

"We got the assessment back," he whispers. "She's a sociopath."

"It's true," says Meg, turning and walking back, having obviously overheard the last part. "But that doesn't mean I'll always do the wrong thing or he'll always do the right one. I don't feel any malice toward you, by the way, Cara. Just indifference," she adds. "And you've kind of grown on me." She winks.

I turn to Meg. "Let's go."

As we get everyone out of the treatment room, Meg seems less antagonistic toward me. She floats to my side as the others lag behind, helping Max.

"Max," Meg says, as we head for the main gate. "I don't get what everyone sees in that guy."

"He had a very troubled upbringing," I explain. "Everything he does is to help people."

"Is it?" says Meg. "Or does he make stupid emotional decisions trying to turn off his own pain?"

Meg's nose wrinkles. "The facts are he was obsessed with some drug treatment so he could be the big man changing the world. He put everyone at risk and allied with a really shady criminal to do it. If you take away how you *feel* about his tragic past and look at what he *does*, Max is kind of a douchebag," she concludes.

"I guess…that's one way of looking at it," I agree. She kind of has a point, I suppose. From a certain perspective.

As we move through the corridor toward the lobby, we pass a shape on the floor. I slow. It's…the battered body of one of the male nurses. He *might* be breathing. I turn to Meg.

"You know anything about that?"

"I have anger issues," she explains, glancing at the unconscious nurse. "Comes in handy from time to time. He'll probably live, if that matters."

"I think…yes. I'll call for help when we get out."

Meg shrugs. "Knock yourself out."

We reach the glass lobby doors. The power cut has stopped them from swinging open automatically. I pick up a fire extinguisher and fling it straight through the glass.

Meg is watching me with something like appreciation as the door shatters and we move through it.

"You've never broken a window before, have you?" she asks.

"Never." I tell her.

"Feels good, right?"

We reach the gates. They hang open.

There are miles of coast behind us. Forest ahead. Nothing. A fresh start.

There's something on the horizon. A car. As it pulls closer, I see an angry face at the wheel. A dark-haired man who looks every inch the gangster. I assume he must be one of Dr. Lutz's criminal contacts. Maybe even his first customer. My muscles tense.

Everyone else has a similar fearful response. So it's a shock when Meg runs up to the man and kisses him.

MEG

Harry's here. I can't believe it's him.

"Harry! How did you get here so fast?" I demand.

He looks sheepish. "I figured you could be in trouble, so…I'd already taken the flight when I last spoke to you."

"Then how the fuck did you even find this place?"

"Ex-cop. Good to see you, kid." He folds me in his arms. For a moment all my problems stand still, and then all the familiar fears bubble up. Because I can't risk Harry.

From nowhere, Max's words come back.

"Why would I give someone the opportunity to abandon me?"

"I suppose, because, sometimes they won't."

Huh. Maybe Max isn't *such* a douchebag after all.

Harry is taking in the group of ravaged faces behind me. "What the hell happened?"

"You don't want to know," I tell him. "How about you take me home?"

"I've only been waiting two years for you to ask, Meg."

"Then do it."

"Well…what about these people?"

I glance over my shoulder. "They could use a ride, I guess. They're…my friends."

He laughs. "Same old Meg, huh? I'm glad rehab didn't change you altogether."

"Me too, Harry."

We're interrupted by the sound of sirens. Two police cars skid to a halt, and Police Chief Hanson and Officer Meyers climb out.

"We came as soon as we could," Hanson says, glancing at Cara.

"Looks like we're late to the party," Meyers adds.

"Maybe," I say, not taking my eyes from Harry. "Maybe not. I'm going to have different kinds of parties from now on."

MEG

It's my regular session with my therapist. Everyone says you should shop around to find a therapist. But there is only one person in the entirety of LA who will consider treating a diagnosed sociopath.

Most therapists are too frightened of us to risk it.

He listens to me at length, nodding in that overly earnest way therapists do.

"I'm done with trying to live like an empathetic person," I told him at our first session, after explaining the insane events of the previous month. "It's…fucking exhausting."

He left a long therapist silence, which I'd finally gotten used to with Max.

"You're giving up on being normal?" he says.

"Pretty much. Think I'm gonna try to be myself. Crazy, right?"

He considered. "No," he said finally. "No, I would say that sounds like growth."

I liked him right away.

"Sociopathy and psychopathy are labels with limited clinical use," he went on to explain. "Your scores would tip you over into the clinical definition of sociopathy. But it isn't 'in or out.' It's part of a wider picture. They're traits on a spectrum of antisocial personality."

"So I'm a sociopath but not a psycho?"

He tilted his head. "I don't consider these terms especially helpful. They conjure a certain view that is derisory. The prevailing characteristic of antisocial personality disorder is an absence of a sense of self."

He sat back in his chair, fingers steepled. "Difficult to have feelings about or for other people if you don't know how you exist separate from them."

"Is that...fixable?"

To my surprise, he nodded. "We can work on your core values. Who you are. Help you feel a far broader range of feelings."

"What if I don't want to?"

"You might not want to," he agrees. "Feelings can be hard. Confusing. They're also a human experience that I'd hate for you to miss."

Nowadays, we do a lot of work together on emotions. The therapist explains it like colors. My emotions are black and white. We're working to broaden my palette.

Good feelings. Devotion. Satisfaction. Loyalty. You can't feel those unless you have your own identity. I'd like to think I had love already. Weak, maybe, but it was there. Just not directed at so many people.

The bad side is I now also feel things I'd rather not. Disappointment with other people. Sadness. Like Dex says. The good thing about recovery is you get your feelings back. The bad thing is you get your feelings back.

We also talk a lot about the qualities I want to keep. Because my purpose is not to become like most people. It's to be myself.

"Many of the qualities of sociopaths are greatly admired," explains my therapist. "A great number of fictional heroes would be sociopaths in real life. Think of the average TV cop. Freethinking mavericks who play by their own rules." He gives a half smile. "Reckless, driven. Often impulsively promiscuous. Most people love these qualities, so long as they're far enough away."

"You're saying I'm a hero?"

"I'm saying you *could* be a hero. With the right mentality. You could also be a very good villain. It comes down to the choices you make. Whether you believe there are people who genuinely have your best interests at heart or you think you're on your own."

I think of Dr. Lutz. Haley too.

"I guess I'm still figuring that out," I say.

"How are you feeling about your sister?"

This is the big question.

"I think…grief," I say. "I think I've got some grief. It's hard," I add. "Feelings are hard."

"Amen to that." He shuffles papers and holds up a sheet.

"Is that why I became addicted?" I ask. "Because I couldn't handle having feelings?"

He considers again. "Only you can answer that," he says. "Addiction issues go hand in hand with sociopathy. Remember, Meg, antisocial personality disorder is a coping mechanism. A way of dealing with unbearable events in childhood. Many relentless traumas that forced you to adapt. You learned that love was unreliable, that adults were cruel and unpredictable, that healthy emotions only led to pain and suffering. As a child, you had no way of knowing how high the cost of losing your empathy was."

I think about this. Until my therapist told me otherwise, I'd always assumed my childhood was fairly normal for Hollywood. Maybe even one of the better ones.

"What I would say," continues my therapist, "is with both disorders, you've come a long way."

CHAPTER ONE HUNDRED FOURTEEN

CARA

The Clinic looks a little different nowadays. I've stripped back a lot of the larger design features. On measure, it's cozier. More inviting, I hope. I was asked to take over sole management by the new investors, who bought the building outright after Dr. Lutz's death.

We fit more guests too. It's a more egalitarian model.

Perhaps most importantly, we don't have triple-secure doors anymore, and patients are encouraged to walk the grounds.

Which is why Police Chief Hanson and Officer Meyers have walked right in without me noticing.

"Miss Morse." Meyers does her delighted smile. Her lipstick looks better, I notice. Maybe she's taking more time for herself. "I like what you've done with the place."

"Thanks. To what do I owe the pleasure?"

Hanson clears his throat with a deep rumble. His giant mustache quivers. "We thought you might like to know. The death of Alexander Frederick Lutz was ruled misadventure. A most unfortunate accident." His eyes flash up to me and back.

"We found out more about his past," says Meyers. "Dr. Lutz discovered his psychopathy by accident. In his early medical career he was involved in a project that mapped the traits of psychopaths.

I think he would have been shocked to discover he fit the data perfectly. And then perhaps…angry at how he would be treated, if anyone knew his secret."

I consider this.

"You were extremely helpful in your testimony," continues Hanson. "Not to mention leading us to all the illegal supplies of fugu so they could be destroyed. We were able to put a lot of what happened together with your help. How Haley's death was faked. Using fugu. We believe Haley broke into the medication room and found the oral dose of fugu that Dr. Lutz intended her to take. Maybe she had a freak-out, or just wanted it over. In any case, she went to the spa where she made one last call to her sister, Megan."

"From what I heard, she left Meg a very confusing message."

"Sounds like Haley Banks, right?" suggests Meyers. "She was…a complex person."

Hanson tilts his head in partial agreement. "In any case, after taking the fugu, Haley goes back to the shared dorm to make sure she's found by as many people as possible. Dr. Max declares her dead at the scene. Haley is taken to the Clinic's own private mortuary," he continues. "Dr. Lutz swaps the body for a dead homeless girl from Seattle."

"How did Dr. Lutz convince the coroner to identify a different body?"

"He didn't," says Hanson. "Four independent witnesses and a respected medic had already identified the victim. Faces look very different when the scaffold of living muscle collapses. Dr. Lutz picked a heroin addict of similar age. Probably fixed the hair, makeup. Tattoo. The human mind sees what it expects to see."

I think about this. "Max didn't know about Haley?" I ask.

Meyers shakes her head. "He was only charged with illegal import of blowfish. Will you visit him in prison?"

"I don't know," I say slowly. "He's out in six months. Maybe I'll see him then. But...I think I'm done with complicated men."

"Good move," says Meyers. "I met my husband right after I made that decision."

I smile.

Hanson strokes his long mustache. "We'll still be keeping an eye on your paperwork," he warns.

"You won't find anything illegal," I tell him. "Just unethical. I have a duty to do the best by my patients," I add. "It all comes down to resources. The more money, the better the chance of rehabilitation."

Hanson nods slowly. "I wouldn't think on the finances too deeply, Miss Morse," he says. "City folk might find us backward out here with our plaid shirts and drip coffee. But we find community can be very effective. Sometimes an apple pie makes all the difference."

"That's a phrase we use hereabouts," fills in Meyers. "Means you check in on someone. That's got very little to do with money, right?"

I think about this. "What I will say," I tell her, "is there is absolutely no pattern to who gets better and who doesn't. People leave here, and you think they're going to make it. Next day they're checking back in. Others you think don't have a hope in hell. They turn their lives around."

"You're talking about Madeline?"

"Something finally stuck with her."

"Sierra?"

"She's taking it a day at a time. Relapsed after she went back on tour with her band. But she's gone solo now, and I personally think it's the best thing for her."

As Hanson and Meyers leave, I pick up the phone to the lab. We're developing a new treatment line with a special ingredient. I didn't lead the police to *all* the fugu supplies. Made sure I kept a little back to start formulating my own research. After all, fugu has the potential to change addiction treatment. I've learned a few things from Dr. Lutz in that regard.

As the police leave, I see another familiar face.

"Hi, Dex," I smile.

It's Dex's fourth round with us. He's done a little jail time. Doesn't want to go back. Today he looks morose.

"What's up?" I ask.

"You know, if this were a movie, I'd have changed, right? Truth is we both know I'm not going to make it. They'll find me in a dumpster one day, Cara. That's just reality. Life doesn't hand out good cards to pieces of trash like me."

I come out from the desk and put an arm around him.

"Hey, Dex?" I say. "We're here for you, buddy. One day at a time."

MEG

I've only been away for a month, but the casino offices look completely different. More colorful. Textured. Guess that's sobriety for you.

I push open the door to Sol's office. He looks up from his desk.

"Hey, Meg. Ready to get back to work?"

"If you'll have me."

He frowns. "Never in doubt. Long as you got your house in order."

There's a pause. "You got sent the doctor's report, right?" I say. "Antisocial personality disorder?"

Sol ducks a quick, awkward nod. "Never did set much store in that psych stuff, Meg. We all got our quirks. Do the job and that's good enough for me."

"OK. But you understand I have problems imagining how other people are feeling. It's not impossible," I add, remembering what I've learned in the past weeks. "But it's harder for me."

"You're saying you don't feel emotions?"

"Common misconception. I feel emotions. I just don't feel yours."

Sol frowns. "Are you telling me you're a weirdo? 'Cause we all knew that about you already, Meg. Case you hadn't noticed, we're all weirdos here. How in hell else we gonna catch the bad guys?"

I laugh. "Sol. About the psych report…"

He raises a hand. "I don't care about it, Meg…"

"I do care about people. Not many. But a few. You're one of the few."

He doesn't look up. "I know, Meg," he says. "Go on. Get back to work."

Harry picks me up after work from the night shift, and we head out to breakfast. A cute little place with table service and no self-serve Bloody Marys. Later we head for a walk along the beach, two regular sober people watching the early-morning fitness freaks pump iron and rollerblade past.

"How's therapy?" asks Harry.

"Good. I think it's good. We talk about you a lot. He thinks you're good for me."

"I am. Who else would have fed your crazy cat for so long?"

I laugh. "I was trying to figure out how this isn't an issue for you. My condition."

Harry thinks for a moment. "Well, for one. I kind of grew up with psychos in the family," he says. "I mean, no one *told* me that Uncle Marco was a bad man or anything. But you got a vibe. Compared to that guy, you're a total sweetheart."

"Thanks. I guess. You still in touch with your mafia uncle?"

"Don't get any ideas, Meg. I don't think he likes me much. I'm not psychopathic enough for his tastes."

"You're still his nephew though, right? He'd avenge your death or whatever."

He shrugs. "Oh, yeah sure. Probably. Family honor. It's not

personal. Which is a little ironic when you think about it. But"—
he raises a finger—"when it comes to fucked-up relatives, I think
it's fair to say you hold the ace, right?"

"With Haley? She didn't kill me," I point out. "She could have.
She killed Tom."

"Nice. The sister who didn't kill you. Keep dreaming big there,
Meg."

"And in the end, she saved my life," I point out. "She did good."

Harry's face creases up. "I think that's a stretch, Meg." He
pauses. "Did you get closure at least?"

My face twists. "Nah. I'm not sure I even believe in it. Haley.
She's part of me. I guess you could call that acceptance. So
maybe I got something better than closure. Maybe I got peace."

Right on cue, my phone rings.

"Hang on," I tell Harry, looking at the number. "I've got to
take this."

His dark eyebrows rise. "Is that who I think it is?"

I nod. Take the call. There are a few seconds while the line
connects. It's a burner phone. I glance at Harry, who has wandered
over to the golden sand and is looking out to sea.

"Hello?" I speak into the phone.

"Hey, Meggy." Her voice sounds different. Brighter. "How's my
favorite kid sister?"

"Hello, Haley. Your only kid sister is doing fine. What's up
with you?"

Haley and I kept it secret. How she stood on the box of medications when she took Dr. Lutz's hand. He was earthed, but she was
standing on a hundred plastic medicine bottles, insulated from the
shock. The current passed right through her, doing nothing much
more than singeing a few hairs.

Haley claims she didn't know this would happen. She stood on the box only to get closer to Dr. Lutz. Her intention was always to sacrifice herself. But I know my sister, and I can't say I'm entirely convinced. Either way, I'm grateful.

Afterward, Haley managed to inveigle Dr. Lutz's criminal contacts into helping her disappear. At least I assume that's what she did. She always was good at getting people to do what she wanted.

"I got a part," Haley is telling me as I hold the phone to my ear, watching Harry kick sand. "Art house movie."

"Really? Who did you have to kill?"

"That would be telling. My agent thinks it's a good role. Could be a big break for a small-town girl from Iowa that no one has ever heard of. That's me," she adds unnecessarily. "Case you didn't figure it out."

"Am I going to get tickets to the premiere?"

"Probably not. Are you going to tell the cops who I really am?"

"Probably not."

We talk for a while, Haley entirely about herself. I encourage her to get therapy. She says she'll think about it. Like always, when I hang up, I'm never entirely sure she's not a danger to society.

"How's your sister?" asks Harry, searching my face for answers. I have been known to spiral after a conversation with Haley. Harry knows the signs to look for.

"It's OK," I reassure him. "I'm not going to get in her way. She's not going to get in mine. It's…how it is with us."

"Right." He looks relieved. "Pleased to hear it. She a sociopath too?"

"I don't know. Maybe. It runs in families. Maybe she's just selfish."

Harry regards me for a moment. "You think it's...curable? This condition you have?"

"I don't know. Why?"

Harry laughs. Pulls me close. "I wouldn't want you to change *too* much, Meg. Although," he grins, waving a finger, "you *have* to admit, it doesn't sound good. 'I'm dating a sociopath.'"

"Guess not."

"But"—he pauses—"my *wife* is a sociopath. Now that has a certain ring to it, right?"

I stop walking. "Harry. Was that a proposal?"

He runs a hand through his curly dark hair and grins at me. "Guess that depends on whether you'll say yes."

I smile. "I might. Probably a good deal for you. James Bond is a sociopath."

"So he is, Meg. So he is."

Truth Is Stranger
Than Fiction

Wondering how much of *The Clinic* is based on fact?

Cate Quinn was inspired to write this book after her own experience in rehab. Read Cate's personal account of addiction rehabilitation and recovery at:

catherinequinn.com/theclinic

Acknowledgments

My first thanks goes the incredible fellow addicts I met in rehab. Each of you changed my life. You know who you are and you're all incredible. Thank you all so much. Seeing such kind people, escaping pain the only way they knew, made me see my own addiction through kinder eyes. The power of the group was to make me reflect; maybe I was like them too.

Not everyone I entered rehab with made it. Less than a year after she finished, Sam, a brilliant young lawyer, attempted suicide in a cry for help. She fell into a coma and was declared brain-dead several days later. Of all the people in rehab, Sam seemed the most likely to make it. She was a smart, beautiful, and incredibly funny person, not even out of her twenties, with a new addiction to exercise and total commitment to her recovery. We all miss her.

It wasn't just rehab that contributed to this book. I had the help of my completely brilliant editors, Celia Killen and Sarah O'Hara at Orion, whose bravery in suggesting edits has made this book so much better than it ever could have been. I am indebted to you both for having faith in me to make big changes. Also to Emad Akhtar whose expertise is always invaluable. My agent, Piers Blofeld, who has been my friend and publishing champion for more than ten years now—we're due an anniversary celebration! I frequently think how lucky I am to have gotten such a great agent so early in my writing career.

In America, my U.S. editor, Shana Drehs, thanks for your hard work and faith in this book.

My incredible partner, Simon Avery, who I love to the moon and back, along with my two children, Natalie and Ben. You are the things that keep me writing books. I wake up happy knowing you are all in my life.

Thanks to copy editor Diane Dannenfeldt for some amazing fixes and pointing out UK-isms that I didn't know existed. Also to eagle-eyed Kelly Burch for the proofing. For the outstanding cover design (everyone loves this cover!), enormous thanks go to Erin Fitzsimmons.

I owe a big debt of gratitude to the neuroscientists who helped with the fugu research part of the book. Neurologist Dr. Jeff Grimm, who pioneers research into drug relapse and has examined the effect of blowfish toxins on the brain, was kind enough to detail his thoughts on the mechanisms outlined in my book.

Groundbreaking neuroscientist Sarah Garfinkel gave insights into alcohol, memory, and emotion.

To the very kind people at the Apogii Clinic in London, who let me freeze to dangerous temperatures (joke! But it felt that way!) in their cryotherapy chamber. Three minutes has never felt so cold. On the other extreme, thanks to Monica Flores in Tulum, Mexico, who let me into her sweat lodge—I really actually thought I was going to die—but it was worth it to feel reborn.

Thanks to the big-hearted people on the northwest coast, who absolutely do not run creepy dangerous rehabilitation centers and took me warmly into their towns and landscapes.

To all the inspirational writers who helped me realize life beyond alcohol was possible. Marian Keyes, the trailblazer for me; Catherine Gray, who wrote *The Unexpected Joy of Being Sober*; Annie Grace, author of *This Naked Mind*; and Julia Crouch, psychological thriller queen.

Finally to the readers. You make it possible for me to do this crazy job, and I wake up grateful every day. I read every one of your reviews and treasure them (or cry about them!). You really are what makes my world turn.

About the Author

© Richard Bolls

Cate Quinn is a travel and lifestyle journalist for the *Times* (London), the *Guardian*, and the *Mirror*, alongside many magazines. Prior to this, Quinn's background in historical research won prestigious postgraduate funding from the British Art Council. Quinn pooled these resources, combining historical research with firsthand experiences in far-flung places, to create critically acclaimed and bestselling historical fiction. Moving into contemporary fiction, Quinn now uses her research skills to delve into modern-day lives and cultures.